Making America's Public Lands

THE AMERICAN WAYS SERIES

General Editor: John David Smith
Charles H. Stone Distinguished Professor of American History
University of North Carolina at Charlotte

From the long arcs of America's history, to the short timeframes that convey larger stories, American Ways provides concise, accessible topical histories informed by the latest scholarship and written by scholars who are both leading experts in their fields and polished writers.

Books in the series provide general readers and students with compelling introductions to America's social, cultural, political and economic history, underscoring questions of class, gender, racial, and sectional diversity and inclusivity. The titles suggest the multiple ways that the past informs the present and shapes the future in often unforeseen ways.

CURRENT TITLES IN THE SERIES

How America Eats: A Social History of U.S. Food and Culture, by Jennifer Jensen Wallach

Popular Justice: A History of Lynching in America, by Manfred Berg

Bounds of their Habitation: Race and Religion in American History, by Paul Harvey

National Pastime: U.S. History through Baseball, by Martin C. Babicz and Thomas W. Zeiler

Wartime America: The World War II Home Front, Second Edition, by John W. Jeffries

Enemies of the State: The Radical Right in America from FDR to Trump, by D. J. Mulloy

Hard Times: Economic Depressions in America, by Richard Striner

Litigation Nation: How Lawsuits Represent Changing Ideas of Self, Business Practices, and Right and Wrong in American History, by Peter Charles Hoffer

We the People: The 500-Year Battle Over Who Is American, by Ben Railton

Of Thee I Sing: The Contested History of American Patriotism, by Ben Railton

American Agriculture: From Farm Families to Agribusiness, by Mark V. Wetherington

Hoops: A Cultural History of Basketball in America, by Thomas Aiello

Years of Rage: White Supremacy in the United States from the 1920s to Today, by D. J. Mulloy

Germans in America: A Concise History, by Walter D. Kamphoefner

American Exceptionalism, by Volker Depkat

Making America's Public Lands: The Contested History of Conservation on Federal Lands, by Adam M. Sowards

MAKING AMERICA'S PUBLIC LANDS

The Contested History of Conservation on Federal Lands

Adam M. Sowards

ROWMAN & LITTLEFIELD
Lanham • Boulder • New York • London

Published by Rowman & Littlefield
An imprint of The Rowman & Littlefield Publishing Group, Inc.
4501 Forbes Boulevard, Suite 200, Lanham, Maryland 20706
www.rowman.com

86-90 Paul Street, London EC2A 4NE, United Kingdom

Copyright © 2022 by The Rowman & Littlefield Publishing Group, Inc.

All rights reserved. No part of this book may be reproduced in any form or by any electronic or mechanical means, including information storage and retrieval systems, without written permission from the publisher, except by a reviewer who may quote passages in a review.

British Library Cataloguing in Publication Information Available

Library of Congress Cataloging-in-Publication Data

Names: Sowards, Adam M., author.
Title: Making America's public lands : the contested history of conservation on federal lands / Adam M. Sowards.
Description: Lanham : Rowman & Littlefield, [2022] | Series: The American ways series | Includes bibliographical references and index. | Summary: "Throughout American history, 'public lands' have been the subject of controversy, from homesteaders settling the American west to ranchers who use the open range to promote free enterprise to wilderness activists who see these lands as wild places. This book shows how these controversies intersect with critical issues of American history"— Provided by publisher.
Identifiers: LCCN 2021046340 (print) | LCCN 2021046341 (ebook) | ISBN 9781442246959 (cloth) | ISBN 9781538125311 (epub)
Subjects: LCSH: Public lands—United States—History. | Public lands—United States—Management—History. | Land use—Government policy—United States—History.
Classification: LCC HD216 .S74 2022 (print) | LCC HD216 (ebook) | DDC 333.10973—dc23/eng/20211206
LC record available at https://lccn.loc.gov/2021046340
LC ebook record available at https://lccn.loc.gov/2021046341

♾️™ The paper used in this publication meets the minimum requirements of American National Standard for Information Sciences—Permanence of Paper for Printed Library Materials, ANSI/NISO Z39.48-1992.

For our children, with hope and confidence in the future they will build.

E. M. S.

B. R. P. and C. C. P.

Contents

Acknowledgments   ix

Introduction: Huckleberries around the Table   1

1   Gathering   11

2   Forming   41

3   Managing   77

4   Balancing   123

5   Polarizing   163

Conclusion: The Promise of the Public's Land   205

A Note on Sources   211

Index   229

Acknowledgments

Like most books, this one shows a single author's name on the cover; however, I could never have written it without the assistance, support, and patience of many others. Acknowledging some of these contributions is a great joy. Thanks begin with series editor John David Smith and Rowman & Littlefield's Jon Sisk. When they contacted me about contributing this volume to the American Ways series, it struck a perfect chord and gave me an important scholarly focus for several years. I am grateful for the initial invitation and all that followed. John David's trenchant commentary and encouragement at critical moments helped sustain both the project and me. Jon's patience and flexibility ensured that this book appeared even after times when I doubted it would. I am lucky to have found them and thank them for all they have done. The rest of the staff at Rowman & Littlefield, especially Sarah Sichina, made certain all the details—from copyediting to marketing—came together behind the scenes, saved me from mistakes, and eased burdens.

A book like this one, which synthesizes a vast literature, depends on nearly uncountable scholars who came before me. Although the bibliographic essay suggests some of the nature of my debts, it is inadequate and surely incomplete. I remain indebted to those scholars and their insights and beg forgiveness of anyone I inadvertently neglected. I also relied on the counsel of historian friends whose work I admire and whose generosity seems boundless. For this project, I called on the extensive expertise of Leisl Carr Childers, Mike Childers, and Jamie Skillen frequently. While I was working on this book, Leisl and I collaborated on a related project during which I learned even more from her. Jeff Sanders is my near-constant sounding board on all things historical, and, once again, I benefited from his commentary, good judgment, and humor. Other historian friends furnished opportunities for me. Doug Sackman asked me to write an overview essay on public lands for the *Oxford Research Encyclopedia of American History* that allowed me to first lay out this long, complicated history. Lisa Brady invited me to write an essay for *Environmental History*, which led me to develop the framework I adapted in this book; that opportunity profoundly shaped this work, and I cannot thank Lisa enough for her support on this and many other occasions. Crawford Gribben brought me to Northern Ireland to share these ideas with Northern Bridge postgraduates, an unforgettable experience that allowed me to think about American public lands in an international setting. I'm fortunate to know these and so many other historians whom I count as friends.

Because the public lands are a vital contemporary issue, I have been able to share some of these ideas in nonacademic forums, which has been an opportunity I have valued and do not take for granted. I have written accounts that appeared in *The Conversation*, *JSTOR Daily*, and *Zócalo Public Square*, which allowed me to reach a public audience distinct from my normal academic one. I appreciate all the editors I worked with. Birgitta Jansen and Craig Deutsche offered me the chance to write an overview of public lands history for *Desert Report*, a publication of the Sierra Club's California and Nevada Desert Committee, which provided a different venue and audience than I am accustomed to having. Rethinking this history on those terms proved valuable, and I remain grateful to them. Most important was *High Country News*. During the drafting of this book, I wrote a periodic column for the magazine, "Reckoning with History," in which I first explored several ideas that ended up here. The erstwhile editor-in-chief Brian Calvert accepted the premise that history can inform our present and made space for me, and that experience has changed how I think about my role as a historian. I am indebted to him. I worked with many editors at *High Country News*, but most often with Emily Benson, which proved to be one of the most helpful partnerships I've known as a writer, and I feel lucky for it. To all the outlets, editors, and readers who helped me hone the history that appears in these pages, I offer my humble gratitude.

Institutional support from the University of Idaho helped me launch and complete this project in various ways. College research grants and a sabbatical contributed to my ability to research and time to think about the history of public lands. My colleagues inquired about the project and showed interest, while students listened and asked questions. Teaching in the university's Semester in the Wild program allowed me to teach in the heart of central Idaho's wilderness, where this history came alive in unique, powerful ways. At a time when higher education suffers in many ways, I count it as my good fortune to have received this support and these opportunities.

Most days when I worked on this book, I did so at home. This means my spouse, Kelley, has lived with this book as long as I have. Her support and patience always sustain me and make the process of writing—and life in general—much better. During the years when I worked on this book, we visited many sites on the public lands and built new memories together. I thank her for indulging my need to see these places to understand them better and helping me to appreciate these lands in new ways. She makes me believe almost anything is possible together, and I love her for that. Although this is a work of history, I have come to believe the public lands are about hope and the future, and so I dedicate this book to the children we have and the world they are making.

Introduction

Huckleberries around the Table

THIS BOOK ON PUBLIC LANDS begins with an inspirational idea from the nineteenth-century American thinker Henry David Thoreau and a metaphor from the twentieth-century philosopher Hannah Arendt. Although Thoreau frequently is found in books and essays concerned with nature, the idea he shared in his final essay, "Huckleberries," which was unfinished when he died in 1862, is seldom remembered compared to many of his more famous lines. And rarely, if ever, is Arendt's work on political action, *The Human Condition* (1958), considered in studies of environmental history. Yet they help frame this book.

Thoreau's essay on huckleberries meanders over several topics but eventually strikes home. After pages of huckleberry natural history, in which he celebrated the fruit's Americanness and its wildness, including its association with Native peoples, Thoreau wistfully recalled his childhood berrying adventures on the hillsides around Concord, Massachusetts. What caused his nostalgia for childhood days was how huckleberry fields had become private property, which Thoreau considered a desecration to the fruit. "It is true," he wrote, "we have as good a right to make berries private property, as to make wild grass and trees such—it is not worse than a thousand other practices which custom has sanctioned—but that is the worst of it, for it suggests how bad the rest are, and to what result our civilization and division of labor naturally tend, to make all things venal." When his beloved childhood huckleberries became simply another commodity to be bought and sold, Thoreau saw a grave downfall for society. Instead of privatizing and pricing everything from land to fruit, he suggested an alternative: common and free areas for "the earth and its productions," as had been the practice among Indigenous peoples.

Town founders ought to have made rivers "a common possession forever," Thoreau thought. "Indeed I think that not only the channel but one or both banks of every river should be a public highway." Not just riverways ought to be open for people to ramble, but towns should also protect beauty, so "more precious objects of great natural beauty should belong to the public." Any mountains or hilltops in a township ought to also be "reserved for the public use . . . [and] left unappropriated for modesty and reverence's sake." Finally, citizens needed to keep parks and forests protected: "I think that each town should have a park, or rather a primitive forest, of five hundred or a thousand acres, either in one body or several—where a stick should never be cut for fuel—nor for the navy, nor to make wagons, but stand and decay for higher uses—a common possession forever, for instruction and recreation." Throughout "Huckleberries," Thoreau sprinkled ideas that imagined a landscape spotted with land set aside for the public—not for their profit or control, but for their learning and inspiration.

It is tempting, if anachronistic, to read a call for the future federal land system in Thoreau's underappreciated essay. He worried that private property took something from nature when it reduced land and what sprung from it as simple commodities. His ideas about common rivers, open beauty, public mountains, and reserved forests presaged concerns about public access, inspiration, protection, and rejuvenation. Although today's public lands are routinely lauded for their role in succoring public life in these communal and noncommercial ways, the system's origins grew more from concern over resource use than preservation in the ways Thoreau advocated. Yet Thoreau, typically a bit outside the mainstream, noted the ways common land might exist outside the capitalist system whose disruption he saw all around him. In truth, the public lands have always included places within the orbit of commodified resources used for private profit and places where the systems of exchange sat somewhat outside that economy. For a nation founded on the primacy of property—both in land and in the terrible, inhuman institution of chattel slavery—these common lands where private property was subordinated to public priorities stood as an unusual institution. From their beginning, they enfolded within them a diverse public's myriad ideals.

Determining those ideals is where Hannah Arendt's philosophy helps. Well known, especially in recent years, for her analyses of the banality of evil and the origins of totalitarianism, Arendt was a political philosopher keenly interested in how people act politically. In her book *The Human Condition*, Arendt theorized how the public realm functions in modern society, and the metaphor she deployed is helpful to understand public lands and will be a frequent touchstone in the pages that follow. The world, in her formulation, is not pure nature but a human artifact. "To live together in the world means essentially that a world of things is between those who have it in common, as a table is located between those who sit around it," Arendt wrote, "the world, like every in-between, relates and separates men at the same time." A table allows people to gather together without "falling over each other." It allows people to be seen and heard from different positions, each with a unique perspective on the thing that gathered them there. Gaining admission to the table does not mean people give up their identities or interests, because what is held in common is not the distinct identities but what brought them together—the table, or, in the case of this book, the public lands. Arendt explained,

> For though the common world is the common meeting ground of all, those who are present have different locations in it, and the location of one can no more coincide with the location of another than the location of two objects. . . . Only where things can be seen by many in a variety of aspects without changing their identity, so that those who are gathered around them know they see sameness in utter diversity, can worldly reality truly and reliably appear.

People who depend on public lands in myriad ways maintain their separate positions but see public places from their distinct vantage point. In other words, if we want to understand the public lands, we need to see how their many managers and users and policymakers see them.

This table metaphor works to guide us through the history of American public lands, and it helps us think about the public lands as part of the democratic experiment that is the United States. It takes no great leap of insight to find faults and failures in meeting the promises of democracy, for the nation is rooted in the dispossession of Indigenous land and the enslavement of Africans. The history of public lands include democratic shortcomings and exclusions just like every other part of U.S. political history. That is partly why thinking about public lands as an element in the democratic experiment is helpful, because we can see who defined the nation's lands and for what purposes, how new ideas supplanted old ones, and how novel understandings complicated traditional views. With the lands themselves as the common object that focuses people's attention—and this book's topic—we learn that this quintessentially American system, like the nation itself, is full of experiments, successes and failures, and promises made, broken, and redefined. Throughout this history, the table and those gathered around it changed and multiplied, guided by evolving laws and science, not to mention shifting political interests. Like a growing family at a holiday dinner incorporating new entrees, the more interests at the table, the more cacophonous and unfamiliar it appeared to those who had been gathering there for generations. This book is an account of how the table changed, which is to say it is a history and not a philosophical treatise or a polemic.

The book attempts to explain how the system came to be and why, as well as how and why it changed over time. The consequences of this system on the land itself and for the people who relied on it, for whatever purpose, remain central to the account that follows. It draws special attention to where constraints and boundaries were redrawn and new political and legal traditions initiated. These moments of transition draw attention to novel arrangements of power and to the land. Frequently, if not always, they were contested, demonstrating that these lands and the processes that governed them mattered to Americans who relied on them. Such disagreements are inevitable and healthy in a democracy when participants were allowed to be involved. This involvement has not always been the case, with some participants directly excluded and some merely perceived their exclusion at other times.

This knotty situation stands out as obvious when considered in basic terms from the genesis. The writer and activist Terry Tempest Williams recently summed up the situation: "Before there were private lands, there were public lands, and before we had public lands, there were Indian lands belonging to more than five hundred sovereign nations in North America." This summation reminds us of the continent's roots in the traditions and sovereignties of countless peoples who have known this place since time immemorial. What Williams does in her eloquent sentence is to de-center our sense of property. There was something before private property, she tells us, inviting us to see the land's history from a perspective and in a longer time frame than typically shapes our national conversations. This book likewise invites us to think about public lands historically, to remember that the way things are now was not foreordained and will not continue forever.

Other books about the public lands often organize themselves around the agencies that govern and administer them, so readers find a chapter on the National Park Service and U.S. Forest Service and the like. Since every agency follows its own logic and is guided by specific institutional missions and policies, this discrete framework is sensible and useful. Nevertheless, history is rarely so freestanding, and lands never are. So this book attempts to tell the history of American public lands chronologically with the aim of showing how broader social and political trends crossed all the agencies and shaped this history.

Certain themes dominate eras to help explain the history of American public lands. A collection of ideas about land and its political purposes emerged in the seventeenth and eighteenth century, preparing the way for the newly independent republic to establish a clear set of rules about the new nation's land. The rules were straightforward: public land should become private land (namely, farms) held by individuals from which they would maintain their economic and political independence. For a growing nation, this ideal depended on acquiring new land by purchase and force and excluding certain people—virtually anyone who was not a white man—from the privileges of owning land. From the start, then, the system was ensured to be a political failure at its heart. Not only did this system fail to fully meet the political ideals it purportedly supported, but ecological conditions also made the legal blueprint unworkable, especially in the American West, with its deserts, semiarid rangelands, and mountainous regions where small-scale agriculture and economic independence were utterly unsuited to the landscape. Cracks in the ideal could not be ignored by the end of the nineteenth century. Chapter 1 tells this story.

Chapter 2 picks up the story of public lands when the nation began to advocate for a permanent public land system. Once reformers recognized the environmental limits that made small landowning likely to fail, they also identified other reasons for reserving some of the public domain from private development. Some places were too scenic to be owned; they should remain accessible to the public as national treasures. Congress established the first national parks to meet this need and keep profiteers from commercializing inspiring places like Yellowstone and Yosemite—or at least preserve the right to determine what the commercial enterprises would be. At the same time, concern about future timber and water supplies prompted Congress to reserve forests for future use, establishing the national forests. Besides writing the laws that permitted this system of keeping lands public, the legislative and executive branches established new agencies to manage these resources, and the courts determined whether the new regime met constitutional requirements.

After establishing these basic elements, the public land system grew beyond its western roots to be a truly national system with national parks and forests, as well as wildlife refuges, crossing the continent in protected islands of scenery, resources, and habitat. Besides expanding the public lands geographically, the decades in the middle of the twentieth century saw the public lands agencies intensify their management of the resources under their jurisdictions. Everything from timber production to tourist experiences was seen as something to maximize under the guidance of professional land managers. This shift toward national and active management produced a frenzy of activity. In the lifetime of one career, a public land manager might have gone from a custodial role as part of a small forest or park staff to growing into managing an operation that built roads and buildings and sprayed chemicals via helicopters while supervising timber sales over thousands of acres or visitor days in the millions. Both trends—the nationalizing and the intensifying—meant that "full speed ahead" seemed to be what characterized the agencies. This transitional and accelerating era is accounted for in chapter 3.

As with Newtonian physics, though, actions produce counteractions, and so by the 1960s and into the 1970s, a revolution in law and policy transformed, even revolutionized, public land management. The new laws seemed to announce new priorities, more aligned with environmental protection and ecological science. The value of wild places was protected in the Wilderness Act (1964) and the continued existence of species was affirmed in the Endangered Species Act (1973). Further, the idea of public involvement was enshrined in laws like the National Environmental Policy Act (1970) that guaranteed opportunities for interested citizens to register their opinions, something for which there had been no requirements and few opportunities during the decades preceding it. In real and important ways, these changes represented victories for environmental and democratic values. However, the agencies, the legislators, and the public were not always clear on whether they wanted new priorities for public land management or simply additional ones. In other words, they often wanted to continue the intensified management and maximum production of resources *here* while more protection might be offered *there*. They wanted their cake and to eat it too, but there was not enough cake and conflicts followed. Chapter 4 describes this period of significant change.

Chapter 5, the book's final one, describes our recent era in which public lands history embodies the same polarization seen more broadly in American political history. The previous era established laws that contained both stricter scientific criteria that agencies were required to follow and more democratic processes that demanded public involvement. Such legislation made it easier to protest extractive use of the public lands, which produced a backlash from the logging, ranching, and mining industries. As environmentalists grew more sophisticated and empowered, they became successful in courts. Radicals in the environmental movement pushed even further in their direct action protests, which prompted a radicalization among resource users who responded in kind. Mutual polarization followed: one provided the gasoline, the other provided the match. In regular intervals, more fuel and more ignition sources were combined. By the twenty-first century, the public lands were among the most contested grounds in the nation with no resolution in sight. One significant result from the endless rounds of protests and stalemates is that public lands agencies often had to refocus their shrinking financial resources on preparing reports and for lawsuits and had less time to protect and administer their lands and wildlife resources. Incremental changes still occurred with additions to the public land system, but the period mostly was characterized by polarizing stalemates that antagonized all interested parties.

The short version of this long and involved history is hard to capture, but the chapter titles attempt to describe this process. It begins with a *gathering* of lands and ideas brought together to form the seeds for the system, which was in place by end of the nineteenth century. It continues with *forming* the system and developing the agencies meant to manage them according to newly defined purposes, which were mostly in place by the second decade of the twentieth century. During the early to mid-twentieth century, roughly the 1920s through 1960s, a hinge in the history of public lands swings. After setting up the system, now the agencies truly started *managing* the land intensively, intervening at multiple scales to an unprecedented degree, from tourists and trees to grazing animals and manipulating wildlife. Such an increase in use and management generated a backlash that also combined with better science and new ways of looking at ecological communities. Rather than using and managing resources, *balancing* uses came to be valued from the 1960s forward with new legislation and procedures that shifted the purpose and administration of public lands. In the end, however, the new balance satisfied few and *polarizing* political conflicts continued as the public land kept changing. We are all wondering what happens next.

Or we can consider the Arendtian table. The metaphor suggests that the lands themselves are the table around which a public gathers to observe and consider it. The initial period saw an uneven audience, and even the table kept shapeshifting. Soon, it took a more solid form with a few powerful people running the meeting. In time, the size of the table and the audience grew, and with that growth came new perspectives and ideas to be considered. A result of that growth was even more people offering quite distinct ideas that challenged the traditional way things were done. For those who had long done things one way, the new conversation around the table felt challenging, even threatening. Soon, the table no longer appeared round but long and narrow, and people could not see everything or everyone. Attention could not be drawn to the same object any longer. This is the crisis we now face: we shout across a divide rather than focus attention and productive energy on shared space.

For most of their history, the public lands were held up by the majority of Americans and the agency managers as a collection of resources to be used wisely. To be certain, a group has always dissented from that narrow view and saw the public lands as places that inspired people. The landscapes of places like Yosemite, Yellowstone, and the Grand Canyon can hardly fail to capture one's breath and imagination and fuel a sense of sublime pride of place. Yet another element of pride emerges in the political character of these lands. The poet Gary Snyder in *The Practice of the Wild* (1990) once explained that "In North America there is a lot that is in public domain, which has its problems, but at least they are problems we are all enfranchised to work on." The writer and activist Terry Tempest Williams put it even better in *The Hour of Land* (2016), a book that both interrogated and celebrated national parks on the National Park Service's centennial: "The integrity of our public lands depends on the integrity of our public process within the open space of democracy." Although Snyder and Williams have shown a great capacity to wonder at the beauty of the land itself, their comments focus our attention to the fact that these lands are enveloped in political systems. The American public is, as Snyder noted, empowered to shape decisions for these lands. And Williams recognized that the corruption of the political system corrupts these lands, that only with a system of public integrity can the lands and their human and nonhuman residents function wholly. This book seeks to capture this spirit, which animates me as a historian and citizen.

A NOTE ON TERMINOLOGY

I sometimes use the term "public's land" when I wish to emphasize this element of the system—its essential publicness, the fact that U.S. citizens own this land. I tend to rely on "public land" but occasionally will use "federal land" interchangeably with it. In the early 2000s, Bureau of Land Management (BLM) land became officially "public lands," but few commentators have used that term in such an exclusive and narrow way. Thus, I'm following common practice where "public lands" refer to the lands currently managed by the U.S. Forest Service, National Park Service, Bureau of Land Management, and U.S. Fish and Wildlife Service. Collectively, I often describe these lands, respectively, as "forests, parks, rangelands, and refuges." When I use "public domain," I am referring to lands not within the public land system and also not yet claimed by individuals or companies. In the nineteenth century, the public domain was vast but shrunk with various homesteading activities and then reservation of public lands. With the creation of the BLM, the public domain effectively was subsumed into the public land system. In this book, I do not examine the much smaller holdings of the Bureau of Reclamation or those controlled by parts of the U.S. Department of Defense, although technically those are "public lands," too.

1

Gathering

INTRODUCTION

THE HISTORY OF AMERICAN PUBLIC LANDS does not begin with the Homestead Act in 1862. It does not begin with the Constitution in 1787 that created the republic. It does not begin with the Northwest Ordinances of 1784, 1785, and 1787 during the period under the Articles of Confederation that established mechanisms to survey and incorporate new territory into the nation on equal footing. It does not begin with the Proclamation Line of 1763 that angered American colonists by preventing them from moving to land west of the Appalachian Mountains and helped to make land a unifying factor for rebellious Americans. True, all of these moments propelled the history of federal land. But a history of American public lands that seeks, like this one, to explain how the nation created the system that now comprises more than six hundred million acres and judge its environmental and political effectiveness must go back further, to the people who have been on the land since time immemorial. That is to say, the territory that the public land system gathers together began as Indigenous land. When creating the system, the American government sidestepped Native claims, ignoring them altogether or manipulating them for the advantages of citizens of the United States. (Native Americans were not universally U.S. citizens until 1924.) Although this book focuses largely on the development of the public land system and not a history of Native Americans and the land, it should be remembered that public lands were *always* Indian lands first, whether Diné or Anishinabe or Niimíipuu. These lands have not remained Indigenous due to a process often called settler colonialism whereby European and later American colonists sought to replace original inhabitants. The current system remains a living legacy of this ongoing process.

Therefore, in any American history that is a history of land, the story is one drenched in blood and broken promises. The English and then American dealings with Native Americans over land is a history of warfare, of conquest, of duplicity and, not infrequently, of interpersonal and state violence. The English love for property shaped how they colonized North America. (Although the French, Russian, and Spanish empires offered alternatives to the British empire, theirs were options that left comparatively small footprints on the legal and physical landscape and need not be a focus here.)

From the new nation's perspective, history grew out of a noble ideal. The land—the table on which the future was set—offered the roots of freedom required to keep the American republic, a world-historical experiment, viable. That viability depended on access to land, according to the worldview that shaped the policies that defined American land. So the nation acquired land to "secure the blessings of liberty to ourselves and our posterity," as the Constitution put it. But those who held the land, which included not only hundreds of Native nations but also eventually the British and Spanish empires, as well as the Republic of Mexico, often lost their liberty for Americans' dream of private ownership of land. This American experiment in land evolved and then foundered. Public lands were the result.

LOCKEAN IDEAS AND JEFFERSONIAN LAND

To understand American history is to consider land as part of the central narrative. Land formed the literal and metaphorical bedrock of the nation's history. From time immemorial, Indigenous lives sunk roots deeply in the land, a relationship that formed cultural identities and spiritual practices, as well as serving economic purposes of subsistence and trade. After a century of exploration, beginning in the seventeenth century, English colonists put their own stake in American ground where they sought both to gain quick riches and to build long-lasting communities from the comparatively abundant resources in North America. Cheap land pulled those colonists willing to take risks and with sufficient resources to travel across the Atlantic Ocean into an uncertain, but promising, future. Competing European empires met long-established Native communities. When conflict erupted, which happened regularly, land and other forms of property often sat squarely at the center. It is no wonder, perhaps, that Puritans conceived of this new place as "nature's nation" (ignoring that it was truly many Natives' nations).

Territorial claims fueled colonization. Land meant possibilities for, if not riches, at least betterment. Europeans sailed across the Atlantic as individuals and families, as part of churches and business enterprises, all aiming to make good in this new place. And making good meant transforming the land materially, to harvest resources from it and to make it yield crops, but first the land needed to be philosophically and legally reimagined as something other than kin as Indigenous peoples understood it. John Locke provided the key American colonists used to unlock a continent. A seventeenth-century English philosopher, Locke famously stated, "In the beginning, all the world was America." The passage fittingly came from the chapter "On Property" within his *Second Treatise of Government* (1690). Locke believed that in a so-called state of nature, all people were free to act on their own accord provided they not hurt others. Further, and crucially for a history of public land, Locke saw nature as originally held in common, unowned. When humans applied labor to the land, they transformed it into property to be held exclusive by owners—that is, by those who labored. Locke's critical passage read:

> Though the earth, and all inferior creatures, be common to all men, yet every man has a property in his own person: this no body has any right to but himself. The labour of his body, and the work of his hands, we may say, are properly his. Whatsoever then he removes out of the state that nature hath provided, and left it in, he hath mixed his labour with, and joined to it something that is his own, and thereby makes it his property. It being by him removed from the common state nature hath placed it in, it hath by this labour something annexed to it, that excludes the common right of other men: for this labour being the unquestionable property of the labourer, no man but he can have a right to what that is once joined to, at least where there is enough, and as good, left in common for others.

In simpler terms: when an individual applied labor to nature, land turned into property held exclusively by that individual. This framework furnished the intellectual justification for colonists acquiring land and dispossessing Indigenous peoples of their homes. To European colonists, conveniently blinded despite obvious contrary evidence, Native Americans provided no labor to the land and thereby did not own it; they merely lived off nature's bounty. (The more religious-minded added providential justification for overtaking Native homes, such as John Winthrop, the first governor of the Massachusetts Bay Colony who wrote in 1634, "For the natives, they are near all dead of the smallpox, so the Lord hath cleared our title to what we possess.") An Enlightenment figure, Locke laid foundations that attracted American intellectuals who found Lockean ideas about property especially irresistible.

Colonists did not privatize all land. Colonial New England villages used common pastures where multiple colonists grazed their livestock. Initially, keeping animals was a community responsibility. The animals themselves were individuals' property, but the common grazing area offered public space. As inequality increased, New Englanders enforced limits on access to the commons. The situation diverged in the Chesapeake region, where colonists devoted themselves so fully and quickly to tobacco that they let their livestock roam in the forests beyond the edge of farms. Colonial Virginians treated this land as open, unowned, public. These spaces in the American colonies were either short-lived or seen as exceptional, however. Land ownership, under Lockean principles, operated as the default system for free white men, and fences crossed the landscape to mark property boundaries. In describing how colonists transformed New England, the historian William Cronon aptly noted, "A people who loved property little had been overwhelmed by a people who loved it much." Perhaps no more astute assessment has been made in so few words to describe the shift from Native homelands to British property.

Thomas Jefferson took Lockean ideas and gave them a distinctly American voice. Jefferson was a Virginian whose Monticello plantation embodied the highest aspirations of the landowning elite; in his parlor, he displayed portraits of those who he believed were the three greatest men ever to have lived: Isaac Newton, Francis Bacon, and John Locke. Long before he became president in 1801 and long after, Jefferson thought seriously about land and its role for America, and he pondered questions about the lands that would compose the nation, because he saw national destiny rooted in the soil.

Jefferson drafted the Declaration of Independence, for example, using language reminiscent of Locke. Some historians have pointed out that American revolutionaries relied on Locke's natural law arguments in claiming independence, indicating that nature itself aligned with Americans' cause. Not only were the colonies far from the English nation, but the American abundance of land also allowed for greater land ownership, which conferred greater economic independence. These factors led to a separate sense of identity for the colonists and gradually weakened bonds with Britain. In addition, when Parliament prohibited American colonists from moving west of the Appalachian Mountains with the Proclamation Line of 1763, American resentment exploded. Accustomed to economic mobility, which often meant geographic mobility, Americans bristled at being contained to the coast, so they cast covetous eyes toward land rolling out toward the western horizon. This grievance, in fact, found its way into the Declaration of Independence, suggesting that the land in the West always guided the nation's dreaming.

Those lands, though, presented complications at the nation's founding. The American Revolution started with skirmishes at Lexington and Concord, Massachusetts, in April 1775. By July 1776, colonists united enough to sign the Declaration of Independence. But these former colonies did not ratify their governing document—the Articles of Confederation—until 1781, not long before the British surrendered at Yorktown. Perhaps predictably, the fate of western lands generated sharp disagreements. The area between the Appalachian Mountains and the Mississippi River lay in dispute and disrupted the process of the nation coming together. Six of the former colonies possessed well-defined western borders; seven had vague and overlapping claims. Led by Maryland, the landlocked states refused to sign on until the rest of the colonies relinquished their western territories. Maryland reasoned that the Revolution was meant to secure these lands from Britain by the sacrifices—the "blood and treasure"—of the thirteen newly independent colonies, and so the nation, collectively, deserved those western lands "as a common stock," as common land. Maryland's reasoning carried the day, and the Articles of Confederation created the American nation. And thus conflict over public lands was in the public square from the nation's inception. Although by no means did this create or even foreshadow the public land system that today covers more than six hundred million acres, it established the principle that the nation held some lands in common (and established the precedent of ignoring Native sovereign claims).

Few people remember much of significance from the short era when the Articles of Confederation guided the nation, but the trans-Appalachian West presented challenges to governing and addressing these issues. Maryland's position was that the public lands "be parcelled out at proper times into convenient, free and independent Governments." In other words, the nation needed a mechanism to create new states out of these territories, and although the Articles of Confederation proved inadequate in most ways, political leaders were up to this task. A series of laws designed to establish an orderly way to incorporate new states were passed. Jefferson's fingerprints covered them and left a lasting legacy.

After their victory over the British, Americans poured over the Appalachian Mountains and invaded the Native territories in the Ohio River Valley. The new nation needed a way to organize the territory being taken from Native nations like the Osage or Shawnee. Administering that far-flung land had confounded the British, and Americans were determined to do better. A series of land laws passed in the 1780s to solve the problem; Jefferson drafted the first, the Land Ordinance of 1784. This law established the principle that unorganized western land would become territories and eventually new states that would enter the nation on equal footing with other states. This law meant that the western part of the nation would not remain political colonies of eastern states. The next year, the Congress of the Confederation passed the Land Ordinance of 1785 and refined it further with the Northwest Ordinance of 1787, which etched Jefferson's ideals into practice, both in the law and on the landscape itself. Most important, the 1785 law established a survey system by which government surveyors would divide American land into square-mile sections that would then be sold by the national government. A simple enough function for government, perhaps, but it marked a significant intellectual and environmental watershed.

The Public Land Survey System squared and commodified the national landscape. Surveyors mapped lines across the public domain, which allowed the national government to sell off parcels to individuals, one of the debt-ridden nation's critical ways to raise revenue. The effort exemplified what the political theorist James C. Scott described as "seeing like a state," an effort by governments to make the world legible so that it might be easier to exert control and govern. This survey process in the early republic fully integrated American land into the market, turning it into property that individuals could buy and sell. The resulting grid pattern, reproduced across the continent—especially clear in the rectangular states in the central part of the continent—subjected ecological systems to a legal logic nonsensical to nature, something abstracted from the material world of life on the land. Rather than following rivers or slopes, American property would follow geometry and reduce the complicated arrangement of flora and fauna across landforms to easily sold blocks of property. This effort reflected the Enlightenment idea that nature should be rationalized and controlled by human intelligence (and governments). The land ordinances and associated surveys codified the national project of turning public land into property. The final punctuation was the Property Clause that was placed in the Constitution, drafted in 1787, that affirmed Congress's authority "to dispose of and make all needful Rules and Regulations respecting the Territory or other Property belonging to the United States."

So long has property been central to Americans thinking about land that it can be hard to remember the purpose behind such a reduction of a place teeming with life and diversity into platted lines to be sold. Again, Jefferson, whom the historian Steven Stoll characterized as an "agrarian philosopher," played a critical role. His only book, *Notes on the State of Virginia,* was published in 1785, the year after the Land Ordinance he authored. *Notes on the State of Virginia* included a faithful description of Virginia's geography, flora, and fauna. Jefferson also offered a deep reflection on the value he placed in land. Besides being an intellectual and a politician, Jefferson was a Virginian planter, and, as such, he found in agricultural life the key to economic independence and republican virtue. He wrote, "Those who labour in the earth are the chosen people of God, if ever he had a chosen people, whose breasts he has made his peculiar deposit for substantial and genuine virtue. It is the focus in which he keeps alive that sacred fire, which otherwise might escape from the face of the earth." The claim vested specific and significant roles for farmers as security for the newly independent nation and pointedly ignored Indigenous claims and practices, as well as the enslaved labor force that made southern agriculture profitable. Only the tillers of the soil, Jefferson argued, could be truly bound to the nation, because they were bound to the soil in ways laborers in factories or urban dwellers could never be. Small-scale independent farmers, known as yeomen, would maintain economic security—rooted in access to fertile land and its transformation into viable farms—and thus be able to promote the public interest rather than selfish private interests. "The small landholders are the most precious part of the state," Jefferson asserted, establishing perhaps an unquestioned preference that lingers even in the twenty-first century rhetoric of politicians and journalists courting rural American votes and voices. Virtue rooted in independent rural life was a central idea of republicanism, America's revolutionary political philosophy. Virtue was necessary for a republic to succeed; it was evident in people who eschewed personal luxury and private gain for the public good; it was safeguarded by economic self-sufficiency. From these republican presuppositions, Jefferson's "chosen people" carried the nation on their shoulders as they cleared and plowed the land and reaped the virtuous rewards of wheat, apples, and cotton.

Jefferson did a lot for land before he became president. When he ascended to the office, he was in the position to do even more. Although he saw himself as a conservative who adhered to a strict interpretation of the Constitution, Jefferson extended his constitutional authority when he thought necessary. And global geopolitics pushed France to present the American president with an unquestioned opportunity to purchase Louisiana, an area that stretched northwestward from the mouth of the Mississippi River to the Rocky Mountains and included virtually all of the Great Plains north of Texas. In 1803, for $15 million, the United States added nearly 530 million acres, roughly 23 percent of today's national land base. No single purchase or treaty settlement in U.S. history was bigger. For Jefferson the agrarian philosopher, Louisiana offered what seemed to be an almost limitless source of land for the yeoman farmers he imagined would be taking up plows and filling in the continent with independent virtue. Although the nation purchased land from France, scores of sovereign Indigenous nations lived and thrived on the plains, from the Sioux in the north to the Comanche in the south, both imperial nations growing in power at the nineteenth century's start. Jefferson and the rest of the U.S. government would not allow Native sovereignty to slow their plans. From Monticello or the White House, the view west into the future appeared to be small farms rolling ever onward, built by independent farmers taking control of the public domain and making it into property. Jefferson's vision and his blindnesses—to Native claims and to the ways this additional land expanded slavery and a decidedly non-yeoman agricultural system—influenced the physical landscape and the intellectual and cultural ways Americans understood the Great West, long outlasting its utility.

ACQUIRING THE PUBLIC DOMAIN

By the time of the Louisiana Purchase in 1803, only twenty-seven years after signing the Declaration of Independence, the American nation had created—by state cession or acquired by purchase—a public domain of more than 766 million acres. Buried beneath this land was a story of Indigenous dispossession, a story by turns duplicitous and violent and always discounting Native nations' sovereign claims. European and American colonialism disrupted Indigenous economic, political, and cultural ways, turning the expansion of the colonial projects into an example of environmental injustice. As historian Louis Warren succinctly explained it, "Only through the violent removal of Indian means to reproduce community and culture, only through destruction of their bodies, could the US turn Native American earth into American land." This land, taken and incorporated into the *American* nation, made the new nation wealthy, and the promise of its transformation into marketable products meant the future looked bright. The Louisiana Purchase initiated a new phase, and for the next six decades the nation experimented with two related activities: acquiring even more land and devising novel ways for it to be turned into the property of Americans.

From the earliest days of exploration, some visionaries imagined the great North American continent under a single ruler. Independence, declared in 1776 and secured by the Treaty of Paris in 1783, seemed fragile at first. The War of 1812 was evidence that the British still cast covetous eyes on their erstwhile colonies. But American victory bolstered national confidence. A treaty with Spain in 1819 brought Florida into American holdings, the last remaining eastern territory that had not been included in the nation as it now exists. A growing economy fueled largely by enslaved laborers growing and harvesting cotton pressed the nation's population westward. Cotton (and tobacco) used up land quickly, and keeping an enslaved labor force busy occupied planters. Meanwhile, the American population grew from four million in the first census of 1790 to nearly ten million just thirty years later. During the first seven censuses, population grew by roughly one-third every decade, an enormous transformation that made even the United States' vast landholdings start to feel crowded.

The South's agricultural expansion was tied to both overuse of land and expanding slavery, while the North's burgeoning grew out of analogous anxieties and other pressures. In New England, some small communities, like Concord, Massachusetts, where Henry David Thoreau lived, had developed a community agricultural system. This achievement sustained growing families for nearly two centuries, but in the nineteenth century, the community was approaching its limits. Population growth and pressures on the land's fertility forced adaptations. Typically, that meant the younger generations relocated westward. Inheritance patterns in which men owned land and gave half the farm to the oldest son only worked for so long before the next generation was pushed off family lands. So by the early nineteenth century, many New Englanders, crowded out of the Northeast, spilled west into the Ohio River Valley and beyond. On the one hand, such migration was a sign of national growth and was celebrated. On the other hand, a highly mobile populace did not constitute the stable, independent yeoman communities Jefferson envisioned and believed were necessary for maintaining virtue and independence.

American reformers launched a small crusade against haphazard agricultural practices. From the earliest colonial era, with so much land available, farmers developed practices of ease, not always of careful husbandry. In the early republic, the fate of the state seemed to rest in its soil. Discussing soil health was another way of considering the nation's fundamental health, economically and politically. Declining soil fertility weakened yields from farmers' fields, and American leaders—not just farmers—grew alarmed.

If Thomas Jefferson theorized the importance of land to a virtuous republic, another president, James Madison, brought some practical insight to the question. After Madison—another Virginian slaveholder and planter—stepped down from the nation's presidency in 1817, he ascended to the presidency of the Agricultural Society of Albemarle in Virginia, an organization Jefferson had cofounded. Madison delivered an address about the serious business of agriculture and the importance of soil. That an ex-president opined on soil indicates how central land and its health remained associated in the minds of leaders with the health of the nation. Madison worried about land impoverishment. Farming poor land or making good land poor through overuse threatened the basis of economic success, and that would undermine national success. In Madison's mind, poor husbandry practices developed when people were not sufficiently rooted to their land. Madison explained the upshot: "Any system . . . or want of system, which tends to make a rich farm poor, or does not tend to make a poor farm rich, cannot be good for the owner; whatever it may be for the tenant or superintendant [sic], who has transient interest only in it. The profit, where there is any, will not balance the loss of intrinsic value sustained by the land." Farmers needed to improve their lands, to develop a more permanent agriculture. For some observers, then and since, yeoman farmers would promote sustainable agriculture because they would not have the means to move to fresh land after ruining their farms. The argument said yeomen knew their land better and were vested more in making it work over generations.

Madison spoke at a formative moment, a time when Americans debated the future of the nation and agriculture. The two were inextricably tied. Madison stood on one side, arguing for improvement, and improvement stood for stability. American abundance, Madison thought, led to poor cropping habits. "In the early stages of our agriculture," Madison described, "it was more convenient, and more profitable, to bring new land into cultivation, than to improve exhausted land." More specifically, Madison and others like him advocated for a closed system in which animals consumed fodder and produced manure that could be reapplied to fields to return nutrients to the soil. This was a mixed husbandry system that colonists brought with them from England and that had thrived, at least temporarily, in New England. The closed, intensive agriculture, as opposed to the open, extensive practices, promised longer-term sustainability. Within just a couple decades of independence, then, an agricultural crisis came to the United States, one that enlisted former presidents.

Madison and similar intellectuals and practitioners worried about the expanding South, fearing the spread of slavery and what it might do to unsettle the fragile American republic. The scale of agriculture there with its production for global tobacco and cotton markets shattered the self-contained farm system, quickly dispensing with anything resembling a self-contained, mixed husbandry farm. Instead, leading southern farmers specialized and produced commodities that brought them great profits. Enterprising plantation owners sought more lands in the West. Texas first attracted their attention, but Texas was part of Mexico. Stephen Austin brought three hundred American families to Texas to colonize the northern Mexican frontier. More Americans immigrated, mostly illegally, to Texas, where Mexican officials soon tired of them, especially since Americans insisted on bringing with them their political economy of slavery. The practice had already been outlawed in Mexico. Trouble kindled and flamed, leading first to the independent Texas Republic in 1836 and then the annexation of Texas by the United States in 1845.

The instability of American borders—their frequent shifts to incorporate Florida and the Great Plains and then Texas—proved important to public lands history, because the existence of the public domain pulled Americans west. Had the Mississippi River been a hard border—if, say, it had functioned like a wall—history might have unfolded differently. But restless and greedy Americans, or simply the growing numbers of them, sought more land. Texas came into the United States not with unanimity. Some in political power consolidated against annexation and the concomitant expansion of slavery. One result was the coalescing of an ideology to justify and promote this type of American expansion as not only necessary but also good. The ideology incorporated ideas about religion and race and came to be called Manifest Destiny. Although much propelled this ideology, it is worth remembering that territory—that is, more land, and specifically more land held by the nation—fed the roots. Manifest Destiny was one of the indispensable tools used to build the table of public lands.

Historians credit an American journalist named John O'Sullivan with the term Manifest Destiny. Certainly the impulse to see white families grow and fill American lands had been evident since colonization, but agricultural expansion and declining soil fertility made this idea of destiny urgent. O'Sullivan merely put into words a common feeling among a certain class of whites. Writing in favor of annexing Texas, O'Sullivan said it would help fulfill the nation's "manifest destiny to overspread the continent allotted by Providence for the free development of our yearly multiplying millions." O'Sullivan did not so much invent the idea that a Protestant God favored the American project of occupying the entire continent as he gave voice to a common belief with roots stretching back to colonial times. Manifest Destiny assumed God's favor and white American superiority and thus ignored existing claims to the land, whether Mescalero Apache or Mexican, Ute or English. Suffused with this sense of superiority and confident in their economic, technological, and military might, Americans entered into a period of great violence and expansionist zeal.

Deploying both war and diplomacy, the nation gathered land to quickly secure its continental empire. In 1846, a negotiated treaty with Britain put the Oregon Country into the United States, an addition of 183,386,240 acres west of the Rocky Mountains and north of Mexican territory. From 1846 to 1848, the United States fought Mexico for its holdings, culminating in the Treaty of Guadalupe Hidalgo in 1848 that brought another 388,680,960 acres to the country. The nation bought some disputed Texas territory in 1850, added a slice of northern Mexico in what is now southern Arizona in 1853, and then purchased Alaska in 1867. This new territory accrued to the public domain more than a billion acres in two decades. By any measure, this was an audacious act.

This period was also marked by racism and violence, promoted slavery and lawlessness, fed dispossession and displacement. Manifest Destiny overwrote Native claims, and its everyday actions crossed into genocide. None of it troubled enough Americans to stop it. Opponents of expanding slavery stymied congressional politics at times, but the idea that the vast continent awaited its destiny to be turned into property by white owners was barely considered and rarely questioned.

DISPOSING THE PUBLIC DOMAIN BEFORE THE HOMESTEAD ACT

In the table metaphor for this history of public lands, the tabletop itself is the land. So, this era after independence, from the Louisiana Purchase to buying Alaska, focused on creating a larger and larger table. And acquiring so much territory constituted a national plan meant to promote virtue, independence, and economic growth. But the nation required a mechanism to transfer that land into individual hands, to make it private property on which individuals would invest labor. The land ordinances of the 1780s were both foundations and blueprints. They allowed for the steady accretion of states to the union, the public land survey making it orderly and rational, albeit ecologically ludicrous: there are few straight lines in nature. For the U.S. government, the nineteenth century was a long experiment in land redistribution, sometimes led by Congress and sometimes by the people (and occasionally by the corporations).

According to those foundational land acts, land would be disposed of at public auctions. However, Americans seldom followed such best-laid plans. Some enterprising farmers preceded the surveyors and squatted on the public domain without purchasing the land. Moving beyond the edge of white governments, these squatters favored just getting started with improving on the land, clearing the forest, building cabins and barns, and growing crops and livestock. These squatters resisted various efforts by Congress to dismiss their claims. So in the first third of the century, preemption became the solution, a largely accepted fact from the people on the land. Defined by land policy scholar Paul Wallace Gates as "the preferential right of a settler on public lands to buy his claim at a modest price," preemption was ultimately a recognition that state power was too weak to restrain farmers from migrating and settling.

In some significant aspects, squatters seem quintessentially American. They were the go-getters, the pioneers, those who became the stuff of ballads and folktales. They plunged across the frontier, out of the clearing and into the woods, and, according to the historian Frederick Jackson Turner in 1893, such people and their continuous westering explained American history. That act of pressing forward into the wilderness—the public domain—created Americans, something unique in world history, so went the patriotic claim. At the frontier, individuals quickly formed communities, in Turner's words, at "the meeting point between savagery and civilization." Democracy sprang forth from these brave men. Turner's story resonated when he told it because it resembled the story those people told themselves. With the gift of hindsight and wider angles of historical vision, we can recognize more myth than history in such a characterization, although the selective frame makes these preemptors no less American. The facts make them arguably even more quintessentially American.

Squatters violated the law. Going west in advance of the surveyors and before the land was for sale was illegal but still common. Doing so led to conflict and war with Native nations. When that happened, white farmers either violently resisted locally or received assistance from state or federal forces, routinely benefiting from state power. Farmers intruding on Indigenous land not only brought troops west but also forced Congress to devise a method to protect the property rights whites believed they had established. Initially, Congress deplored the legal mess squatters created. In 1807, it passed a law explicitly making them trespassers; however, local governments rarely enforced it. By the 1820s and 1830s, with more representatives in the House from states created out of the former public domain, congressional attitudes lightened, and legislators passed laws that exempted squatters. The House Public Lands Committee viewed these trespassers as "benefactors, not malefactors," as two public land history specialists, Samuel Trask Dana and Sally Fairfax, put it, "whose enterprise and contribution to the development of the country should be regarded by permitting them to buy without competition the land on which they had settled." Although this is not how Turner had portrayed American democracy proceeding on the frontier, by forcing military assistance and making Congress accommodate them, squatters did propel American democracy, again at the expense of Indigenous rights.

The preemption laws facilitated westward (dis)possession. But initially they were few, and preemptions never reached even 100,000 total acres for a single year in the 1820s. The more comprehensive Preemption Act (1830) boosted the process. It permitted settlers who squatted on land without a legal claim to buy up to 160 acres for $1.25 an acre. The law rewarded those who had jumped ahead of surveyors and other legal institutions. It also set up a political pattern. Followers of Jefferson, who by the 1820s largely fell into the Democratic Party, favored the law, seeing in it a way to support the yeomanry and prevent concentrated economic power. It united westerners and southerners who shared an interest in expanding into western territories with as few restraints as possible. Their opponents, the National Republicans who became Whigs in the

1830s led by Senator Henry Clay of Kentucky, thought such legislation encouraged the riffraff to migrate and both rewarded and resulted in fraud and speculation. From 1830 to 1835, preemptions shot up and averaged almost 350,000 acres annually, while sold land averaged more than five million acres over that half-decade.

In 1841, Congress passed another Preemption Act, much like its earlier counterpart to give squatters rights to the land, but with more expansive conditions. The earlier laws had all been limited in time (one year) or space (certain states only). The 1841 Preemption Act allowed 160 acres for $1.25 an acre to heads of households, widows, and single men at least twenty-one years old who were citizens or who had declared their intention to become a citizen. These qualifications meant that African Americans and Native Americans were excluded and, though widows and heads of households might include women, all preemption laws (indeed, all land laws) overwhelmingly were designed for white men.

The Preemption Act of 1841 accomplished and reflected several things. One, it reified republican preferences for stable land ownership in comparatively small plots. It made ineligible people who owned 320 acres or more and those who left their preemption land to take up residence on other parts of the public domain. Two, it showed that land policy emphasized a vision for society that was agrarian and white. Three, it accepted facts on the ground—the settlers possessing and developing land—despite preferring an orderly development of land following Enlightenment principles as represented by the grid from the Northwest Ordinance. Finally, the 1841 law recognized indirectly that the federal plan to raise money from selling off public lands in large tracts at auction had failed. Instead, reluctantly, squatting no longer was seen as illegal but, in Gates's words, "an honorable step in the pioneering process toward farm ownership." Nevertheless, problems persisted. Fraud was common, because land speculation could be a route to wealth quicker than a route to republican virtue. The legal requirements for improving the land and establishing residency were easily met and even more easily, in Gates's words, "evaded by false testimony," which led to a "growing disrespect for land law enforcement that reached its extreme in later years." In other words, some used preemption to get rich and acquire more land than the law intended, weakening the system's foundation.

In the age of Manifest Destiny, it was not uncommon for ideals to succumb to more troubling realities. The heady political rhetoric of democracy that propelled American movement westward actually eclipsed the democratic rights of those already living in the West. The idealized agrarian republic following rational plans that emerged in Jefferson's mind and Congress's laws became imperfect realizations on the ground in the footprints of squatters and in the bank accounts of speculators. But inconsistencies and politics fit together like hand in glove. A renewed sense of idealism pooled in the 1850s and spilled over in full expression during the 1860s as the nation tore itself apart.

The prize of the Mexican-American War was the greater Southwest. Because of its Spanish and then Mexican history, land law functioned differently with legacies that continued once the United States acquired the region. Rather than sell or give off parcels of 160 acres, large land grants—up to a million acres and more—went to individuals who would promote settlement. These grants functioned as an incentive to bolster population in areas far from colonial or national centers of power. Some of that land functioned explicitly as a commons for the community to use, while the rest went to enterprising farmers and ranchers, defined not in a grid but by natural features. The priority for common benefit and geographic specificity offered a strong contrast to the tradition in the rest of the United States. The 1848 Treaty of Guadalupe Hidalgo guaranteed land rights for Mexican citizens who chose to remain. However, land titles often were hard to prove to the satisfaction of American legal officials, who were frequently not disinterested parties. Conflicts over this land and whether it was truly in the public domain or whether it was part of a long-standing community's right continued well into the twentieth century.

For public lands history, the Oregon Country offered a more representative laboratory. In the 1830s, foreign missionaries, like Marcus and Narcissa Whitman and Henry and Eliza Spaulding, had arrived to convert the Native peoples. Their conversion strategy included introducing agriculture in forms that would have been familiar to Europeans but not to the Cayuse or Nez Perce. A federal official, Elijah White, traveled to Nez Perce country in 1842 and dictated eleven laws, the main purpose of which seemed to establish the idea of property and protect the missionaries and other European Americans who claimed it. One rule, for example, read, "Anyone harming crops or taking down a fence so livestock could come in would pay damages and suffer twenty-five lashes." The existence of this enterprise—of Christian conversion, of agricultural conversion, of property conversion—predated American acquisition of the Northwest. (At the time, the United States and Great Britain agreed to jointly occupy Oregon Country.)

As soon as the nation secured the region, Congress induced Americans into the Northwest with the Oregon Land Donation Act in 1850. The law confirmed land grants made over the previous several years to the amount of 320 acres per white husband and another 320 acres for his wife. The law allowed married white couples 320 acres total if they arrived between 1850 and 1854, a provision meant to encourage migration of families to Oregon and that reinforced the white nuclear family as normative in the republican experiment of widespread farming. As historian Peter Boag has explained, Jefferson's republicanism "did enshrine a certain set of values about sexuality, the primacy of the male-female couple, the family, and gender behaviors and roles and their relationship to the land." Besides imposing certain cultural expectations on the land, the Oregon Land Donation Act also undermined an existing social order. The federal government had not yet negotiated with the Tribal Nations in the Northwest; thus this generous land donation act dispossessed Native peoples of their territories. The legislation called for negotiating treaties, but treaty councils occurred in 1854 and 1855 only as the law was expiring. The law secured 2.5 million acres from the public domain into private ownership and served as a model for the Homestead Act a few short years later.

THE HOMESTEAD ACT

Although Congress passed dozens of laws to shift the public domain into private hands, the Homestead Act of 1862 remains the largest in political and cultural imaginations. It is, as it were, the centerpiece on the table. So it deserves some careful consideration.

Homesteading rested on the idea of improvement, a term that possessed both legal and symbolic meanings. Most simply, for legal requirements, "improvements" for land being preempted or homesteaded meant settlers built fences, a cabin or home of sorts, planted crops, and the like. Wilderness—raw land—in this formulation was bad or incomplete and needed to be improved or even redeemed. Improvement also was associated with the sort of intensive farming James Madison advocated. Adding improvements to a farm meant the farmer could stick it out, rather than having to strike out for new land. Improvement offered signs of permanence, as the historian Steven Stoll concluded in his study of soil and society: "Permanence of society, landscape, and home was the paramount value of improvement." As Madison's presence foreshadowed, politics found a home in discussions of land and improvement.

In the years leading up to the Civil War, party politics reflected these ideas refracted through the lens of slavery. In 1848, struggling to contain slavery—specifically, to keep it from extending into the lands acquired from Mexico—the Free Soil Party formed. After running presidential candidates in 1848 and 1852, the party collapsed, only to be reconstituted into the Republican Party by 1854. Slavery undergirded the parties' positions, but the free soil elements of the new Republicans explicitly connected land and slavery. Although Jeffersonians had long seen smallholder agriculture as the embodiment of American republicanism, the Republicans identified slavery with poor land and agricultural practices, an added element to the emerging antislavery arguments. Frederick Law Olmsted, who went on to fame as the designer of New York City's Central Park, traveled through the South and in 1856 observed, "Labor is the creator of wealth. There can be no honest wealth, no true prosperity without it." The Lockean foundation to Olmsted's perception was clear. And Republicans in Congress aimed to build up a policy apparatus that supported what they viewed as a proper society grounded in free labor, as opposed to slave labor, and free land, as opposed to aristocratic plantations.

The Republican Party promoted a vision of free labor yeomanry in which the West could become a bulwark against expanding slavery and extend the traditional Jeffersonian ideals. Some Republican leaders argued that slavery destroyed soil, which would thwart the development of American civilization. In 1850, William Seward spoke in the Senate and declared that free settlement in the West would "bless the earth, under the sway of our own cherished and beneficent democratic institutions." In Seward's mind, the land itself would benefit from extending free labor, because enslaved labor exhausted soil, but free labor would be likely to improve it. To exemplify this belief, one abolitionist reformer set up a community of black farmers in the Adirondacks to test this vision of dual improvement: of land and of people. The free labor ideology meant stable communities, according to its acolytes.

No one typified that view better than Abraham Lincoln, the first Republican president. Although both became presidents, Lincoln and Jefferson came from different social stratas: Jefferson from a family with vast landholdings, while Lincoln was born in a one-room cabin. Jefferson theorized about the importance of land and improvement; Lincoln embodied that idea, working land personally and seeing improving nature and improving oneself as of a piece. So, Lincoln became an ideal vehicle to extend the Republican ideals of improvement across the nation. Secession furnished the opportunity.

Once voters elected Lincoln in 1860, southern states began seceding. Since the Confederacy literally left the country, the Democratic Party's strength, which rested in the South, could no longer offer effective resistance. That allowed the Republican Party to pass long-stalled legislation to advance a social vision with land transformation at its heart. In 1862 alone, Lincoln signed the Pacific Railroad Act, which established the governmental support necessary to sponsor a transcontinental rail line that would link free labor agricultural communities across the nation, and the Land Grant College Act (also known as the Morrill Act), which donated land, often taken from Native peoples, to states to fund agricultural colleges where scientific research could be conducted and disseminated to support agricultural improvement for community stability; he also authorized the creation of a cabinet-level Department of Agriculture (USDA) designed to promote agricultural interests, which were seen as, in one advocate's words, "the very foundation of our national greatness and prosperity." These developments created a system that grew—an economic lifeline in the railroads, an educational and research apparatus in the land-grant colleges, and a governmental arm with the USDA. These laws together reflected how Republicans committed the federal government to promoting economic development, consistently at the expense of Native American lands and opportunities.

Those measures were necessary arteries, but the heart—for the people—beat with the Homestead Act, a plan to quickly turn the public domain into small farms. The initial proposals had been bipartisan. The first proposed homestead law came in 1844 from an Illinois member of Congress, Robert Smith, a Democrat. Even in 1862, when the debate over the law was in full flower, William S. Holman, an Indiana Democrat, stated, "In my judgment, the policy of applying the public lands in such manner as to increase the number of independent farmers, of secure and independent homesteads, decentralizing and diffusing the wealth of the nation, is of the very first importance; vital, indeed, to the ultimate stability of the Republic." Meanwhile, the Republican Speaker of the House, Galusha A. Grow, noted that the law had "the unmistakable approval of the popular will." With bipartisan support and popular favor—not to mention the fact that the opponents were by this time in the Confederacy—the law passed on May 20, 1862.

The law was so popular in part because of its generous terms. For heads of households, the law provided 160 acres to citizens and those who declared their intent to become citizens. For immigrants, the law offered a pathway to Americanization. Homesteaders, then, Americanized the land while the land worked to Americanize the immigrants. (However, African Americans and Native Americans need not apply, other than rare exceptions.) The land would be free as long as the homesteader lived on the land for five years and improved it. Legally, improvement meant "actual settlement and cultivation," to prevent absentee ownership or speculation, which violated the democratic spirit and intent of the law. Improvement bundled up a set of Jeffersonian ideologies that enshrined free labor and argued that applying reason and labor to the natural environment would ensure success for self and nation, an experience President Abraham Lincoln exemplified through his own life.

Always, the homesteading ideal served practical and ideological goals. During the Civil War, Republican leaders saw the Homestead Act as meeting certain practical ends: it was a way to develop farms and increase revenue from internal taxes. However, the law's larger significance in American society and economy would be to develop the West and integrate (with the help of the growing railroad networks) the region with the national economy. The mid-nineteenth-century economic vision of the Republican Party was on full display here. The government's responsibility was to facilitate economic development by enabling laws that, in the words of one scholar, "released individual freedom." After facilitating that release, government would step back and allow individuals to generate economic growth. The Homestead Act is the quintessential example of this ideology and has long been celebrated as such, covering over its exclusions and dispossessions.

How should we ultimately understand the consequences of the Homestead Act from the perspective of public land and environmental history? For the public domain, the Homestead Act accomplished its work well, getting somewhere between 270 million and 285 million acres into individuals' hands. In the past, some scholars used faulty data and premises to argue that homesteading constituted only a minor role and that the majority of homesteads failed to "prove up," the term used to designate that someone satisfied the requirements to obtain a free and clear title. However, recently scholars have reexamined data and calculated that in the West, about two-thirds of new farms between 1863 and 1900 originated as homesteads, and these met the act's obligations between five and six times out of ten—a slight majority. The Homestead Act continued the odyssey of transforming land into property, America's vast space into farms, public land into private fields. It symbolized the nation's agrarian logic, an idealized economic and social program, but that logic would founder on the shoals of a challenging environment.

CRACKS AND ADJUSTMENTS

Homesteading could not meet all the grand dreams theorists and policymakers imagined for it. Conceived by a nation whose center of gravity lay in the East, it faced ecological challenges when transported out of the Ohio and Mississippi River valleys. The 160-acre homestead prize worked well for family farmers in the well-watered Midwest but ran aground on some environmental challenges west of the 100th meridian, where rainfall came more sporadically and in less quantity than most American farmers were able to accommodate. Although a majority of homesteaders across the West "proved up" their claims, sizable numbers did not, and in certain states failure rates were high.

When government surveyors imposed their invisible lines over the arid West's parched landscape, cracks appeared. The land ordinances from the 1780s, for all their brilliant prospects, failed as a universal blueprint. That was the message of John Wesley Powell, a Civil War veteran who lost part of his arm at the Battle of Shiloh and who in 1869 led the first river expedition down the Colorado River through the Grand Canyon. Congress instructed the West be explored and surveyed in preparation for systematic resettlement—after shoving aside or killing many members of the West's Native nations. This process would precede the next step of developing resources. Congress named Powell the head of the Geographical and Geological Survey of the Rocky Mountain Region (known usually as the Powell Survey), where he thoroughly explored the Colorado Plateau. His numerous expeditions through the West beginning in 1867 through the 1870s made Powell the leading expert on the West's lands and peoples. In 1879, he published his *Report on the Lands of the Arid Region of the United States*, a radical assessment that flew in the face of received wisdom and offered alternatives, something that writer Wallace Stegner called a "blueprint for a dryland democracy" in his classic biography of Powell, *Beyond the Hundredth Meridian* (1954). Powell's *Report* doused the fires of enthusiasm that homesteading should march westward across the plains, over the mountains, and through the interior West on its way to the Pacific coast and a continental empire.

Powell recognized in the West a diverse landscape, one with different ecological characteristics that demanded distinct laws to govern them. The Northwest Ordinance made no sense as a universal, self-replicating property-making machine; 160 acres made no sense as a universal unit designed for optimal agricultural success for a yeoman farm family. Observing Utah, Powell found a land in transition with a future different from what preceded it in Illinois, where he had spent much of his life. Members of the Church of Jesus Christ of Latter-day Saints, more commonly called Mormons, migrated to the Great Salt Lake Valley in 1847 and launched successful communities based on an irrigation enterprise that was cooperatively built and maintained to deliver just-adequate water to small farms averaging between 10 and 50 acres. That communitarian spirit, combined with a realistic approach to scarce water resources, inspired Powell, who envisioned the region adopting new land laws to guide the West along similar pathways. Rather than carving up the public domain in a 160-acre pattern, Powell called for two new laws, one each for governing irrigable and grazing land. For the former, a group of at least nine people would organize an irrigation district and each person would obtain no more than 80 acres. Each would have guaranteed shares of water, delivered by a system they together made, since "aggregated capital or cooperative labor will be necessary," he explained. "Here, individual farmers, being poor men, cannot undertake the task." Similarly, for grazing land, Powell proposed grazing districts where homesteaders would control at least 2,560 acres, a significant increase from the Homestead Act's 160-acre limit since feeding livestock off sparse rangelands required much more space. Helpfully, Powell drafted the legislation to do this and enlisted a few congressional allies. By 1890, his thinking had evolved further when he argued that the West ought to be governed by cooperative commonwealths defined by watersheds, since water was the limiting factor for settlement.

Powell's revolutionary plan to reorient the mechanisms to extend the Jeffersonian dream failed to generate enthusiasm. Stegner believed it was because Powell was too radical. His *Report*, in Stegner's words, "was a complete revolution in the system of land surveys, land policy, land tenure, and farming methods in the West, and a denial of almost every cherished fantasy and myth associated with the Westward migration and the American dream of the Garden of the World." But even more than being revolutionary, Powell challenged "political forces who used popular myths for a screen, he was challenging the myths themselves, and they were as rooted in the beliefs of religion." In this telling, Powell's was a brave, prescient voice raising an alarm about a federal policy framework doomed to fail in the West.

Powell was not alone but a part of an emerging group of conservationists who diagnosed problems with American land use and began reaching toward some tentative solutions. No one was more significant than George Perkins Marsh, a Vermonter and diplomat, who helped create an intellectual and scientific context for ideas like Powell's and further reforms. In 1864, Marsh published *Man and Nature; or, Physical Geography as Modified by Human Action*. The book marked a watershed in American thinking, as it presented a view of nature changed dramatically and negatively by humans and their economies. In one of his most famous lines, he summarized human tendencies: "[M]an is everywhere a disturbing agent. Wherever he plants his foot, the harmonies of nature are turned to discords." Having served widely in the Mediterranean

Basin, Marsh observed the terrible consequences of deforestation and more general environmental degradation there, and he saw signs of this decline developing in the United States. *Man and Nature* offered a clarion call, awakening in Americans a sense that environmental destruction followed human activity and that such transformations might be permanently deleterious. He recommended maintaining forests to protect watersheds. Marsh helped American link forests and water together and tie them with conservation in a vision of a balanced landscape.

Marsh's ideas and Powell's plans to revolutionize the public land system helped reformers pressure Congress. The legislative branch was not quite ready for revolutionary change, and Congress still remained primarily interested in making private property out of the public domain. With the Homestead Act failing in more than four out of ten attempts, Congress tried to adjust the means to get to the same ends. These efforts reveal a willingness, even a necessity, to adjust Jefferson's methods but without reassessing the yeoman dream.

Congress offered a series of changes in the public land system, changes that both simply adjusted existing patterns and rewrote them. While Powell explored the Colorado Plateau, Congress tinkered with the existing ideology and its implementation that the public domain needed to be transferred to private hands for economic development. Policymakers recognized deficiencies in the western environment. The Great Plains had too few trees, so they passed the Timber Culture Act in 1873, doubling the size of homesteads to 320 acres if colonizers would plant 40 of those acres in trees. The West also had too little water, so in 1877 Congress passed the Desert Land Act, giving married farmers up to 640 acres if they promised to irrigate it. (Single farmers received only half that, still doubling the Homestead Act's provisions.) Then Congress belatedly recognized that some western land was not suitable for small-scale farming, so legislators passed the Timber and Stone Act in 1878 that allowed the purchase of 160 acres for logging and mining. As a whole, these laws poorly met their goal of advancing economic development. According to the public land scholar Paul Wallace Gates, only 25 percent and 26 percent of the acreage claimed under the Timber Culture and Desert Land Acts respectively proved up. Meanwhile, the Timber and Stone Act quickly became notorious for its use of so-called dummy entrymen who, for a fee, quickly signed over their acreages to timber, mining, or railroad corporations. In such schemes, the land became private, but not for the Jeffersonian family farm.

By the end of the 1870s, the nation's public domain stood at a crossroads. After nearly a full century, the national policy was found wanting, or at least incomplete. By opening up the door for adjustments, though, Congress and conservationists tacitly admitted that the universalizing land ordinances from Jefferson's age might not work in every place.

CONCLUSION: PUBLIC LANDS COMMISSION

By the final third of the nineteenth century, some Americans questioned the land system as it existed in the United States. While some saw evidence of wastefulness, a profligacy with natural resources, others who were often aligned with larger corporate interests—mining companies, ranching conglomerates, timber interests—wanted access to even more land or resources. The beginning of debates stirred at the public lands table that had been assembled with relatively little change in its ideology since the republic's dawn. The writing had been on range, so to speak, for a while. Congress had amended homesteading laws—the Desert Land Act and the Timber Culture Act for instance—to respond to apparent failures and to attempt to create a system better adapted for the West, which presented a complicated climate and difficult landscape for standard agricultural practices. Such changes and challenges confused what had once seemed a fairly straightforward process.

Worried about its ignorance of facts on the ground, Congress authorized a Public Lands Commission in 1879, something that land policy experts Samuel Trask Dana and Sally K. Fairfax called "the first explicit congressional recognition that a comprehensive public lands policy might be necessary or appropriate." Congress directed the commission primarily to systematize federal work in the western public domain. The commission was to codify the laws for surveying and disposing of the land and to standardize land classifications (e.g., pasturage, irrigable, timber). In addition, Congress wanted the commission to recommend "the best methods of disposing of the public lands of the western portion of the United States to actual settlers." These instructions still assumed the highest purpose of the public domain focused on privatizing that land in individual hands. The phrase "actual settlers," however, suggested a concern about fraud that put the public domain into the hands of corporations, absentee owners, or speculators, problems that soon gained much attention. But the commissioners generally assumed that Congress was asking for assessments that would lead to, at most, a "readjustment" rather than "sweeping changes" of "a radical character." Consistent with this assumption, the commission announced that it still considered the chief role of public land policy "to secure bona fide occupation and utilization by actual settlers" and that large concentrations of acreage in individual hands was "not only unrepublican, but . . . essentially unjust." For the most part, the commissioners concluded that the system "generally reached" those goals, "though not without occasional failures." These "occasional failures" included individuals amassing more land than Congress intended.

In addition, a sizable portion of western lands did not fit with the laws currently written, for settlers could not settle and survive in many timbered regions or on many open ranges with a 160-acre claim. The commissioners explained, "A very great proportion of the land of the west cannot become settled and pass into private ownership, because under the terms of existing laws it is not desirable to the settler to acquire them." This simple, matter-of-fact statement undermined the foundational assumptions of American public land law. As such, it landed on Congress with a thud. Land was supposed to become property. What was the commission saying? What did it mean for the region's future? Problems seemed destined to foul up the future even more.

As instructed, the commission produced their *Report of the Public Lands Commission* (1880), surpassing eight hundred pages, the vast majority of which included the testimony of various public officials and statistics about federal land laws. Noting that Congress had passed some remedial legislation (e.g., the Desert Land Act), the commission objected to these piecemeal correctives, arguing for a "perfectly harmonious and congruous part of a symmetrical whole." This commission hoped to rectify this fragmentation problem by classifying lands. The system then in place assumed all land was arable, something belied by the mountainous and arid West, so the commission recommended designating land into categories—Arable Lands, Mineral Lands, Irrigable Lands, Pasturage

Lands, and Timber-Land—and each of these land types required new laws that addressed their specific geographic and economic realities.

One of the commissioners, John Wesley Powell, saw his influence in the report's recommendations to solve at least some of the dilemmas the commission had uncovered. After his 1878 *Report on Lands of the Arid Region*, he now found another opportunity to make his case that much of the West could not support agriculture as practiced elsewhere. And that meant Congress needed to adjust land laws. Following Powell's earlier ideas, the Public Lands Commission recommended selling tracts of 2,560 acres where the environment seemed solely suited for grazing. Another notable recommendation included classifying timberlands and then *withdrawing the land from sale*, retaining them under federal control. Local settlers could use the timber to build, but not for commercial purposes. The government could sell timber only on alternating sections but must keep trees smaller than eight inches to ensure reproduction of the forests.

These recommendations were nothing short of revolutionary, a radical break from the status quo and the beginning of a new era. As Dana and Fairfax put it, the *Report of the Public Lands Commission* marked "the beginning of the end of the all-land-is-the-same, 160-acre-parcel approach to resource management." In other words, the commission argued that geographic or ecological specificity should be reflected in the nation's land laws.

This commission and its report set an important precedent and pattern. Congress's call for a commission acknowledged that all was not well with the public domain. Periodically, every couple of decades, Congress would empanel commissions or ask for studies to report on the public lands and make recommendations. These studies drew on recognized experts, typically from within the federal government. As such, they tended to act from a position of power and expertise believed to be rooted in scientific understandings, at least as adequate as available. Yet, as inherently political figures, they operated within constrained circumstances. Commissions like this one usually recognized shortcomings in federal management, and yet their solution was almost always more (but better) federal management, often through the adjustment of laws and the further application of scientific management. Any radical recommendations rarely reached a receptive Congress because the legislative body was conservative, often favored other values, and preferred short-term thinking over long-term. Still, the various public lands commissions and studies did inform Congress—and by extension the public—of the state of the public lands.

By the end of the nineteenth century, then, public resources split into two tracks. On the one hand, the liberal policies of the government continued. In fact, homesteads increased. On the other hand, another policy framework edged in. Seeing wasteful use of resources and being concerned that some lands could not sustain what up to then was seen as "normal" economic development, the federal government recognized the need for adjustments and restraints. This became the conservation movement, a reform effort that tried to take stock and reorient the way the state and the public interacted with public resources. It was born out of both fear and confidence. Conservation reset the table.

2

Forming

INTRODUCTION

AFTER TRAVELING IN THE SAME PATHWAYS for a century, public land policy was difficult to divert. Difficult, but not impossible. Critics like George Perkins Marsh, reformers like John Wesley Powell, and everyday farmers and miners and ranchers saw shortcomings in the existing system and agitated for change that might establish a legal regime that more effectively facilitated their use of public resources—or their protection. Furthermore, signs from the land itself signaled problems. Fires, floods, and erosion remade the land and reduced ecosystems' resilience. This deterioration in nature was visible to the naked eye, often from miles away. These factors pushed Americans together, around their public land table, to consider different ways to think about the nation's lands and how to use and administer them.

The table had been created in the colonial era making land a key part of the nation's destiny, but destinies evolve. In this new era, the table setting changed. It was as though the nation set the small kitchen table for a family dinner, but guests arrived and compelled them to move to the larger, formal dining room that remained unfinished. Accordingly, the piecemeal arrangement led to many arguments. In fact, the conversations about resources and conservation during these years cycled through waves of idealism and confidence, on the one hand, and then through contention and debate, on the other. So tracking this history requires close attention to the ways history's trajectory veered off and how that veering also split into competing factions. Sitting around that table, in those days, meant endless conversations and debates.

BEYOND PRIVATE PROPERTY

Given the cultural and political values Americans had invested in land and its power to secure and represent independence, a strong countervailing and equally inspiring impulse would be needed to change even part of this trajectory. A tragedy unfolding on the Great Plains and two uniquely scenic landscapes inspired the shifts and set important precedents.

Two things impressed Europeans and Americans when they first encountered the Great Plains: the lack of trees and the abundance of bison. In the early nineteenth century, when Americans began their steady invasion of the homelands of the Lakota and Kiowa and more, they were witnessing the recent results of a nomadic revolution that had occurred among many plains nations. The horse's return provided an opportunity for new mobility, something many (but not all) tribes chose. This cultural and economic adaptation pressured bison populations and perhaps by the mid-nineteenth century already halved the number grazing on the plains. In the aftermath of the Corps of Discovery's successful continental crossing, more hunters and trappers crisscrossed the region. After millennia of dominance, the bison faced increased pressures from humans and their animals like horses whose habitats and food sources overwhelmingly overlapped with bison.

The center of the continent experienced an ecological revolution. And signs of collapse—both cultural and animal—appeared early. Beginning in the 1830s, observers remarked on the declining bison herds. A famous American artist, George Catlin, traveled to the plains being most interested in capturing American Indians on canvas before what many predicted to be an impending and inevitable disappearance. But Catlin's anxiety encompassed bison, too. In "melancholy contemplation," Catlin lamented the "noble animal in all its pride and glory," the American bison, "so rapidly wasting from the world." Catlin's main concern was the Native American population, but he recognized how deeply entwined were the plains tribes' culture and economy with the bison. So, in 1832, Catlin advocated government action, a policy to preserve "in their pristine beauty and wildness, in a magnificent park, where the world could see for ages to come, the native Indian in his classic attire, galloping his wild horse, with sinewy bow, and shield and lance, amid the fleeting herds of elks and buffaloes. . . . A nation's Park, containing man and beast, in all the wild and freshness of their nature's beauty." Catlin's idea was arguably the first national park proposal. Few among early advocates of preserving nature paid any attention to Native Americans, although his idea of sequestering tribes within a park presented some ethical problems. Yet his proposal reminds us that all the public lands and their histories are wrapped up with the history of the nations who first called the continent home and the ways land protection was bound up with the dispossession of tribal lands.

The destruction of the bison was one of the main dramas of the nineteenth century, but the Civil War struck a more discordant human tone. Amid the most devastating carnage of American lives in war, and just after Abraham Lincoln received for the second time the official nomination for president from the Republican Party in June 1864, Congress passed a short law having to do with a valley in California, seemingly far from Civil War battlefields. Lincoln signed it, giving to California a slice of the public domain—Yosemite Valley and the so-called Mariposa Big Tree Grove. The law required California to dedicate the land to "public use, resort, and recreation" and to provide for the "preservation, improvement, and protection of the property." The simple law did not even fill a single page in the *U.S. Statutes at Large*, but it signaled something new, a novel role for the federal government: establishing nature parks.

Not everyone welcomed this revolution, and the resulting conflict revealed a fracturing consensus around republican and Republican land policy. Removing land from the public domain meant removing it from the possibility of "improvement" as defined by a republican faith in transforming raw land into farmland through free labor. But throughout the 1850s, Frederick Law Olmsted and others had developed a new rationale for improvement, a way that public parks could offer civilizing influences too. In Olmsted's mind, public spaces open to all benefited society, just as did education or aid to children, so "the state ought to assist these sorts of things," Olmsted wrote in 1853. Many still argued that only actual settlers should be taking land from the public domain, but a new strand of thinking encouraged state involvement in various activities, including promoting parks.

Yosemite under state management proved to be contentious. The enabling legislation put a board of commissioners in charge, and it faced controversy over its handling of James Mason Hutchings, who claimed lands under preemption rights within Yosemite Valley and would not leave. The ensuing legal contest ended up at the U.S. Supreme Court in *Hutchings v. Low* (1872), in which Justice Stephen J. Field, a New Englander who had relocated to California during the Gold Rush, found against Hutchings. Field affirmed that the congressional power used to create Yosemite preserved "a wise control in the government over the public lands, and prevents a general spoliation of them under the pretence [sic] of intended settlement and pre-emption." In other words, Congress could preserve public land for purposes of park preservation, an effort apparently needed to prevent it from potential "spoliation." Republicans concluded that state control of Yosemite had failed, since the commissioners proved unable to remove Hutchings and establish a park along the lines Olmsted imagined. While the California conflict brewed slowly, the federal government grew as it finished a civil war and began reconstructing the former Confederacy. These tasks enlarged the scope and strengthened the capacity of the federal government, which made conservation easier in ensuing decades.

As Hutchings fought for his rights to stay in Yosemite Valley, government surveyors traveled throughout an area of northwestern Wyoming called Yellowstone. Reports from Lewis and Clark's party and stories from fur traders had dribbled out of the West of this wondrous place with strange geographic phenomena, including geysers and boiling springs, tinged with fantastic colors. Because it was the world's first true national park, its origin story often carries with it more than a whiff of myth.

The story often told explains how of a group of men sitting around a campfire in 1870 discussed all the possibilities of developing Yellowstone for the tourist trade, something just then taking off as part of national culture. Recognizing the specialness of the landscape, these men decided that no individual should own such a fabulous landscape. It should belong to everyone. In describing this fantasy history in 1905, one of the men, Nathaniel Langford, recalled the party debating whether to file individual claims or whether to pool them together when Cornelius Hedges Jr. expressed his disapproval: "There ought to be no private ownership of any portion of that region, but that the whole of it ought to be set apart as a great National Park, and that each one of us ought to make an effort to have this accomplished." Maybe.

This selfless story first appeared more than a quarter-century after it purportedly occurred and deflected some critical details. Members of the expedition, known usually as the Washburn-Langford Expedition, were not disinterested. Langford had been hired by the Northern Pacific Railroad's financier Jay Cooke to publicize the region to generate enthusiasm—and traffic—for the NPR line. And although today we associate Yellowstone country with beauty, in 1870 several in this party found it more unusual than beautiful, a "marvelous freak of the elements," according to one observer. This landscape was at least equally bewildering as inspiring. When Langford published his account of "The Wonders of the Yellowstone" the following year in *Scribner's*, a major American magazine, the descriptions seemed so incredible that not everyone believed them to be true. But it sparked public interest.

Ferdinand V. Hayden, the head government surveyor, had his curiosity piqued and persuaded Congress to fund an expedition the year following the Langford-Washburn trip to check on these rumors. The survey included scientists, as well as visual artists. The photographs from William Henry Jackson and the oil paintings from Thomas Moran helped convince the public that Langford's unusual descriptions were not fantasy. Whereas Langford struggled to incorporate the wild landscape into American culture and more than once named things after the underworld, such as Devil's Slide, Hayden's group resurrected the weird landscape and placed it in the context of God, not the Devil. The language of the sublime became common, suggesting a sense of awe. Moran's paintings especially captured this emotional valence. Now Yellowstone could speak to Americans in a cultural language they could appreciate. In no time, Yellowstone became a quintessentially American symbol.

In 1872, Congress made it official, passing the Yellowstone Park Act. In language consistent with the earlier Yosemite law, the legislation declared that the area, some 2.2 million acres, was to be "reserved and withdrawn from settlement, occupancy, or sale under the laws of the United States, and dedicated and set apart as a public park or pleasuring-ground for the benefit and enjoyment of the people." Meanwhile, the Northern Pacific Railroad certainly had played a role in promoting the region and amassing interest for the place. The railroad hoped to monopolize traffic to the area. Federal preservation helped further Cooke's goal, because as a national park, the greater Yellowstone region could not be broken up or controlled by competitors. Despite the corporate interests that helped guide the creation, the fact remained that Congress declared that "regulations shall provide for the preservation, from injury or spoliation, of all timber, mineral deposits, natural curiosities, or wonders within said park, and their retention in their natural condition." These passages announced something new in American land policy: preservation and retention of natural areas. Some of the public domain at least would remain permanently public protected by a transformed and powerful federal government.

Objections numbered fewer than a twenty-first century American, steeped in public land controversies, might suspect. The primary reason for few obstacles was Yellowstone's ecology. What made the area so spectacular and unusual made it an unlikely locale for heavy settlement and profitable business. Its strange geology and geysers would have wrought havoc on farmers' fields. Besides, its high elevation meant heavy snows and short growing seasons. Making a living in Yellowstone beyond fur trapping would be rough going, although it had been used as a hunting ground for millennia and the persistence of Native people hunting and traveling through Yellowstone prompted conflicts in subsequent decades. These conditions at Yellowstone (and several other early parks) led one historian to posit that the parks were "worthless lands" in the eyes of most enterprising Americans, making them relatively noncontroversial. Moving forward, of course, things became more complicated.

THE CALL TO RETAIN PUBLIC LAND

Concern about bison and the precedents at Yosemite and Yellowstone—as powerful as they were—were not sufficient to change the republic's long-standing practices for the national estate. As the change of the century approached, several trends converged to create a national conservation movement. As this history unfolded, those living through it could hardly have anticipated how conservation would converge at a reset table.

For many Americans, the inspiring, sublime landscapes of the West, such as Sequoia National Park, offered the hope that the nation might reconcile after the Civil War. These western places *might* allow for a *national* focus on healing. Promotional literature emphasized this nationalist mood and suppressed attention to racial and class conflicts. American intellectuals had long felt insecure in their nation's cultural output. European cathedrals and literature had a long head start on the United States (since Native homes and traditions were routinely dismissed), so Americans searched for alternative sources of identity. In nature, they found something that matched—even surpassed—Europe. For scale and beauty and meaning, few things could compare to the Grand Canyon, and the Grand Tetons held their own against the Alps. After the first railroad crossed the continent in 1869, tourists could get to these landscapes more readily and a campaign to "See America First" helped define the nation by its monumental landscape.

But inspiration from scenery alone could not carry the load all the way to conservation. Problems with the economic relationship between Americans and their land provided the spark to inspiration's tinder. George Perkins Marsh shared alarms first and most loudly, but he was not alone in identifying wasteful extraction practices. A scientific critique emerged from Marsh and others, purporting to explain the fundamental misalignment between Americans' economic activities and the land's capacity to withstand it. Logging, ranching, and mining all beat up the land in the nineteenth century, and not on a small scale. The extractive nature of these industries assaulted the public domain, reaping profits while the public received only a deteriorating environment in return. There were no fees or royalties collected for taking timber or minerals or using range resources. The period after the Civil War often is called the Gilded Age, because fabulous fortunes accrued to a few in a growing industrial economy while that prosperity masked gaping inequality and widespread poverty just beneath the thin veneer of success. The wealth acquired from natural resources often came from devastating the resources and the working communities left behind. A backlash started forming against the rapacious business practices that destroyed landscapes.

This backlash took several forms. Hunters and anglers concerned with declining wildlife published *Forest and Stream*, which raised concerns for a national literate public, while a similar constituency formed the Boone and Crockett Club to promote a set of "proper" attitudes and practice toward sport hunting. (This was full of exclusions based on race, gender, and class, but it also promoted conservation of game.) The state of New York created a forest reserve to protect watersheds. But more than private clubs and local government action, most effort to rethink the public domain centered at the federal level and focused on forests.

As early as 1873 the American Association for the Advancement of Science convened a committee to study forest protection. The American Forestry Association formed two years later. The first federal forester, Franklin Hough, was appointed in 1876 to study the nation's forest conditions. His *Report on Forestry* (1878) opened with his fears, having watched "the wasting of supplies and the complete exhaustion of one forest region after another with an anxiety natural with those who look forward to the provable conditions that must necessarily exist in another generation, and who feel the responsibilities of the present with regard to the future." That eye toward the future marked one of conservation's most important insights, but property traditions made protecting forests hard. Private landowners had no obligation to serve the public interest, and governments—local, state, or national—were in no position to plant and manage trees, especially since, unlike in Europe, there were few trained foresters to administer forests. If the United States lacked land and foresters to manage them, Hough thought, perhaps governments might at least prevent "depredations" and trespassing, in effect becoming a security guard of trees to stop "timber-thieves," who had the bad habit of setting fires to hide their work. Ideally, Hough believed forestry needed to be improved in the United States as both a scientific and a political practice. Reserves could protect against timber famine and give the government a concentrated area to guard against abuses.

Hough's report signaled increasing interest among government agents, who were coming to identify a common portrait of public domain forests, and that picture was not cheery. Just the year before Hough's *Report on Forestry*, Secretary of the Interior Carl Schurz's annual report devoted space to the problems of American forests, too, stating that he also favored reserving forests for fear of what was commonly believed to be a coming timber famine and tired of "depredations"—the key word many used to describe wasteful use of public domain forests. To stop the wastefulness he and others saw so evident, Schurz proposed, "All timber-lands still belonging to the United States should be withdrawn from the operation of the preemption and homestead laws." Other government departments, as well as the Public Lands Commission, assessed the West's forests in similar terms.

Evidence of problems accumulated, and reform pulsed in the air. But Congress is a slow deliberative body, not a fast-moving one. In 1885, Congress introduced six unsuccessful bills to create public forest reserves with similar results in 1888, 1889, and 1890. In 1891, finally, Congress passed a law—the General Revision Act—that charted a new path forward.

So much fraud attended to public domain timber that Congress recognized a need to repeal and revise certain measures. It repealed the Timber Culture Act and revised similar public land laws. But besides rolling those laws back, the legislation pushed forward with Section 24, a provision that merits attention. The entirety of Section 24 is short:

> That the President of the United States may, from time to time, set apart and reserve, in any State or Territory having public land bearing forests, in any part of the public lands wholly or in part covered with timber or undergrowth, whether of commercial value or not, as public reservations, and the President shall, by public proclamation, declare the establishment of such reservations and the limits thereof.

This section, only a sentence long, reversed the long-standing trend established in the 1780s of selling the continent's land. Now, the legislative branch gave the executive the power to carve off sections of the public domain to reserve forests. It was a significant precedent, one embedded in a larger reform impulse.

It is noteworthy that the purpose of these forest reserves was not specified. Nor was any managing agency identified. Though vague, the law found a willing president right away. Within a month of signing the bill, President Benjamin Harrison proclaimed the first reserve—Yellowstone Forest Reserve—adjacent to the first national park. By the end of 1892, thirteen million acres of forest land was protected. Then the next president, Grover Cleveland, added another five million acres. With an area nearly the size of South Carolina contained in public forest reserves, government officials needed information to establish a set of guiding principles.

MAKING DECISIONS FOR RESERVED LAND

After granting the power and then creating millions of acres as "reserves," neither Congress nor presidents clarified what these reserves were to be managed for. As reserves grew in number, the need to establish clear authority for them became a pressing need. Reformers called for thorough investigations with clear recommendations, and in time ad hoc arrangements grew into bona fide institutions.

In 1896, the National Academy of Sciences appointed a National Forest Commission to investigate western forests and recommend action. The commission headed west to study the problem of forests around a set of questions, ecological and political: (1) Can fire be excluded, and should forests be permanently reserved to protect timber supply? (2) What are the broader influences of public domain forests on climate, soil, and water? (3) What legislation is necessary? Charles Sprague Sargent, a Harvard botanist and publisher of *Garden and Forest*, led the commission that included other eminent and experienced scientists. A young man, Gifford Pinchot, joined the commission as its secretary. Pinchot had studied forestry in France and envisioned that profession with almost unlimited potential for reform (as Hough had presaged), and this appointment marked a significant career break for him. A well-known California conservationist and writer, John Muir, joined the commission informally, so that he might influence its findings but not be bound by them. Throughout the summer, the commission traveled through forests in Montana, Oregon, and California before heading east to the Grand Canyon in Arizona, then New Mexico and Colorado. Along the way, Pinchot and Muir delighted in each other's company, sneaking off on their own to sleep outdoors and revel in the West's forested mountains. Yet for all their personal affinity, Pinchot and Muir diverged when the commission wrote its report. The majority of the group, including Muir and Sargent, believed the only way to protect the forest reserves was to foreclose them to development and guard them with soldiers. Pinchot maintained that the forests needed to be used and managed by a professional forest service yet to be created in the United States. Acrimony bubbled up; however, Pinchot muted his criticism so that the final report appeared with a misleading veneer of consensus.

The National Forest Commission recommended a strong federal force to protect the forests from fires and corporate timber theft—the twin menaces of American forests at the time. The commission called for "A special fire force of a most elastic nature should be organized, capable of easy expansion and reduction, since for more than half the year there would be nothing to do in that line. . . . A protective force would be required to guard against theft in the localities where stealing is going on." The commission did not object to local settlers using forests, arguing that "Public timber [is] to be open for the use of settlers under a license system with nominal charges. Under the license the settler [is] to have some responsibility regarding fire, etc., and to be given a direct interest as against large corporations." These passages reflect the thinking at the time. The forests were threatened by natural hazards—fire—and corporate malfeasance that could only be matched by federal strength, a governing philosophy becoming more popular and powerful. The small-scale and local approach to using the forests was also emphasized. In creating these reserves, the commission concluded, the federal government remained partly consistent with the historical trend of the public domain helping small-scale economic enterprises and partly inconsistent by creating a space outside the private property grid long central to American political geography. Although the commission members disagreed on some central questions, they recognized that corporate timber interests were devastating forests and also worried about the devastating effects of grazing, strong enough concerns about environmental damage that a federal counterforce seemed necessary.

One of the National Forest Commission's main recommendations led to significant changes on the land and in both politics and policy. "All lands fit for timber reservations should be withdrawn" from settlement and corporate ownership, they urged. When the report made its way to the president's desk, Cleveland created another thirteen forest reserves amounting to slightly more than twenty-one million acres, on George Washington's birthday, just before he left office. Known as Washington's Birthday Reserves, these forest reserves sparked controversy. Westerners saw Cleveland's action as economically restrictive and devastating. A California newspaper close to one of Sierra Nevada reserves north of Lake Tahoe explained that they would slow, "if not wholly arrest, the development of the county's resources." Not content to complain about economic constraints, the Seattle Chamber of Commerce likened this situation to revolutionary days: "King George had never attempted so highhanded an invasion upon the rights" of Americans. The *Rocky Mountain News* claimed that "theorists, enthusiasts, and cranks" conjured this idea, anathema to actual westerners who knew the conditions on the land. Objections like these were common in the West, where locals bristled at easterners—almost always depicted as ignorant and arrogant—making policy, the ramifications of which they did not understand.

Western economic interests and newspapers were not alone in their criticism, though. Western senators passed a bill restoring the forests to the public domain, only to have an enraged President Cleveland veto it. However, because Cleveland declared these reserves ten days before his term ended, he soon left scene. Congress still had to respond, and it did so decisively. The resulting law, the 1897 Organic Act, guided federal forest management until the significant environmental reforms of the 1960s and 1970s. The Organic Act sought to establish federal power "to regulate . . . occupancy and use," a departure from the weak regulatory state that amounted mostly to turning a blind eye, allowing westerners to use the public domain freely. Public anger toward large timber companies (and, to a lesser degree, livestock operations), along with fears about diminishing timber stands and watershed quality, buttressed policymakers who aimed to better manage these national reserves. According to the law, the stated purpose of forest reserves was "to improve and protect the forest within the boundaries, or for the purpose of securing favorable conditions of water flows, and to furnish a continuous supply of timber for the use and necessities for citizens." Timber—"dead, matured, or large growth of trees"—could be sold, under Interior Department regulations and supervision. The new president, William McKinley, signed the law reinforcing the president's power to make the reserves and clarifying the purpose of the reserves, a result cheered on by the National Forest Commission.

Yet Congress had not been unanimous, and the debate revealed important fault lines in the West. Written into the bill were provisions that good agricultural land or mineral deposits would not be part of the forest reserves, making it clear that when farming or mining could happen, private property would still reign supreme. In addition, the suspension of the

Cleveland reserves remained in effect until March. This delay allowed owners to transfer their claims from within the reserves and select new land, an allowance that gave many timber owners better forest land. But these compromises did not satisfy all western interests. John Shafroth, a representative from Colorado, called conservationists "brazen" for their assertion of power over western resources: "This proffered guardianship over Western local interests we most earnestly protest against. You may have the power, but it is not right. The Western senators and representatives know full well what is for the permanent welfare of their states, and they are far more eager to advance the welfare of their states than other representatives can possibly be." Such a sentiment was widespread, if not universal, and versions of it would be heard continually.

Knowing how the reserves functioned locally helps reveal reasons for supporting or opposing them. Opposition in Colorado was particularly intense, as historian G. Michael McCarthy showed in *Hour of Trial* (1977). In Colorado at least, the federal government did little in the first years of the forest reserves to block access to them or to limit their use by local residents. But tensions mounted leading up to 1897 because according to law, entry to the reserves was barred for grazing or firewood collecting or mining. The reserves' existence stymied development, a fact compounded by the widespread belief that the General Land Office hired incompetent administrators who could not be trusted to follow regulations to protect forests from fire and timber trespass. Frustrated by this situation, Coloradans simply ignored the rules and used the reserves however they pleased. According to McCarthy, "Presidential proclamations, acts of Congress, and rules and regulations were all meaningless technicalities. The government could be damned; the forest reserves simply did not exist." Changing such attitudes and stopping actions that flowed from them—cutting timber commercially, for instance—seemed beyond the federal government's functional capacity at the time.

So when the 1897 law went into effect, federal conservationists faced a dilemma. On the one hand, much of the public (and Congress) were genuinely concerned and alarmed by the negative conditions of forests and convinced of the need to assert federal authority to protect these resources. On the other hand, small-scale local operators who relied on the reserves for timber for fences and construction materials and for grazing their stock continued their opposition. Large operators also felt shut out of the commercial potential the growing forest reserves represented. Meanwhile, the federal agency needed to improve its management to demonstrate its worth. And along the way, resources continued to deteriorate, especially the rangeland that blanketed the western foothills and mountains, leading to further controversy.

The 1897 Organic Act finally clarified the purposes of the forest reserves, assuming the Department of the Interior would continue managing the resources. But changes were coming. In 1898, Gifford Pinchot was elevated from special forest agent in the Department of the Interior to head of the Division of Forestry in the Department of Agriculture. Pinchot proved an effective administrator and bureaucrat. When he took over the forestry division, it employed sixty people; by 1905, it included five hundred. In 1901, Theodore Roosevelt became president, and the two developed a close friendship and partnership, rooted in conservation. In these years, Pinchot built up the political power to achieve a bureaucratic transfer of the forest reserves from Interior to Agriculture. The mismatch—where federal forests were in Interior but federal foresters were in Agriculture—had long been recognized but not resolved. The Transfer Act bridged this gap in 1905, and Pinchot became the chief of the newly created U.S. Forest Service (USFS), housed within the Department of Agriculture; in 1907, forest reserves were renamed national forests.

More than simply a bureaucratic change of address, the move symbolized the ways Pinchot and other foresters saw forests and their job. Trees were crops to be managed for productivity and for use of Americans. Pinchot once simply said, "To grow trees as a crop is forestry." To frame his task, Pinchot wrote a letter on the day of the transfer for his boss, Secretary of Agriculture James Wilson, to give the new chief forester. Known as the Pinchot letter, or the Wilson letter, it established an ideal for the national forest system that guided the agency for decades and still matters. It is worth quoting extensively:

> In the administration of the forest reserves it must be clearly borne in mind that all land is to be devoted to its *most productive use for the permanent good of the whole people*, and not for the temporary benefit of individuals or companies. All the resources of forest reserves are for use, and this use must be brought about in a thoroughly prompt and

businesslike manner, under such restrictions only as will insure the permanence of these resources. The vital importance of forest reserves to the great industries of the Western States will be largely increased in the near future by the continued steady advance in settlement and development. The permanence of the resources of the reserves is therefore indispensable to continued prosperity, and the policy of this department for their protection and use will invariably be guided by this fact, always bearing in mind that the *conservative use of these resources in no way conflicts with their permanent value.* You will see to it that the water, wood, and forage of the reserves are conserved and wisely used for the benefit of *the home builder first of all,* upon whom depends the best permanent use of lands and resources alike. The continued prosperity of the agricultural, lumbering, mining, and livestock interests is directly dependent upon a permanent and accessible supply of water, wood, and forage, as well as upon the present and future use of their resources under businesslike regulations, enforced with promptness, effectiveness, and common sense. In the management of each reserve *local questions will be decided upon local grounds*; the dominant industry will be considered first, but with as little restriction to minor industries as may be possible; sudden changes in industrial conditions will be avoided by gradual adjustment after due notice; and where conflicting interests must be reconciled the question will always be decided from the standpoint of *the greatest good of the greatest number in the long run.*

These general principles will govern in the protection and use of the water supply, in the disposal of timber and wood, in the use of the range, and in all other matters connected with the management of the reserves. They can be successfully applied only when the administration of each reserve is left very largely in the hands of the local officers, under the eye of thoroughly trained and competent inspectors. (emphases added)

Several critical themes emerge. The reserves are to be productive—that is, they are to be used, settling any question about whether they were to be locked up and the public kept at bay. They were to be permanent, not opened for private ownership. They also were to be permanently used, so that any harvesting needed to occur on conservative grounds, not altering their long-term value. The reserves focused on helping the home builder, not the timber corporation. This plan would secure a self-sufficient operation, much akin to the long-touted Jeffersonian ideal.

The reserves hoped to serve local communities and decide in local favor, a promise those angry Coloradans and other westerners wanted but were skeptical would be kept. The famous line "greatest good for the greatest number in the long run" became the rhetorical shorthand that guided the Forest Service's management orientation and goal. Even today, much of the public still identifies with it. Drawn from nineteenth-century philosophers Jeremy Bentham and John Stuart Mill, such utilitarianism meant to serve as many as possible. Finally, as legal scholar Charles Wilkinson has noted, the letter evinces both Pinchot's populism in standing for "the whole people" and his anti-democratic tendencies with a strong belief that scientists and other experts could and should manage resources without input from politicians as proxies for the people. This bifurcation is reproduced within the agency itself with a strong Washington, DC, presence and also a decentralized structure in local ranger districts. The Pinchot letter thus encapsulated all the hopes and paradoxes and seeds for growth and conflict that would challenge and characterize federal forestry ever since.

In the years immediately after forest reserves became an arrow in conservation's quiver, Congress was slow to quell public controversy by providing clearer definitions and directions for the new reserves. Initial restrictions had irritated local users who ignored them as best they could and used their political allies to frustrate reform. In short order, though, Congress and officials in the executive branch asserted authority and redirected history on the public lands, ensuring political debate accompanied any decision for conservation.

FIGHTS OVER THE RANGE

Although the *Forest* Service seemed primarily focused on trees, grazing became one of the initial challenges to its authority and the resource base it administered. Despite all the homestead laws that privatized much of the West, millions of acres remained unclaimed and rested in the public domain or, after 1891, were controlled by the federal government in forest reserves. Although there were no individual owners, the land was being exploited. Stockgrowers used vast acreages of the West to fatten their cattle and sheep. Although gold rushes and homesteads made for better stories, their presence were limited by comparison. Grazing extended widely across the West, and in the wake of millions of hoofprints came a wrecked range.

In the late nineteenth century, a common story was acted out. Here is how one rancher remembered it, a few decades after the fact:

> In those days we had everything in Creation we wanted. The grass was stirrup-deep and green all the year around. There was plenty of water and lots of rain. The steers got fatter on the range then, than they do now in a feeding pen, and we always had a good market for them, and for the cows too, if we'd wanted to sell them, for there were soon plenty of fellows trying to start outfits. But we didn't want to sell, for the country was ours as far as we could see, and nobody could come in and tell us what to do to make it better, or worse.

An Arizona rancher's nostalgic recollection, this story was a wishful reverie of thick grasses, abundant water, fat animals, thriving markets, easy opportunity, and unfettered access. Contemporary reports of the same area reported a type of paradise with plentiful grasses and abundant water. But in 1926, a forest ranger in this same part of Arizona assessed the range as having reached "the ragged end of it all." What had happened between the 1880s and 1920s? The simple answer was livestock.

Colonizers and missionaries had brought cattle and sheep, along with horses and goats and pigs, to the Southwest and California in the eighteenth and nineteenth centuries (a couple of centuries after horses pushed up to and beyond the southern plains), but the main thrust of the western livestock industry dates from the mid-nineteenth century. The destruction of the bison cleared the Great Plains of its most plentiful herbivore, opening up an ecological and economic niche that cattle quickly filled; in the historian Richard White's memorable phrasing, "Cattle grazed among the ghosts of bison." By 1880, some four million cattle grazed on the western plains pushing up to the eastern flank of the Rocky Mountains, a number that nearly doubled in a mere half-decade. Ranching offered good profits, in part because land for grazing cost nothing. Cowboys drove cattle across the plains using the public domain as free fodder.

With such good, open conditions on the range, rapid growth for the livestock industry followed, attracting some smallholders but also large capital concerns from both the East Coast and Great Britain. With little legally to limit them, such as having to buy or lease land, livestock operations grew and grew until two ecological disasters converged to force reconsideration. Ranges became overstocked. Grasslands on the southern plains deteriorated in the face of overgrazing. Across the 1870s, the land base required to feed a single steer—five acres—increased tenfold—to fifty acres—even as herds grew and compounded the issue. By the mid-1880s, in some places in the northern plains, ninety acres were needed to keep a steer fed.

Just as more animals had to spread across more land, the second disaster came: the winter of 1886–1887. After a drought that made the overstocked range even more vulnerable, blizzards and bitter cold descended over cattle country and left animals adrift, cold, and starving. Perhaps 30 percent of herds died, in some places more. The large Montana livestock operator Granville Stuart explained, "This was the death knell to the range cattle business on anything like the scale it had been run on before. . . . A business that had been fascinating to me suddenly became distasteful. I wanted no more of it. I never wanted to own again an animal that I could not feed and shelter."

In the aftermath of the Great Die-Off of 1886–1887, ranchers recognized limits to nature's ability to continue feeding these animals. Stockgrowers saw the need to secure ranch properties where they could make hay to feed their herds through winter. Although these home places still received free lands from the federal government through homestead provisions, having to make hay, which often included irrigating fields, meant the stock industry no longer relied solely on the free grass available on the public domain. The emerging system included small homesteads owned by families with good water connected to much vaster ranges where their livestock could graze for several months with minimal investment of labor.

The subsidy of free grass and free land, however, created conflict between different economic interest groups and worsened range conditions that would set the stage for government reforms. Well-capitalized cattle companies fenced in land on the public domain, an illegal act of excluding others from the public domain. By the late 1880s, after Congress passed the Unlawful Inclosures Act (1885), the government acted against almost four hundred such enclosures that had fenced 6.4 million acres, although few leading ranchers faced indictments. Large companies also competed against smallholders struggling to establish their own ranches or farms. The most infamous example came in Wyoming's Johnson County War in 1892. This episode generally is used to illustrate western vigilantism, but it reveals critical dynamics of public domain ranching. Large and powerful ranchers were organized in the politically dominant Wyoming Stock Growers Association and controlled large areas of the territory. They hired men to kill small ranchers accused of rustling cattle. These smallholders homesteaded and owned their land in the well-watered Powder River country, their presence disrupting the WSGA's dominance that relied on the open range. Typically, this history is shared as an example of class violence, but competition for environmental resources also increased and produced violence.

A final set of conflicts emerged on western ranges when sheep arrived. Public domain grass was as free to sheep raisers as it was to cattle growers and attracted flocks as readily as herds. The animals were economic engines, as Richard White put it: "Cattle and sheep were so many machines to turn grass into meat, hide, or wool, all of which could be readily turned into dollars." Because the main product sheep furnished for markets—wool—did not require slaughter, the animals multiplied even faster than cattle. In New Mexico territory, for instance, 619,000 sheep in 1870 grew to nearly five million in less than two decades. Most often, these growing sheep populations followed cattle onto the public domain. As such, they entered a rangeland already grazed and often already overgrazed. Quickly, cattle ranchers and others came to associate the presence of sheep with degraded grasslands. John Muir, who helped found the Sierra Club, famously referred to sheep as "hoofed locusts," capturing the contempt many felt toward the animals. Such an epithet, though, paled compared with cattle interests who organized against the sheep interests. In the Northwest, cattle interests organized the Oregon Sheep Shooters Association. A secretary of one regional subset, the Crook County Sheep-Shooting Association of Eastern Oregon, wrote to the state's leading newspaper, the *Oregonian*, declaring in part:

> We are the direct and effective means of controlling the range in our jurisdiction. If we want more range we simply fence it in and live up to the maxim of the golden rule that possession represents nine points of the law.... When sheepmen fail to observe these peaceable obstructions we delegate a committee to notify offenders.

These mild and peaceful means are usually effective, but in cases where they are not, our executive committee takes the matter in hand, and being men of high ideals as well as good shots by moonlight, they promptly enforce the edicts of the association. . . . In some instances the Woolgrowers of Eastern Oregon have been so unwise as to offer rewards for the arrest and conviction of sheep-shooters and for assaults of herders. We have therefore warned them by publication of the danger of such action, as it might have to result in our organization having to proceed on the lines that dead men tell no tales. This is not to be considered as a threat to commit murder, as we do not justify such a thing except where the flock-owners resort to unjustifiable means of protecting their property.

Perhaps tongue-in-cheek, perhaps legitimate threat, this missive revealed a deep divide on western ranges where violence bobbed to the surface with little provocation.

Sheep damaged the range with overgrazing (as did cattle), but they also earned enmity because of the economic, ecological, and social practices of pastoralism. In the ancient Mediterranean world, herders practiced transhumance, a system in which shepherds took their charges to the mountains in the summer because lowland plains could not sustain large flocks. The constant movement disrupted private property, left a wide swath of grazed land in their wake, and generally mowed down mountain pastures. As ecological pressure increased on western ranges, competition to get to fresh ranges increased. Arriving ever earlier, animals often consumed grasses before they could set seeds and reproduce, exacerbating the overgrazing problem. Their hooves disturbed and compacted soil, which prepared the way for weeds to overtake the range and hastened erosion. Finally, social prejudice attracted opposition to the sheep industry on the western public domain. Herders came from marginalized groups—commonly Native Americans, Mexicans, Basque immigrants. For many of the most powerful economic interests in the West, sheep and their keepers represented degradation and instability in social, ecological, and economic ways.

By the 1890s, many portions of the western public domain could no longer sustain itself. Perennial native plants could not reseed. Livestock operations went bankrupt. Animals starved. People moved on. Yet the idea that, with a little capital and a few animals, a small operation might grow into a great one remained alive. Faith, as much as reality, fueled that idea. A critical element of this imagined state, though, depended on free access to land, and in much of the West homesteaders could not acquire sufficient land to raise profits because they would need so much land to feed a herd large enough to build sufficient wealth. Even large operations recognized the economic problems of the industry they led. The Wyoming Stock Growers' Association, a powerful political and economic force in the territory, opposed selling the public domain to them. They feared land taxes would eat away their profits. If the richest cattlemen in Wyoming could ill afford to pay for grazing land, imagine how difficult it would have been for small operators. The subsidy of free government grazing land thus proved central to the western livestock industry. But the profligacy with which the industry weakened the range spelled growing problems.

So by the time forest reserves and the U.S. Forest Service were created, the ranges required attention. In 1898, the secretary of the interior forbade grazing on the forest reserves, except in Washington and Oregon. At the time many ranges were overstocked, and conflict between sheep and cattle interests—not to mention battles between grazers and downstream farmers—devolved too often into violence. Pinchot, who then was the head of the Bureau of Forestry in the Department of Agriculture, aimed to understand both the range condition and the position of ranchers. He embarked on an inspection tour of Arizona in 1900, for instance, after which he hired one of the local leaders, Albert Potter, to study range problems more closely. Observations from Pinchot, Potter, and others helped to formulate new policies.

Although range damage was widespread, Pinchot came to believe that regulation, not prohibition, would suffice to revive public rangelands. This approach matched his broader approach to conservation: wise administration by experts. The secretary of the interior had called for permits to graze on the forest reserves in 1901, an effort to control the timing and the numbers of cattle and sheep grazing the mountains. Without regulation, ranchers overstocked the range to maximize production and to keep competitors out. For similar reasons, they trailed animals up to the mountain regions before forage was strong enough to withstand the grazing pressures, consequently ruining the capacity of plants to regenerate. Government agencies developed a permit system, but many stockraisers hoped to create a leasing system, something that would give them more control over what they did on the range. By never adopting a leasing system, the government maintained stronger control, although it could be difficult to exercise it.

The next administrative step was a grazing fee, first announced by the USFS in 1906. The fees seemed modest: 20 to 35 cents per head for cattle and horses for the summer, 35 to 50 cents for the year, 5 to 8 cents for sheep in the summer, and 8 to 10 cents for goats. Special reductions were allowed for smallholders and "home builders" close to the forest. Still, however modest, the fees proved controversial. The American National Live Stock Association (ANLSA) approved of the fees, but the organization did not represent all ranchers. Smallholders especially saw the fees as a way to push them off the range. Ranchers objected to the fees, calling them a tax and refuting the agency's constitutional authority to impose them. Furthermore, the USFS determined that many ranchers ran too many animals and demanded they reduce their herds. These conservation measures implemented by the Forest Service to manage and improve the range challenged the status quo and riled up the opposition.

Conflict like this headed inevitably to court. Two cases ended up in the U.S. Supreme Court in 1911. In the first, Fred Light defied a court injunction and ran five hundred head of cattle on the public domain, but they wandered onto the Holy Cross Forest Reserve in western Colorado, something the Supreme Court declared that "he expected and intended that they would go upon the reserve to graze thereon." Light essentially encouraged the trespassing. Local ranchers organized as an anti-tax force and refused to pay the fees the Forest Service levied. A local paper characterized Light as "the most cantankerous of all the kickers against the forest reserves," and the Colorado legislature paid the legal fees Light incurred, a reminder of how strong were anti-conservation forces in Colorado. Light relied on mountain meadows to feed his cattle and had done so for years. He argued in court that if the government could charge a small fee and regulate when cattle could graze, it was but a short, slippery step to confiscatory fees and wholesale restriction that would ruin his livelihood. Light represented the anxiety public land ranchers often felt, a dependency on the federal agencies that controlled the land they used but did not own. The courts, including the Supreme Court in *Light v. United States* (1911), disagreed, affirming the right of the Forest Service to regulate the range.

Meanwhile, Pierre Grimaud was caught running an illegal band of sheep in Sierra South National Forest in California near the Nevada border. Grimaud, a Basque herder, argued that the United States had no power to regulate his actions. Sheep raising relied on the ancient practice of transhumance, moving the animals into mountain ranges during summer, and caring little for property distinctions (much less government restriction). One California critic complained, "There can be no doubt that sheepmen are a curse to the state; they penetrate everywhere, destroy the roots and seeds of the grasses; in traveling over the hills they keep the rocks and earth moving, destroying vegetation and denuding the hills of soil." While this critic complained for environmental and economic reasons, the *legal* issue in *United States v. Grimaud* (1911) focused on whether the Forest Service had the power to restrict activity in the national forests. In short, Grimaud's lawyers maintained that rules and regulations, including those that restricted grazing by requiring a permit, were an unconstitutional delegation of legislative action to the executive branch. Congress could not allow the Department of Agriculture to carry out what was, in effect, a legislative function. Grimaud's was not the only case, and courts across the region were deciding in different ways, heightening the importance of clarity from the Supreme Court. In a unanimous decision, the Supreme Court declared Forest Service restrictions were constitutional. The Court put it simply: "The authority to make administrative rules is not a delegation of legislative power."

When the USFS began exercising its authority, the agency aimed to address the problems of grazing, not timber cutting. The vast range, characterized by deteriorating ecological conditions and few rules guiding its use, taxed the agency's capacity. The USFS tried to restrict and define access and recoup some costs needed for administering the national forests and range improvement projects. Accustomed to free rein and range, stock interests were wary or downright oppositional. Their challenges stretched from informally grazing their animals where they had no right to formal contests over the Forest Service's constitutional authority. By 1911, grazers lost the legal fights, but the Forest Service continued to face a whole set of problems. The heady days that ranchers longed for were gone; crises were brewing.

VALUE OF CONTROL

This period in public lands history focused mainly on recognizing problems with the status quo, studying them, and devising legal and policy means to address them. Private property was not practicable everywhere; unregulated use and exploitation of resources could not be tolerated if the American people were going to have those resources to use and benefit from into the future; the federal government asserted its authority to control land and regulate the use of resources. This culminated in a wave of activity that started in the late nineteenth century and crested in the first decade of the twentieth. Governing power grew as part of a general era of reform. It also developed out of close attention to a natural world that showed signs of decline. Last, it spawned from a set of values, rooted in ideas about the relationship between humans and the natural world, values that fell under the aegis of control. Two examples show how government agencies dispensed control on to nature: fire and varmints.

Like a Rorschach test, fire came to represent whichever conservation challenge the observer wanted it to. Some experts criticized the practice of deliberately setting fires—an ancient practice that occurred anywhere conditions allowed for it—as an unscientific and irrational tradition that was unbecoming a modern society. Some observers found fires economically wasteful, as they burned up standing timber that could have been converted to homes or factory walls, as well as diminishing the next generation's stock of trees. So foresters like Gifford Pinchot aimed to eliminate the threat of forest fires, and, true to form, he was confident it could be done. In his 1910 book, *The Fight for Conservation*, Pinchot explained:

> I recall very well indeed how, in the early days of forest fires, they were considered simply and solely as acts of God, against which any opposition was hopeless and any attempt to control them not merely hopeless but childish. It was assumed that they came in the natural order of things, as inevitably as the seasons or the rising and setting of the sun. To-day we understand that forest fires are wholly within the control of men.

Pinchot's statement must be read as aspirational, if not foolishly overconfident, especially as during the year in which it was published the agency faced an enormous test of its mettle.

Among the northern Rocky Mountains and their western foothills near the Idaho-Montana border, the summer of 1910 brought a harsh drought. Dry forests in a region where thunderstorms regularly formed spelled a combustible disaster, particularly because it was also a time of industrial expansion, including mining and railroad enterprises pushing into the backcountry and adding numerous ignition sources. Scattered fires throughout July brought firefighters into the woods; by August, U.S. Army soldiers joined them and thousands of men tried to beat back the flames. Still, the fires grew until August 20, the Big Blowup, when they all seemed to merge. They swept over mountainsides taking everything in their path. When they reached towns, buildings burned, and people escaped—sometimes—on trains. Chaos scattered the best efforts of firefighters.

A symbolic moment stood in for all the other anonymous moments with Edward Pulaski. He was a Forest Service ranger from Wallace, Idaho, a town that was evacuated, nearly destroyed, and placed under martial law. Pulaski was taking forty-five of his crew back to Wallace when the flames blocked them. The ranger directed them into a small mine opening along the West Fork of Placer Creek. Frightened by the chaos outside and feeling trapped, one firefighter tried to leave but faced Pulaski at the opening with a revolver drawn; the firefighter stayed. Smoke and exhaustion left everyone unconscious. When they revived early the next morning, one man reported to the others that "the boss is dead," but Pulaski roused: "Like hell he is." Through his actions, he saved all but five men, a credit to fast thinking and luck. The story became central to the founding lore of the Forest Service and rallied the young agency.

The 1910 fires helped secure the Forest Service's founding psychology and established important precedents. Although easily forgotten today, the USFS was a controversial creation, its longevity not secured in 1910. A senator from northern Idaho, Weldon Heyburn, who lived in the heart of the burned areas, had been a particularly vociferous foe of the agency. But the firefighters became heroes after 1910 and their activity unassailable. In those years, a debate raged within the forestry community about whether good management might include deliberately setting fires in some forests. Indeed, the August 1910 *Sunset* magazine featured an article from a private forester arguing in favor of light burning;

worse timing for such an appeal could not have been arranged. The burned-over northern Rockies solidified the idea that the Forest Service would be a fire control agency, an identity it developed with impressive single-mindedness for decades. It helped that the next several chief foresters experienced the 1910 fires in some firsthand way. The Big Blowup burned suppression into the agency's DNA. With nearly eighty firefighters dead, three million acres burned over, and seven to eight billion board feet destroyed, the 1910 fires gave the Forest Service a sense of clarity and moral purpose. Fires were to be extinguished, banished from the forests. If the agency was successful, it would be in control. This idea animated the Forest Service for decades, even if nature continued to resist such human conceits.

Other agencies joined the Forest Service in its effort to control the natural world. The Bureau of the Biological Survey, the forerunner to the U.S. Fish and Wildlife Service, waged a war on predators that showed an analogous desire to control the living world. The Bureau's first chief, C. Hart Merriam, wanted to study natural history but Congress wanted the agency to offer practical benefits for farmers—the sort of mission mismatch common in conservation history. Beginning in the 1880s, farmers in the West asked for help controlling predators and rodents. States had already begun extermination programs, handing out poison and passing bounty laws. But to farmers' frustration, those efforts had not solved the problem, so they turned to federal agencies. The Forest Service employed trappers to kill predators like mountain lions and bobcats. In 1907, the Bureau oversaw the killing of 1,800 wolves and 23,000 coyotes. Congress appropriated $125,000 in 1914 to continue supporting this work the following year. Western politicians earned the thanks and support of western livestock interests with this investment. By the mid-1920s, predator control amounted to a quarter of the bureau's budget; by 1931, it was three-quarters. Killing animals seen as nothing but "varmints" gave no one pause.

An agency that originated to study animals had morphed into something that killed creatures defined as undesirable. And the Biological Survey and its allies did their work efficiently, and efficiency was perhaps the most powerful word in conservationists' lexicon. If part of predator control programs was meant to protect livestock operations, another part focused on safeguarding desirable wildlife. Yet eliminating predators disrupted ecological relationships. One of the most famous examples came on the Kaibab Plateau, north of the Grand Canyon and part of a national forest and game preserve. In 1904, there were four thousand deer. Predators were eliminated, and by 1922 deer populations neared one hundred thousand. This magnificent increase set up a tragic collapse in following years from malnutrition after the booming population ate itself out of its own habitat. Wherever carnivores were removed, faunal and floral relationships were disrupted, sometimes dramatically. Scientists offered competing explanations, in part because the debates never simply examined scientific evidence but were shot through with human values. The control of nature—fire or predators—was about asserting human dominance for human ends, not ecological ones.

One last mode of control might be mentioned as a postscript and transition. The bureaucracies born in this era and designed to manage public lands asserted their control within government. To have an effective voice, conservationists and scientists needed departments and bureaus and services to ask for money and administer programs to meet the goals of conservation as established by Congress and demanded by conditions on the ground. Federal bureaus established their influence. Yet those agencies could and did run afoul of each other because differing missions, interpretations, and priorities pushed government entities into each other. That competition and conflict may have been necessary to help define the outlines of the public lands and their purposes.

HETCH HETCHY

One of the most famous conflicts that illustrated this element of control and competition in public lands history focused on Hetch Hetchy, a beautiful valley near Yosemite Valley and contained within the national park. There, over the course of a decade in the first part of the twentieth century, competing ideas about conservation clashed. Ever since, Hetch Hetchy's history has been used as a parable.

The story is deceptively simple. San Francisco wanted a cheaper, reliable supply of municipal water. The Tuolumne River flowed through Hetch Hetchy Valley and public land, making it a cheap source the government would not have to purchase. Many elite and middle-class travelers enjoyed the scenic beauty in Yosemite National Park, including Hetch Hetchy, John Muir chief among them.

Muir was a Scottish immigrant and Midwestern transplant to California in 1868, and he spent his adulthood exploring and extolling the Sierra Nevada for the spiritual sustenance the mountains provided and the wild counterpoint they offered to the growing urban and industrial taint of turn-of-the-century America. In 1892, Muir cofounded the Sierra Club and presided over it, leading wealthy club members, women and men, to excursions to the mountains. "Going to the mountains was like going home," he wrote once, although he disdained the Miwok who called the Sierra Nevada home. Learning of plans to dam the river and flood Hetch Hetchy Valley activated Muir's political side. Working with his friend Robert Underwood Johnson, who edited the leading *Century Magazine*, Muir publicized the plan for the dam in some of the most memorable prose ever issued forth in favor of wilderness.

Muir cast his rhetoric with all the subtlety of a landslide, framing the cause as one of good versus evil, selflessness versus selfishness. He concluded an essay, "Hetch Hetchy Valley" (1912), with two powerful paragraphs:

> These temple destroyers, devotees of ravaging commercialism, seem to have a perfect contempt for Nature, and, instead of lifting their eyes to the God of the mountains, lift them to the Almighty Dollar.
>
> Dam Hetch Hetchy! As well dam for water-tanks the people's cathedrals and churches, for no holier temple has ever been consecrated by the heart of man.

Such language continues to echo problematically in environmental campaigns. But Muir wrote them amid a clear battle, exaggerating his virtue and his opponents' vices. In the stories told later, Muir was cast as a preservationist, one who wanted to leave nature alone. In fact, he welcomed a road, even a hotel, to help people be able to appreciate Hetch Hetchy. And the opponents, usually called conservationists, wanted nothing more than to line their pockets.

Meanwhile, those facing water problems in San Francisco saw things differently. The preeminent city in California, San Francisco enjoyed advantages of an excellent port but a poor supply of water and vulnerability due to the likelihood of earthquakes. A series of water companies that started in the 1850s eventually consolidated and was named Spring Valley Water Company by 1904. Questions over reliable service, exorbitant rates, and elite ownership plagued the company as early as the 1870s when some advocated municipal ownership, a rising trend across the nation. As the city grew, so did the dissatisfaction with water. The massive 1906 earthquake and subsequent fires, caused by ignited broken gas lines and not stopped sooner because of broken water lines, were used as further evidence of the San Francisco peninsula's water insecurity. Securing the water supply in Hetch Hetchy Valley promised to bring abundant water to the city, controlled by an impartial city government, and serve a greater good. But the subsequent campaign demonstrated, on a national stage, how difficult defining the greater good could be.

The moves and countermoves by local and national governments ping-ponged for more than a decade. Congress included Hetch Hetchy Valley in Yosemite National Park in 1890, but even as the twentieth century got underway, what was allowed and disallowed in national parks remained murky. In 1901, Congress passed a Rights-of-Way Act, allowing dams within national parks, national forests, and other public lands. San Francisco applied for water rights in Hetch Hetchy along with nearby Lake Eleanor almost immediately afterward, and then applied in 1903 to build a dam. But Secretary of the Interior Ethan Hitchcock denied the request on December 22, an early Christmas present for park purists, arguing that the national park status required him to protect natural scenery. Later the secretary wrote to President Roosevelt that "if natural scenic attractions of the grade and character of Lake Eleanor and Hetch Hetchy Valley are not of the class which the law commands the Secretary to preserve and *retain in their natural condition*, it would seem difficult to find any in the Park that are unless it be the Yosemite Valley itself" (emphasis added). The phrasing here maintained fidelity to the statute establishing the first national parks. If the parks were to mean anything, Hitchcock was saying, their scenery must be preserved and protected. San Francisco interests in the mountain valley did not abate, and the politics evolved. James Garfield replaced Hitchcock at Interior, and Garfield's close friendship with Gifford Pinchot, whose heart beat with a utilitarian rhythm, promised a different attitude, one more open to dam-building in national parks. Meanwhile, Muir appealed personally to President Roosevelt, who subsequently suggested to Garfield that development in Hetch Hetchy Valley might be "unnecessary." Despite Roosevelt's equivocation, Garfield accepted San Francisco's petition. The dam would be built, but that is not this story's end.

Muir, his allies in the Sierra Club, and sympathetic audiences throughout the country wrote articles and letters and generally agitated in the first national popular campaign for preserving public lands. They emphasized beauty, rendering Hetch Hetchy in words that described a paradise on earth. Here, they fell into an unresolvable trap. They needed people to know and appreciate the place, so they encouraged visitation. This very strategy became wired into the national parks' DNA. Gaining support for the parks required people to visit them, which demanded some degree of development, including roads and hotels and other creature comforts. Park partisans also emphasized how ugly the reservoir would be when its levels dropped and nothing but mud would be visible along the shore. Their story was of beauty ruined. In this rare place saved from civilization's negative effects, allowing a dam was like inviting soldiers to a peace rally.

The conflict brought out heated rhetoric. San Francisco's city engineer lampooned opponents to the dam as "long-haired men and short-haired women," a gendered insult marking out clear roles being transgressed. But mainly, the dam proponents told a story that boiled down to an argument about majoritarianism. The oft-trumpeted phrase and conservation's slogan—the greatest good for the greatest number—was trotted out as de facto evidence of superiority. A dam might supply water to more San Franciscans than the number who would gain soul-sustenance from a wild valley off the beaten path. The U.S. Constitution set up a government meant to protect minority ideas while enacting majority ideas; it has always been a tricky balance to keep the majority from running roughshod over the minority. Hetch Hetchy saw this basic governing question at the heart of controversy.

Beyond this central issue, Hetch Hetchy represented an important moment historically. In most respects, the effort to defeat the dam proposal was the first nationwide campaign to stop construction for something resembling wilderness. That the dam opponents drew from Martinez, California—where Muir lived—to Boston and Washington, DC, indicated the growth of aesthetics in conservation. In addition, the story became a morality tale. It offered a stark divergence—preservation or conservation—that has bedeviled conservation history. The entire framework came to dominate historical understandings to such a degree that nuance was shunned. Even worse, perhaps, this dichotomy does not account for the important way the Hetch Hetchy conflict generated discussion and strengthened conservation broadly, something historian Char Miller has noted: "Without such tension, the idea of conservation would not have emerged as one of the most important of Progressive era credos." When framed as Muir against Pinchot, preservation versus conservation, or wilderness opposed to urbanization, divisions were highlighted, and thus areas of agreement were hidden. The rise of industrial-scale logging and other extractive industries in the public domain—by those Roosevelt referred to as land skinners—pushed activists and reformers together against that fundamental threat.

The political response (not just the rhetoric) to Hetch Hetchy was lasting. National park advocates pushed for a federal bureau to match the U.S. Forest Service. Too much confusion existed among the public who thought national forests and national parks were synonymous. The lack of a federal agency dedicated to building and protecting the parks fed that uncertainty. Frederick Law Olmsted Jr., a famous landscape architect whose father had done pioneering work in Yosemite, favored an agency dedicated to parks, pointing out that both parks and forests allowed for recreation, but distinct purposes guided them:

> The National *Forests* are set apart for economic ends, and their use for recreation is a by-product properly to be secured only in so far as it does not interfere with the economic efficiency of the forest management. The National *Parks* are set apart primarily in order to preserve to the people for all time the opportunity of a peculiar kind of enjoyment and recreation, not measurable in economic terms and to be obtained only from the remarkable scenery which they contain—scenery of those primeval types which are in most parts of the world vanishing for all eternity before the increased thoroughness of the economic use of the land.

This position largely prevailed. In 1916, Congress created the National Park Service, housing it within the Department of the Interior, further distancing it from the USFS within the Department of Agriculture. The Park Service's Organic Act established a purpose: "to conserve the scenery and the natural and historic objects and the wild life therein and to provide for the enjoyment of the same in such manner and by such means as will leave them unimpaired for the enjoyment of future generations." Providing for enjoyment and leaving parks unimpaired has proved a challenging balancing act in the century since.

COSTS OF CONSERVATION

The conservation movement undeniably achieved much. Protecting certain scenic treasures—Yellowstone, Yosemite, Grand Canyon—from development ranked high among national achievements, to the point of articulating a sense of cultural nationalism. Starting a permanent public land system in which experts would study and plan for long-term sustainability of resources offered something new for the republic. Yet expertise had drawbacks, and not all Americans were included closely in these developments. And costs could be counted. These costs included abridgments of liberty, an erosion of democracy.

Experts closely guarded their domains. As the public lands agencies grew, employees sometimes grew deaf to perspectives other than their own. Their beliefs about how forests worked or how wildlife fit in environments took on the hue of ideology. For example, the historian Nancy Langston's study of the Forest Service in the Blue Mountains of northeastern Oregon, *Forest Dreams, Forest Nightmares* (1995), showed foresters working hard to understand the unusual forests they were charged with managing, but they often were slow to recognize their ideas were ill suited to that place. Because these agencies remained family-like, with experts connected in tight circles, often educated in the same institutions, new ideas broke through slowly. Managers not toeing the line about stopping all fires and eradicating predators found it difficult to get a hearing. With few exceptions, agencies listened poorly when other values or ideas popped up.

What was more problematic and tragic was the way park and forest preservation intersected with dispossession of Native American lands. The public land policy of the nineteenth century encouraged the movement of American citizens and immigrants onto Native lands. The U.S. Army devoted great resources to killing opposition, and the Bureau of Indian Affairs developed reservations to confine Indigenous nations away from the vast majority of the continent. This process was essentially complete in 1890 when the massacre at Wounded Knee in South Dakota marked the end of armed Native resistance. This was also the year when Yosemite became a national park. In many ways, they were parts of the same process of confinement.

The explorers who traveled in marvelous landscapes like the Northern Rockies or Southwestern deserts often remarked how the lands seemed untouched by humans. The trope of seeing the land fresh, as the first to set eyes on it, appealed to these men. For example, George Bird Grinnell, a scientist, traveled through the region now contained in Glacier National Park in 1885. He remarked on the "absolutely virgin ground . . . with no sign of previous passage." Yet he followed Natives' trails and saw their hunting parties. Grinnell was one of many who could simultaneously describe and erase the Indigenous presence on the land, developing a myth of pristine and unpeopled land. This story helped make these landscapes "wild," even though they had long been used. Grinnell's (and others') rhetorical erasure of obvious human impact became a model for how Americans thought of national parks: as nature unadulterated, unpeopled, untouched.

As American tourists visited the parks and saw Native Americans, confusion set in, along with fright and indignation. When the U.S. Army and the Nez Perce warred in 1877, the tribe retreated through Yellowstone, frightening some tourists. By 1886, the cavalry administered the park, patrolling against fire, poachers, and Native Americans. Three large reservations were not far outside Yellowstone at the turn of the twentieth century, and tribes used the park to hunt, a practice that led to a legal challenge in 1896.

Complaints grew about Native hunters, especially from the Lemhi and Fort Hall Reservations in Idaho, west of the park. Race Horse, a Bannock leader from Fort Hall, killed seven elk in Jackson Hole, out of season, and surrendered to authorities as part of a test case. This was not within the national park boundaries, but it did focus on treaty authority and public lands. The U.S. Circuit Court Judge in Wyoming found that the 1868 Fort Bridger Treaty applied; the treaty guaranteed the right to hunt on public lands in Wyoming. Had it stood, the decision would have clarified treaty rights and allowed the Bannock and other nearby tribes to freely exercise their hunting rights on public lands, including

Yellowstone. The U.S. Supreme Court in 1896, though, decided differently. In the same torturous logic the Court often used in cases related to racial discrimination, it argued that treaties were created as an expediency with the expectation that "the march of advancing civilization foreshadowed" a future where reservations would be "settled by the white man." Therefore, "the right to hunt given by the treaty clearly contemplated the disappearance of the conditions therein specified." In other words, the right to hunt did not exist, because the treaty makers did not expect the Bannock, and others, to still be hunting.

Besides hunting, the land out of which parks were made also prompted controversy. North of Yellowstone, hugging the Canadian border, the Blackfeet Reservation encompassed the northernmost Rockies in the United States. The federal government grew interested in an 800,000-acre parcel whose western boundary would have been the continental divide. In 1895, after tense negotiations, the Blackfeet ceded the land for $1.5 million but retained the rights to continue cutting timber, hunting, and fishing in the ceded area as long as it remained public land. It soon became a forest reserve, and in 1910 Congress created Glacier National Park. Although Blackfeet artifacts graced the grounds and hotels at Glacier, their presence and subsistence practices were not embraced. As in other parks in this age, Native Americans were removed from a permanent or seasonal home, limited in their access, denied their traditional and established treaty rights, erased from the history, and eventually confined away entirely.

All public land had been Native territory, but conservation's management did not only strip Indigenous people of their rights or accustomed uses. Rural people, especially those who lived close to poverty, could be targeted by certain elite ideals about how people should live with nature and were also among the most vulnerable to the power of the state when it exercised that authority in conservation. Wealthy hunters, like Theodore Roosevelt, developed a code of conduct for sport hunting they believed all should follow. Killing wildlife, including birds, for the market or for food represented low character in this version of conservation that became enshrined in organizations like the Boone and Crockett Club. Yet hunting for their larders served critical functions for many rural Americans and immigrants.

One of the leading conservationists of the day, William T. Hornaday, who played a critical role in bringing bison back from extinction's brink, expressed full-throated bigotry in his classic book, *Our Vanishing Wild Life* (1913). The book celebrated wildlife and mourned the losses that mounted while also engaging in facile stereotyping. With sweeping generalizations, he noted that the sandhill cranes in Minnesota were "being killed by Austrians and Italians, who slaughter everything that flies or moves." He included an entire chapter called "Slaughter of Song-Birds by Italians," characterizing this immigrant group as a "scourge" to birds. (Hornaday could barely contain himself in his animosity and xenophobia: "The Italians are spreading, spreading, spreading. If you are without them to-day, to-morrow they will be around you. Meet them at the threshold with drastic laws, thoroughly enforced; for no half way measures will answer.")

With such attitudes prominent in some circles, it was easy to discriminate on public lands. Fining immigrants who hunted out of season or who did not have the proper licenses could lead to charges that amounted to more than a month's wages. During labor struggles in the mines near Superior National Forest in northern Minnesota, for instance, mine owners colluded with game wardens to strictly enforce game laws. By making it harder to get food from the public lands, striking miners were more apt to go back to work. In such ways, conservation became a tool to control working-class men and hurt their families. Although conservation aimed primarily at maintaining something like a productive sustainability for the public's wildlife and resources, its regulations could be deployed to discriminate against the already vulnerable.

CONCLUSION

A new era had formed, although it still was in a fruitful period of sharpening its definitions. According to the new governing vision, part of the nation's estate would remain public, managed by expert government employees. That meant part of the national table would be open to all—at least theoretically, as some restrictions applied. Those restrictions kept those sitting at the table relatively uniform in perspective, seeing things through a limited set of interests. To be sure, debates were common, as some interests clashed over details and emphases; however, a host of alternative interests remained uninvited. But conservation grew as a movement and public lands agencies grew in power, fueling an ambitious future in which the system expanded to the East and moved to maximize its efforts. Emerging out of this formative age found the public lands to be sites for experiments in new management. The table, more solid than ever, gathered together confident managers who believed they could meet any need.

3

Managing

INTRODUCTION

THE PUBLIC LAND SYSTEM kept growing, and so did the confidence of its managers in the four decades after World War I. Innovations in policy and management developed as well, fueled by a faith that increasing production—of timber, of forage, even of recreation—could be met by applying scientific ideas carefully. This strategy strengthened the power of managers, making these decades something of a golden age for them, especially with the additional money invested during the New Deal response to the Great Depression. These public agencies moved out of their custodial role and into long-term planning and intensive management. However, sustaining the environment and sustaining the economies that depended on public resources increasingly conflicted, while management plans often failed to meet scientific expectations. Conserving and protecting natural resources remained at the heart of the public lands agencies, but maximizing them through intensive management often meant that the power of commercial interests forestalled greater reform or restrictions on economic activities.

With few exceptions, those with interests in the public lands—whether from the agency side or from the clientele side—remained from a close social circle with a predictable set of interests. Most all were men. Most all were white. Most all were professional in the agencies, and most all were "capitalist" in the public. Most all agreed that natural resources were to be used to benefit society, but that could be calculated most simply using economic measures only. This introduced enough possibilities for controversies, but the relative sameness meant they settled around a table of mutual concern with reasonably consonant worldviews.

ADDING EASTERN FORESTS

For two decades, forests reserves and the Forest Service remained solely western phenomena; however, concerns about the state of eastern forests had prompted reformers in the late nineteenth century to think seriously about managing forests differently. George Perkins Marsh's *Man and Nature* (1864) proclaimed the need for better forest management lest New England towns face a shrinking resource base unable to sustain communities and economies. The worsening conditions in the East that catalyzed critics had not diminished. Meanwhile, natural disasters in the East and West dislodged congressional inactivity and created an eastern complement to the western national forests. The process moved slowly with varied strategies in play but resulted in a notable shift in the public land table on which conservation politics played out.

In the late nineteenth century, Americans in the eastern half of the continent felt many of the same concerns that eventually led to the national forests in the West: anger about devastating logging practices, fear about forest fires, and worry about unsustainable economic, environmental, and social practices. In the White Mountains of New Hampshire and the southern Appalachians where Tennessee and North Carolina meet and scattered spots in between, residents fretted over the growing harm caused by rapacious logging, which often led to fires in the aftermath when piles of slash caught a spark and spread.

Concerned citizens did not see how to regulate the privately owned forests, though. New York tried a state-level approach, creating the Adirondacks Forest Preserve in 1885, soon adding an amendment to the state constitution that designated this land "as now fixed by law, shall be forever kept as wild forest lands." Other statewide groups aimed to establish clear priorities for their forests, but unlike the forests in the West, the trees of the East were owned by individuals and corporations. Any role for the federal government, then, would be new and controversial. Despite being outspoken proponents of states' rights (especially in matters of race relations), several southern states, led by North Carolina, passed laws in 1901 authorizing the federal government the right to purchase private forests in their states. The first step was taken.

To walk further along conservation's road, advocates approached Congress with myriad strategies where enthusiasm met skepticism. Speaker of the House Joseph Cannon believed "men with a forest fad like yours to be nuts," a comment that pointed out some of the obstacles conservationists faced in getting laws passed. Undeterred, legislators developed legislation and held committee hearings. At first New England and the South followed separate paths, which slowed progress. So advocates worked to unite the legislation and emphasize the national significance. Still, opposition stayed strong; Cannon once proclaimed, "Not one cent for scenery!" An opportunity appeared when Cannon appointed John Weeks to the House Agriculture Committee in 1907, telling Weeks that with him, "as a business man [sic]" on the committee, it might be able to create a forestry bill Cannon could accept. Cannon's act acquiesced to the sense of inevitability that some bill would eventually be successful and might as well have some practical force behind it.

But all the action did not stay in Congress. Indeed, not all the action was even human. In the spring of 1907, a major flood on the Monongahela River in West Virginia and Pennsylvania devastated a wide area, causing a $100 million in damage and at least fourteen deaths. In no time, commentators identified deforestation as the key culprit. A West Virginia newspaper explained, "Twenty years ago two inches of rain would have done little else than make a big river. Today it caused the second largest flood in history of the valley. The barren hillsides are responsible for it." State government agencies issued similar declarations, decrying deforestation and its role in exacerbating flooding. Marsh's warnings, more than four decades old, were coming true. Help from nature only went so far, though.

Throughout the East, leading citizens often adopted conservationist ideas. Organizers traveled around the region to raise awareness and cultivate a conservation ethic that could mobilize voters, who pushed for conservation votes in Congress. Ministers and doctors joined scientists and politicians to champion for the region national parks, forest conservation, or hiking trails. Organizations like the Appalachian Mountain Club helped citizens get out to the country, and speakers or organizers in local communities, such as Maria Louise Sanford from Minnesota, shared their ideas through women's clubs or local papers. Philip Ayres, a forester with the Protection of New Hampshire Forests, developed a presentation that included color glass slides for a Magic Lantern projector, much like latter-day slide projectors, to illuminate (literally) the lands being destroyed by bad logging and devastating fires. By the first decade of the twentieth century, a nascent conservation sentiment permeated all points east of the Mississippi River. Joining the regional contingent of conservation-minded citizens were national organizations, such as the American Forestry Association and the American Association for the Advancement of Science, which announced support for eastern forest reserves. Popular and professional support swelled across the East and combined with what seemed obvious signals from the land that something needed to be done.

The context that propelled the eventual Weeks Act, then, combined economic and ecological devastation caused by a seemingly careless logging industry with growing political interest and popular agitation throughout the East, with a natural disaster as a final catalyst. Congress had been working on various drafts, which eroded Speaker Cannon's opposition. The House finally passed the bill in a close 130–111 vote in June 1910. The Senate dallied, as opponents marshaled their power to stymie again. One senator from Idaho, Weldon Heyburn, characterized it as the "most radical piece of fancy legislation" ever considered in Congress, a striking exaggeration. Meanwhile, Heyburn's home was on fire. The massive 1910 fires along the Idaho-Montana border captured Americans' attention and garnered the necessary support for the Weeks Act, which the Senate got around to passing in February 1911. President William Howard Taft signed on March 1.

The Weeks Act included a series of specific, practical elements to develop a federal conservation presence in the East. Its stated purpose showed Congress's intent to protect "the watershed of navigable streams, and to appoint a commission for the acquisition of lands for the purpose of conserving the navigability of navigable rivers." Forest conservation was tied up with water supply, something that focused on or limited where the commission could recommend acquiring private lands—only at headwaters of sizeable streams. Most of the lands targeted were cut over, abandoned, and often tax-delinquent. Within a decade, the USFS oversaw two million new acres in the East, creating a second type of national forest—one created from private lands, not carved out of the public domain as in the West. The Weeks Act made the agency truly national.

But as Congress primarily aimed to acquire brutalized land for protection and rehabilitation, the Weeks Act also carried a firefighting role.

Congress authorized funds to be transferred to states that developed fire protection plans in accordance with federal guidelines established by the Forest Service. This part of the Weeks Act allowed the agency to build cooperative arrangements for firefighting and improved the capacity of national, state, and even private forestry to mutually respond to fires and helped standardize protection. The provision made the Forest Service the leader in the firefighting establishment and helped pull along often reluctant and stingy state appropriators, starting or significantly improving state forestry efforts. With the Forest Service as a leader, the agency's article of faith that all fires should be extinguished was extended to the South, where a long history of deliberate burning would strike a contrasting vision of forest and fire management at odds with most of the agency. The following decade, Congress added to the Weeks legacy with the 1924 Clarke-McNary Act, extending the functions of the Weeks Act by allowing the agency to acquire land for timber and not just watershed protection. Clarke-McNary showed the continued recognition that forests existed within larger landscapes and jurisdictions that depended on cooperating agencies and landowners.

The Weeks Act and subsequent legislation signaled a number of important precedents. Among them, simply getting the federal government to purchase land for national forests was most significant. But it also responded to ecological problems more prominently than earlier conservation measures. Western national forests already attempted to forestall timber famine, in part because of worries over overcutting. However, these reforms responded more directly to concerns over deforestation's ecological disruptions to watersheds and to develop a stronger firefighting apparatus. So science was gradually becoming a more important factor in conservation legislation. Yet, of course, other interests also moved eastern conservation forward.

CREATING EASTERN PARKS

Expanding the national forest system in the East required new legislation and long-standing concerns about deforestation with timely pushes from Mother Nature in terms of floods and flames. Expanding the national park system in the region required a different set of prompts. This growth became a priority not long after Congress created the National Park Service. But the lack of a sizeable public domain made creating parks just as complicated as the national forests. The history of the early campaigns in the East shows many themes similar to what happened in the West, such as displacing people, but it also included philanthropy, which was a new strategy but soon became widespread. Thus, the East Coast analog seemed familiar, but with a difference. Eastern national parks helped set new trends.

Efforts prior to the 1930s were scattered. What became Acadia National Park was the first eastern national park. Mount Desert Island, off the Maine coast, had become a retreat for the wealthy in the late nineteenth century. Two residents, George Dorr and Charles Eliot, combined forces to create a trust and then set out to acquire land. By 1916, they had secured five thousand acres and gave it to the federal government. Insufficient then to be a national park, Woodrow Wilson declared it the Sieur de Monts National Monument in 1916. Soon, John D. Rockefeller Jr. joined forces with Dorr and Eliot and donated $3.5 million to the trust and quadrupled the acreage. In 1919, Congress changed the name again and created Lafayette National Park, the first national park in the East and the first made entirely out of former private land. (It was renamed Acadia in 1929.) Almost a century after its creation, the writer Terry Tempest Williams, more known for her celebrations of Utah than islands off the Maine coast, characterized Acadia as a "breathing space." She continued reflectively, "Perhaps that is what parks are—breathing spaces for a society that increasingly holds its breath." This apt phrase captures an essence of the national park system—a place apart for its quietude, even as that escape often hides the roiling politics involved to create and manage such places.

Stephen Mather, the director of the Park Service from 1917 to 1929, turned South for far more complicated park complexes that opened a new and often contested chapter in national parks history. In 1926, Congress authorized three new parks in the South—Mammoth Cave in Kentucky, Shenandoah Mountains in Virginia, and the Great Smoky Mountains in North Carolina and Tennessee—but prohibited the federal government from buying land for them. The states or private philanthropists would need to foot the bill, and this would require patience and persistence. In the interim, in 1934, Congress authorized a national park for the Everglades in southern Florida. None of these parks were finalized for at least a decade. One reason for the long delays was because people occupied these landscapes. Winning over or accommodating local leaders or, alternatively, using the power of eminent domain and shoving local residents aside took some time.

The Great Smoky Mountains furnish perhaps the most revealing example. Long home to the Cherokee—the Eastern Band withstood the Indian Removal Act in the 1830s and remained in the mountains and valleys along the North Carolina-Tennessee border—the Smokies were a biodiverse hardwood forest. Joining the Cherokee in those colorful mountains were white farmers who developed semi-subsistence agriculture among the forests. About seven thousand residents lived there at the turn of the twentieth century when foresters came to survey the grand spruce and chestnut forests and began to reenact a common environmental history. Building railroads into the valleys, lumber companies commenced to stripping the mountains of their valuable timber. Fires followed from the spark-prone equipment and the piles of slash. Floods followed the fires. The landscape deteriorated and made the subsistence farming, long practiced on the barest of margins, even harder. Lumber companies made no long-term plans. In the face of all these trends emerged a surprising movement to create a national park in these same Smoky Mountains. Tourists had arrived in the Smokies around the same time as lumber companies, seeking escape rather than profit. Local boosters formed the Great Smoky Mountains Conservation Association in 1923, and enthusiasm coalesced for a national park.

Two problems existed, one intellectual and one practical. The intellectual one was how to understand the scenic landscape that was obviously inhabited, for tens of centuries in the case of the Cherokee and for tens of decades among white farmers. Partly, park advocates moved around this issue by envisioning these mountain people as part of the park in the form of "picturesque" additions. The Cherokee in particular would be "objects of interest" to visitors. More obviously than in most national parks, the Smoky Mountains park would be a wilderness created out of other peoples' homes. And that was the second problem: removing property owners. Using the power of eminent domain, park commissions at the state level bought 1,132 small farms and 18 large tracts of land, removing an estimated 5,665 people, who left their cemeteries behind to be maintained by the National Park Service. John D. Rockefeller Jr. again helped tip the financial balance, donating $5 million for purchasing these acres. He also demanded timber cutting be stopped immediately and dedicated the Smokies to his mother. The process coerced people away from the mountains where they had forged a strong sense of place. In a reversal of what had typically happened in the West, Cherokee communities remained outside the park boundaries when drawn and did not suffer (further) removal.

The Everglades offered related but distinct experiences. Two elements are of particular note in the origins of Everglades National Park in southern Florida. First, there were the residents. Beginning in the 1870s, market hunters had destroyed bird populations for the plumage used in women's fashion. Then real estate developers concocted plans to drain and develop the Everglades. Meanwhile, the Native Americans who lived in the Everglades, the Seminoles and Miccosukees who had descended from the Creeks, found it increasingly difficult to survive in the region because of the same pressures that were transforming the Everglades ecology—development and drainage of the wetlands. As the NPS began investigating its prospects in south Florida, the fate of the Indigenous people focused government attention. The main questions were whether the Native people could live within the park and if they would be allowed to hunt and fish. Secretary of the Interior Harold Ickes delivered a radio address in 1935 in which he argued that "the Seminoles ought to have the right of subsistence hunting and fishing within the proposed park." Ickes continued, telling the history of Seminoles in Florida—not a cheery one—suggesting that the park and adjacent reservation might, "in some degree, make up for the sufferings" at the hand of the United States. Despite the high-minded rhetoric, federal policy shifted, and officials encouraged relocation instead of incorporation. Long in the planning, Everglades National Park finally was dedicated by President Harry Truman in 1947. Park superintendents established strict restrictions on Natives' activities within the park, and controversies have popped up periodically ever since.

Second, the Everglades offered a new park model, one influenced by ecology more than simply scenic grandeur. NPS Director Mather first suggested investigating the Everglades as a potential park in 1923, but the effort gathered interest slowly. Some observers raised objections to the Everglades, barely eight feet above sea level, as hardly matching the West's grander scenes. The early parks had been so monumental—looming mountains, deep canyons—some people found it hard to put the Everglades into the same category. When debated in Congress, one opponent called it a "snake swamp park on perfectly worthless land." Perhaps its fiercest advocate was Marjory Stoneman Douglas, whose classic book *The Everglades: River of Grass* (1947) helped transform the image of the Everglades as a swamp into something magnificent. "The grass and the water together make the river as simple as it is unique," she wrote. "Yet within that simplicity, enclosed within the river and bordering and intruding on it from each side, there is subtlety and diversity, a crowd of changing forms, of thrusting teeming life." Douglas announced a quieter beauty worth protecting, contrasting it with the showy monuments like Rocky Mountain National Park. That thrumming life included scores of birds and reptiles not common elsewhere. The "river of grass" helped solidify the notion that parks were for environmental protection and not just scenery.

Creating Shenandoah National Park in the Blue Ridge Mountains of Virginia followed essentially the same path as Great Smoky Mountains National Park: condemnation and removal of local residents. These acts, made in the name of the public good, pushed some of the public out even if they needed and welcomed the money they received. Resentment often followed, especially because national parks catered to recreation for well-to-do city dwellers. The park's central feature, Skyline Drive, symbolized this situation, for the 105-mile road was about moving through scenery, not living on it. The initial park visitors imagined this road being the uniting force for the park. When President Herbert Hoover visited the mountains, he marveled at the views and reportedly (and perhaps apocryphally) declared, "This mountain top is just made by God the Almighty for a highway." Scenic drives through stunning scenery had become popular in the 1920s, with automobiles then more affordable for many Americans. And in the Great Depression building such roads became key public works projects to provide relief for unemployed men. The popular Civilian Conservation Corps (CCC) during President Franklin Roosevelt's New Deal provided some of the labor to construct these roads, which ensured easier access for touring Americans. Locally, however, Skyline Drive closed existing county roads to preserve the park's sense of undisturbed wilderness.

Roads became an important symbol for conservation in the East. The Blue Ridge Parkway connected Shenandoah National Park with Great Smoky Mountains National Park and was itself a national park, with national forests often flanking its sides. But it is useful to remember that in 1910, none of this existed: no ridgetop roads, no national forests, no national parks. In three decades, the promise of a conservation landscape in the East had been fulfilled, or at least begun. Its trajectory—relying on private land and philanthropy, using eminent domain and condemnation, taking a decade and more between authorization and dedication—looked different than in the West with its vast public domain. The enthusiasm, though, prompted reconsideration. On the side of the road in these very mountains, a group of men articulated a new goal for conservation: wilderness.

WILDERNESS AND RECREATION

During autumn 1934, the American Forestry Association met in Knoxville, Tennessee, in the valley below the new Great Smoky Mountains National Park. The meeting gathered leading foresters, including a number who criticized typical forestry management. A field trip offered the opportunity for a handful of people to pull off to the side of the road and discuss something that had been on their minds. Too many roads stabbed the wild hearts of remote mountains, they thought. To counter this trend, they decided to build an organization dedicated to wilderness.

A few years before, one of those foresters, Robert Marshall, wrote an article called "The Problem of the Wilderness" (1930), in which he called for just such an idea. Another one, the regional planner Benton MacKaye, drafted a constitution for such an organization, anticipating the opportunity to meet with like-minded reformers. After agreeing on the basic idea, they invited a few others into their fold. In January 1935, they officially formed the Wilderness Society, marking the organizational beginning of a new idea about wilderness: that large areas of federal lands ought to remain roadless, a system of public lands without development. Besides Marshall and MacKaye, the founders included Harold Anderson, Harvey Broome, Bernard Frank, Aldo Leopold, Ernest Oberholtzer, and Robert Sterling Yard. All of them had been involved, and would remain involved, in significant conservation initiatives beyond wilderness. The founding of the Wilderness Society, though, helped to focus attention on wild spaces and agitate for their protection at a federal level. Getting from that roadside meeting outside Knoxville to what became the National Wilderness Preservation System in 1964 took some time. And the trails that wrapped around that journey showed how important recreation in myriad forms had become to public lands politics.

After the turn of the twentieth century, automobile ownership and roads expanded dramatically across the nation and into the public lands. The federal lands agencies struggled to determine how roads and automobiles would shape the areas under their control. The Forest Service took halting steps in the late 1910s and early 1920s. Arthur Carhart, a landscape architect working for the Forest Service, was tasked with developing recreation plans, including second homes and cabins in picturesque places. At Trappers Lake in the White River National Forest in northwestern Colorado, Carhart proposed limiting development within half a mile of the lakeshore because he worried that too many summer homes along the shore, occupied by private citizens, would monopolize this space and prevent public access. Although the Forest Service accepted Carhart's idea here, he soon grew tired of the lack of support and left the agency. Still, his plan for Trappers Lake has come to be recognized as one of the origins of wilderness recreation on public lands, a decision for restraint.

Carhart's contemporary in the Forest Service, Aldo Leopold, generally gets more credit. Leopold began working in the Southwest in 1909. In 1921, Leopold published his first essay on wilderness, "The Wilderness and Its Place in Forest Recreational Policy," in the *Journal of Forestry*. He articulated an idea, floating in rare corners of the agency, that some lands within the national forests would serve their highest function not for timber or forage production but for recreation. Some recreation would be developed with roads and designated campsites, Leopold explained. But the agency ought to leave some recreational opportunities wilder, defining wilderness as "a continuous stretch of country preserved in its natural state, open to lawful hunting and fishing, big enough to absorb a two weeks' pack trip, and kept devoid of roads, artificial trails, cottages, or other works of man." Many parts of the national forests satisfied that definition, but Leopold saw that as a small proportion of the system and in jeopardy. The agency would find it "much easier to keep wilderness areas than to create them," so he urged planning and putting some areas off limits for more roads. He continued to refine his ideas for decades, making Leopold an essential member of the Wilderness Society's founders with experience rooted in national forest management.

In his original wilderness essay, Leopold directly noted that national parks did not fit his ideas for wilderness recreation, because hunting was prohibited. But roads were not. Although cars were not permitted immediately into national parks, it did not take long. In 1908, Mt. Rainier National Park was the first park to officially allow automobiles on roads. They spread quickly, if controversially at times, through the system, and without question, seeing the parks by car was how most tourists saw them—what one historian aptly called "windshield wilderness."

Both the Park Service and the Forest Service developed their recreational capacity, recognizing the public's appetite for scenery and nature as part of the emerging consumer economy. But they developed a rivalry as they pursued different tracks. The Park Service started with few pre-existing parks. To grow—a bureaucracy's driving need—it needed more parks, and those sites almost invariably came from existing national forests. In the first couple of decades of the Park Service's existence, under the leadership of its first two directors, Stephen Mather and Horace Albright, park growth was coupled with Forest Service losses. Grand Canyon, Zion, and Grand Teton all became national parks out of Forest Service land, and other parks, such as Mt. Rainier and Rocky Mountain, grew at the expense of national forest acreage. Undoubtedly, too, the Forest Service took recreation more seriously because the Park Service had become a competitor. The agencies developed distinct recreational programs, but the net result was a significant increase in recreation on the public lands—something that thinkers of the early republic would have hardly imagined.

Besides the NPS-USFS rivalry, another sign of recreation's importance was the National Conference on Outdoor Recreation, convened in 1924 and 1926 by President Calvin Coolidge, to define and establish a federal recreation policy. Its mere existence indicated the importance of outdoor recreation in an increasingly urban and industrial nation, but that masks the diverse interests involved. Reformers seeking to connect outdoor recreation to Americanism and its martial purposes spoke alongside wildlife advocates and good roads boosters. Within that cacophony, Leopold once again pleaded for wilderness as part of the federal response to the acknowledged need for recreational policy. Consensus eluded conference-goers, and other ideas proliferated, too.

Also in the 1920s, the idea of the Appalachian Trail (AT) emerged. In 1921, Benton MacKaye, a founder of regional planning, first articulated the idea of a linked trail from Georgia to Maine. Its roots, however, went back to the nineteenth century. The AT developed in piecemeal fashion, growing from local groups of hikers who, as the urban-industrial complex arose, saw walking as an inoculation against the deleterious effects of dirty cities. Walking and hiking offered positive health effects, connections to nature, and a sense of communalism in groups like the Appalachian Mountain Club, the nation's first hiking club founded in 1876. Local clubs promoted hiking and built and maintained trails, while advocating for public access in the mountains and building relationships with local landowners to allow access across private property. When the federal government began acquiring cutover lands in the East after the Weeks Act, a new dynamic of public-private partnerships developed.

More than anyone, MacKaye developed the idea of connecting all the local paths for an Appalachian-wide trail. He envisioned the trail as a "retreat from profit," an experiment in regional planning where "Cooperation replaces antagonism, trust replaces suspicion, emulation replaces competition. An Appalachian trail, with its camps, communities, and spheres of influence along the skyline, should, with reasonably good management, accomplish these achievements. And they possess within them the elements of a deep dramatic appeal." This vision represented a thorough rethinking about land, its purpose, and how recreation might fit within a larger regional plan, with public land as a central thread. His vision required close cooperation between communities and the federal government, between private and public lands. It demanded careful zoning among recreational, rural, and industrial land uses. It paid close attention to environmental conditions, hoping to match land use with the land. All of this necessarily intensified the role of land managers, a leading trend in this period.

The Great Depression profoundly changed the circumstances and discussion surrounding federal recreation. The rural economy started crashing in the mid-1920s through much of the West; by the time Franklin

Roosevelt took over the presidency in 1933, many people were desperate. Roosevelt's sprawling plan for relief and recovery, known as the New Deal, included substantial investment in public lands. The Civilian Conservation Corps became one of the most prominent and popular examples of federal relief. The CCC took men and put them to work on conservation projects in the national forests and elsewhere in the rural landscape. The money they earned, the majority of which was sent home to parents, stimulated the economy while the labor they provided transformed landscapes (and themselves). The CCC built roads, bridges, and campgrounds; they reforested the land, fought fires, and slowed erosion. In the final report that chronicled its achievements from 1933 to 1942, the CCC director quantified the corp's efforts:

- 2 billion trees planted
- 40 million acres of farmland treated for soil erosion
- 800 new state parks
- 10,000 small reservoirs
- 46,000 bridges
- 13,000 miles of hiking trails
- Almost 1 million miles of fence
- 1 million fish stocked in rivers
- 400,000 predators eliminated

All told, 118 million acres had been affected, an area larger than California. The CCC scattered across the nation and included projects on private and public land, but its long-term influence was strongest on public forests and parks where, even today, people drive on roads they constructed, sleep in campgrounds they established, and walk on trails they built.

In national forests, where fires had long been a scourge, the CCC provided a larger firefighting force than the USFS had ever been able to muster. The CCC built 3,116 fire lookouts and hung 88,000 miles of telephone wire to connect them, along with 68,000 miles of firebreaks and about that many roads. This fire infrastructure and the CCC's presence in such numbers on the fire scene helped the Forest Service formalize in 1935 its long-term ambition to extinguish every fire. The agency announced its 10:00 a.m. policy, stating that every fire would be extinguished by 10:00 the next morning, or the next, until they achieved the goal. The idea to kill every fire as fast as possible was not new to the Forest Service, but the CCC and the lookout network developed gave the agency a workforce to make the idealistic 10:00 a.m. policy plausible. And it extended the policy as a universal prescription across all federal forests.

However, at the same time, cracks appeared in the Forest Service's armor. In 1934, in the Selway River country near the Idaho-Montana border, just south of the main site of the 1910 fires, another massive fire swept through the northern Rockies. Elers Koch, a forester who had distinguished himself in the agency from its beginning, observed this burn closely. The Selway Fire burned 180,000 acres. Koch knew the country and regretted that the Forest Service had punctured its wilderness character with roads and telephone lines and airstrips and other intrusions meant to protect it. When the fires came and the CCC stood powerless to stop them, Koch suggested Forest Service policy and practice were a "ghastly mistake like plowing up the good buffalo grass sod of the dry prairies." Later in his essay "The Passing of the Lolo Trail" (1935), published in the *Journal of Forestry*, he continued, "The whole history of the Forest Service's attempt to control fire in the back country of the Selway and Clearwater is one of the saddest chapters of the history of a high-minded and efficient public service. In the face of the most heroic effort and the expenditure of millions of dollars and several lives, this country has been swept again and again by most uncontrollable conflagrations." The agency had little to show for the millions of dollars it spent on fire prevention. It might as well let it remain wild and allow fire a free rein. Such a position seemed a downright radical one, emerging as it did from within the Forest Service.

Critics of the CCC voiced concerns beyond the failure to stop big conflagrations. All the infrastructure the CCC built and many of its other projects transformed the land. Leopold complained that many efforts harmed wildlife. Timber stand improvements removed nests in Wisconsin; drainage projects on the East Coast emptied marshes, which provided critical habitat for waterfowl. He pushed for a better biological basis to CCC work, publishing such ideas in many essays in professional journals. Soon critics used ecological language in their own public arguments.

While Leopold published essays for academia and occasionally the broader public, Bob Marshall worked within government bureaucracies and grew frustrated by the roads the CCC built. Marshall was a government forester who bounced between the Forest Service and the Bureau of Indian Affairs throughout his career, and he had been asked to scout a route in the Great Smoky Mountains to extend the skyline drives so popular along eastern mountain ranges. Believing that people benefited from the quiet spaces of wilderness, Marshall condemned all the roads that punctured the roadless tracts that remained. Marshall was a driving force behind the roadside meeting that launched the Wilderness Society idea and then bankrolled it with his family's wealth. The Wilderness Society was not alone; other organizations, such as the Sierra Club, the Izaak Walton League, and the National Wildlife Federation announced similar objections to some road-building projects in the public lands of the West. More than stopping logging or overgrazing, protecting wild places in this period meant keeping roads and the machines that drove on them out.

Marshall worked on reform within the Forest Service. Beginning in the 1920s, local foresters could set aside parts of the national forests they administered in categories meant to protect them for recreation, typically called primitive areas. They could just as easily redefine the areas and open them up to roads or logging. In 1937, USFS Chief Ferdinand Silcox put Marshall in charge of the agency's new Division of Recreation and Lands. Promptly, Marshall developed a series of stricter rules called the U-Regulations, where no commercial timber cutting or roads for motorized transportation were allowed. Under Regulation U-1, the Forest Service chief could recommend "wilderness" areas larger than one hundred thousand acres to the secretary of agriculture who could then establish them, and public notice and hearings were required for any policy change; Regulation U-2 created "wild" areas between five thousand and one hundred thousand acres under the chief's authority alone; and Regulation U-3 designated "roadless" areas that allowed some timber cutting and other uses (above one hundred thousand acres, authority rested in the agriculture secretary, and below that with the chief). By vesting power for these decisions higher in the bureaucracy and, in some cases, requiring public input, wilderness preservation became more secure. With these new regulations, the USFS was limiting the development of infrastructure like roads, seeing in some areas potential for large, unobstructed space with the freedom to wander, to establish scientific baselines, and to maintain a type of primitive America that many celebrated as the nation's roots.

In their first two years in operation, the U-Regulations were used only twelve times by the Forest Service in increasing the protection of primitive areas into wilderness areas. These included a wild tangle of mountains in the North Cascades near the Canadian border, the rugged mountains in the Rockies of western Montana now known as the Bob Marshall Wilderness Area, and the Selway-Bitterroot Wilderness Area where Elers Koch recognized that fighting fires was a losing proposition. Generally, though, reclassification was slow. And in 1939, just after the U-Regulations went into effect, Marshall died, and then so did Ferdinand Silcox; Europe exploded into world war; and the wilderness cause within the agency suffered for lack of champions in a time now focused on other great matters.

When World War II broke out, much changed for recreation of any kind on public lands. For obvious reasons, the federal government's attention turned overwhelmingly toward the war effort. At times that meant undermining, or at least threatening to undermine, conservation policies designed to protect scenic treasures.

For example, the Park Service could not maintain the personnel that the CCC and other Depression-era programs supplied. The first six months of U.S. involvement in the war saw the Park Service drop from just under 6,000 employees to roughly 4,500; by June 1944, it was down to a little under 1,600. All told, in about three years, Park Service personnel dropped by 75 percent. Park visitors, facing rationing and shortages of gas and rubber, dropped by more than half. Meanwhile, the agency director at the time, Newton Drury, said he managed the parks on a "protection and maintenance basis." Troops stayed sometimes for recovery and rehabilitation in parks, using former CCC facilities. Other parks held valuable resources, and the need (or temptation) was too great to resist. Secretary of the Interior Harold Ickes allowed salt mining in Death Valley and tungsten in Yosemite, both deemed especially critical to the war effort.

In northwest Washington, Olympic National Park was targeted by the Department of Defense, which wanted the park's Sitka spruce stands for use in airplane manufacturing. The Olympic Peninsula was heavily timbered. In 1909, President Theodore Roosevelt created the Mount Olympus National Monument, nominally to protect the glaciers in the mountains and the habitat for elk, named in his honor: Roosevelt elk. In 1915, President Woodrow Wilson whittled down the portion of the most heavily timbered area by half, almost three hundred thousand acres. By the mid-1930s, conservationists wanted it back and proposed a largely roadless national park to keep the isolated Olympic Mountains an object to experience with eyes and feet, not tires. In 1938, Congress created the park. The war turned covetous eyes back toward those wooded river valleys on the west side of the park. The Park Service prevailed during the war, but lost afterward when logging occurred in remote parts of the park, using the excuse of removing windblown timber or clearing inholdings for salvage contracts that continued into the 1950s.

Wartime exigencies might be forgiven as a temporary aberration, but before the war recreation had become a leading part of the public's relationship on federal lands, a relationship Americans wished to resume. But threats to the parks continued. In 1953, Bernard DeVoto, a writer with an acerbic pen and a national audience with a column in *Harper's*, wrote a scathing article called "Let's Close the National Parks." The most popular parks were showing signs of wear and tear after record crowds visited the parks in the immediate postwar years. Roads were filled with potholes. Buildings needed repairs. Rehabilitation broadly was required. According to DeVoto, some of the most popular parks included "true slum districts," and he noted that this "priceless heritage . . . [was] beginning to go to hell." He blamed not the Park Service nor the public, but Congress, which was forcing the agency to rely on "financial anemia." Since Congress would not adequately fund the parks, DeVoto reasoned, the parks should be "temporarily reduced to a size for which Congress is willing to pay." His efforts to shame Congress were read widely, for *Harper's* was one of the leading magazines in the nation. It would not be the last time that DeVoto rallied the national public to controversies on the West's public lands. That the shape of national parks and public access to recreation opportunities graced national magazines demonstrated the existence of a new constituency that would increasingly shape public land policies more broadly against agencies that intensified their management priorities, even for leisure.

GRAZING THE PUBLIC LANDS

Just as advocates for recreation sought a more vigorous role for public lands agencies, so did scientists and managers of western rangelands. Managing those ranges had become a persistent challenge for the Forest Service, especially after World War I when the ecological deterioration from overgrazing was obvious to everyone. The power exercised by livestock interests exceeded other economic sectors, and resistance to change—especially regulation—continued. Although small changes in grazing regulations imposed by the Forest Service in its earliest years provoked cattle and sheep ranchers, the agency established its undeniable constitutional authority to manage the land and regulate livestock operations. Amid a broad agricultural crisis of the 1920s and the drought and worsening depression of the 1930s, experts and land managers grew concerned about the continuing deterioration of the western ranges. After years of neglect, politicians and land managers sought to control and manage the unclaimed public domain to bring order to a disordered situation. In addition to some of these administrative changes, including the creation of a new agency—the Bureau of Land Management—scientific ideas and practices informed range management and revealed the difficult ways science folded into public land management. On these public ranges between the world wars, federal resource managers brought a stronger, more intensive type of land-use regulation that often produced a more contentious environmental politics.

Although two decades old, the Forest Service was still trying in the 1920s to learn about the lands under its jurisdiction. Across the West, the grasslands and ranges showed unmistakable signs of decline. In central Arizona's basin and range country, for example, two different USFS employees assessed the land in similar ways. Fred W. Croxen, a district ranger on the Tonto National Forest, which protected the watershed of Phoenix, visited with long-time ranchers and reported what he had learned at a grazing conference in the 1920s. According to the ranchers, compared to the abundant grasses of the 1880s, the range was at "the ragged end of it all." The other observer, far better known, was Aldo Leopold, who had surveyed much of the Southwest and identified overgrazing as the culprit for changes on the land, which included invasion of brush and increased erosion. Few people observed landscapes as well as Leopold, and he was able to see their human and natural history. He explained what happened simply: "When the cattle came the grass went, the fires diminished, and erosion began." Grazing had been present there for half a century, had enriched some ranchers, and established an important economic sustenance and cultural identity for many. But by the 1920s, cattle and sheep had taken an ecological toll and were gradually undermining the ability of the pastoral economy—and the rangelands on which it relied—to continue.

While Croxen's remark pointed at a dramatic endpoint, Leopold's suggested a historical explanation. Grazing destroyed grasses and helped introduce exotic annual plants that replaced heartier native perennials. The practices of ranchers also disrupted long-standing patterns of burning the range, which had the effect of replenishing nutrients in the soil. Livestock reduced ground cover through their grazing and their trampling, hastening erosion. What Croxen and Leopold described proved consistent across the West—in northern New Mexico's mountains where sheep trailed, in the northern Rockies where large ranchers ran vast herds, in the mountains not far from the Pacific Coast where livestock introduced changes that unraveled ecosystems as the Forest Service took over.

During World War I, the Forest Service had temporarily increased the permits available for animals on national forests. Between 1916 and 1918, cattle increased by almost four hundred thousand and sheep by more than six hundred thousand to make more meat and wool available for Europe and the American war effort. Many observers even at the time saw signs of overgrazing, but once the temporary increases settled in, the agency found it hard to reduce them. The Forest Service up to that point had tried supporting small-scale ranchers, true to its stated mission and long-standing agrarian traditions. After the war, though, cooperation between large-scale ranchers and USFS personnel increased. In 1921, Will Barnes, the agency's new grazing chief, maintained that "the large owners are more interested in their stock and the use of the range, give their stock far closer supervision than do the little men, obey our regulations much more willingly, and in every way make what may be considered ideal users of National Forest range." The 1920s saw this type of coordinated organizing across many industries, a mark of the modern era. Its effect was a step toward marginalizing small-scale ranching, the sort of independent ideal long enshrined in American thinking and political culture, in favor of larger operations.

Meanwhile, the Forest Service could not ignore the obvious range damage and sought remedies. Agricultural expansion during the world war quickly led to overproduction and weakened ranchers' economic position. So when the Forest Service attempted to raise grazing fees in the mid-1920s to move them closer to market value, livestock operators protested. Some of the fee increases topped 100 percent, causing understandable alarm. Congress, not the Forest Service, was behind the fee increase, arguing that the current system subsidized western livestock groups who were not paying market value for the privilege of grazing. The national organizations—the American National Live Stock Association and the National Wool Growers Association—opposed the fee changes. In the debates that followed, western ranchers argued their position forcefully. They began to use the language of rights—that is, they had the right, rather than the privilege, to run their livestock on the public lands—and argued the Forest Service had overreached its administrative authority.

Range scientists offered what they saw as scientific proof of the need to change grazing regimes and influenced how the Forest Service and other agencies understood the landscapes. Ecology had existed in some form for decades, but by the 1910s and 1920s, the discipline had established its strength. The leading figure in American ecology was Frederick Clements, a grasslands specialist whose vision of how nature worked dominated the field for decades. Clements saw plant communities as organic entities, organisms themselves, that moved through predictable stages of development until reaching a climax state determined mainly by climate and held in equilibrium. Only disturbances could thwart this successional process. Nature was, in Clements' view, properly understood as predictable and stable; any instability arose from disturbances. A balance of nature should be maintained, then, by keeping disturbances minimal. He did not allow for disturbances, like fire, to be incorporated as part of or necessary to maintaining particular plant communities, such as many western rangelands.

The applied management that flowed out of Clements's science meant, basically, protecting plant communities and allowing them to bounce back "naturally" without interference. Fence plants in and fence disturbance out and all would be well, so went the logic. This philosophy meant suppressing fires, already the organizing principle of the Forest Service, but also restricting grazing when ranges appeared overgrazed. Managers had to determine grazing numbers and timing within the successional framework, as ecologists understood it. To further this research, the Forest Service opened several range experiment stations, including the Santa Rita (Arizona) and Jornada (New Mexico), where scientists aimed to discover how to determine carrying capacity and stocking levels. But blind spots sometimes kept them from seeing how the range and grazing worked in larger ecological, economic, and administrative systems. For example, their observations of the plant succession process through the 1920s did not match the predictions, and giving up their expectations proved difficult given how administrative and economic preferences pushed managers toward policies within a Clementsian successional framework. Succession seemed simple: stop harmful disturbances. Reality was messier. According to one scholar, "Succession in range science was less a theory than a policy." That is, it spoke to administrative needs rather than scientific processes.

Forest Service managers aimed to understand the West's rangelands to determine how to match livestock numbers and range carrying capacity. Range conditions, researchers consistently explained, varied dramatically year by year, especially in the driest parts of the West, which invariably were places where ranching and not much else played an economic role. But managers and ranchers both wanted to develop stable stocking levels, especially because livestock operators needed that clarity to secure credit from banks.

Given the massive task, the hundreds of millions of acres needing attention, doing the job accurately and efficiently were prime administrative goals. But success eluded the Forest Service. James Jardine, the agency's grazing inspector, sent out employees on range reconnaissance, and after a decade he reported about 23 million acres surveyed, a mere 20 percent of national forest rangelands. Quickly, too, the USFS learned from both its experimental ranges and the reconnaissance practices that individual ranges determined grazing capacity. That is, rangeland science could only offer specific observations about particular places, but generalizing about how nature worked more broadly would not lead to clear answers. Determining proper stocking levels could only be accomplished on a case-by-case basis with frequent reassessments, a far slower approach than either managers or ranchers wanted. Similarly, carrying capacity, a concept that guided management goals, was a problem. It was an abstract measurement applicable everywhere without considering local conditions and was needed for administrative and economic purposes. However, carrying capacity proved almost useless for true ecological understanding. Still, in these interwar years, countless range scientists and managers tried to understand how Forest Service lands functioned so that they could manage them better, an enterprise that took only halting steps given the powerful economic questions involved.

The national forests were not even the most controversial grazing real estate, nor were they in the worst condition. Vast acreages of unclaimed land on the public domain remained largely unmanaged, and ranchers used these ranges with few restrictions or rules. The debate over grazing fees on federal lands became a useful wedge to rethink and to challenge more fundamental elements of the western grazing regime, including an argument around states' rights and the fate of these public rangelands.

In 1929, President Herbert Hoover convened a Committee on the Conservation and Administration of the Public Domain of 1929–1931, the third public lands commission. While the previous public lands commission appointed by Theodore Roosevelt in 1903 concluded that national control was essential to orderly economic development of the vast western range, Hoover's commission held different political and economic principles and came to different conclusions. Hoover and the commission he created believed that "private ownership . . . should be the objective" for grazing lands, a departure from the widespread use of the public domain by livestock growers. To move toward private ownership, the commission proposed granting the public domain to the states—some 235 million acres—after which the states would presumably auction off the land to the highest bidder. The federal government, though, would maintain subsurface mineral rights. The states balked at that proposal. Such a gift, thought Senator William Borah, an Idaho Republican, was akin to giving the states "an orange with the juice sucked out of it." In many cases the minerals held the superior value, in addition to generating income for the federal government.

States accurately saw the public domain as largely a degraded rangeland, potentially a huge burden to administer and costly to rehabilitate after decades of overgrazing. Utah's governor pointed out that states already controlled similar acres that generated no revenue; why would they want more? What western states wanted, he said, was federal range rehabilitation: "Our ranges are being very seriously depleted and deteriorated, and they have got to be built up, and built up right away, or else they will be beyond repair." Meanwhile, those who favored smallholders thought the idea of auctioning off lands to the highest bidder contradicted the long-standing putative purpose of public lands to help support small operators. The commission itself divided deeply over the issues and recommendations, so much so that former USFS Chief William Greeley refused to sign off on the final report. The commission's idea to grant lands to the states failed to ignite state interest, but its descriptions of degraded resources and the urgency with which westerners asked for help indicated just how dire the situation seemed.

Although the results from the third public lands commission might not have been what the Hoover administration anticipated or wanted, the commission's very existence was a sign that the status quo could not continue. Two landmarks demonstrated this continued problem with public grazing lands: the Taylor Grazing Act and *The Western Range* (1936), a study being prepared by the Forest Service to assess the nation's grazing lands.

Ranchers' operations were insecure because they did not hold rights to the land; at the same time, government managers worried about unquestionably declining range quality. Congress prepared to address public-domain grazing with the Taylor Grazing Act, which went into effect in 1934. The law provided federal oversight on millions of acres by the new Division of Grazing (to become the U.S. Grazing Service in 1939). This agency would help to rehabilitate range conditions (to help the ecology), could authorize ten-year permits (to give ranchers some stability), and collect grazing fees (to help pay for it all). In deference to livestock interests, the law's authority rested with local ranchers who constituted grazing districts that exercised great influence in administering this new system. The grazing districts established rules and determined who enjoyed access to ranges. In return, the ranchers gained more security for their operations, because they were allowed to continue grazing their customary ranges and their grazing permits were recognized as collateral for loans—an important recognition of property relations for them that heretofore had been undefined and always at risk. The legislation also effectively ended homesteading on the public domain.

Yet the Taylor Grazing Act did not do much to arrest the degradation of public lands—the legislation's first stated purpose—because the forces doing the degrading remained in charge. Advocates for the law hailed the local advisory boards as representing "democracy on the range" or constituting "home rule," allaying some resistance to federal authority. When the two main purposes of the law—stabilizing the livestock industry and stabilizing the range—conflicted, the grazing boards supported industry. The weak federal presence deferred almost universally to the advisory boards composed of local ranchers. One study pegged that deference at 98.3 percent of the time. Furthermore, these boards assigned fees, defined stocking levels and access, and implemented other rules, all of which assured that large-scale livestock interests dominated and locals retained their customary ranges. In other words, the Taylor Grazing Act helped maintain the status quo. Improving the ranges' ecological condition happened haphazardly, mostly as an afterthought, and only when it did not interfere with profitability. Despite those weaknesses, the law asserted a stronger federal presence, an intensification of its authority, even if ranchers still enjoyed predominant power.

When Congress was debating the Taylor Grazing Act, dust clouds from the Great Plains were carried on the wind and darkened skies and symbolically showed legislators what was at stake: the health of the West's groundcover. At the same time the Taylor Grazing Act was going into effect, the Forest Service was preparing a report, begun in the early 1930s and released in 1936, that assessed the western rangelands more thoroughly than ever. *The Western Range* claimed that forage on the western rangelands had been depleted by about half, and the public-domain ranges—those areas under the Taylor Grazing Act's jurisdiction—had declined by two-thirds, the worst category of all the lands surveyed. By contrast, Forest Service lands were down by about one-third. The document served as a political bludgeon. Secretary of the Interior Harold Ickes wanted to take over the Forest Service's rangelands and create a new Department of Conservation. *The Western Range* was the Forest Service pushing back against the political threat. As such, many have dismissed it solely as a political document in a contest of bureaucratic power. The general trend it identified, though, spoke to a significantly depleted resource. One of its findings, for instance, said that 98 percent of the available public domain—some 150 million acres—was "eroding more or less seriously." Such problems and neglect posed a serious problem for rangeland ecology and any economy based on it. Livestock interests kept overstocking the range, while the range's capacity kept declining. The prognosis appeared poor.

Politicians imagined political solutions and managers dreamed of technical ones. In 1946, as part of a general bureaucratic reorganization, President Harry Truman created the Bureau of Land Management by combining the General Land Office and the U.S. Grazing Service, both agencies within the Department of the Interior. The move gave the BLM responsibility for more than 520 million acres of land in the West and Alaska (essentially all the public domain not claimed by individuals or administered by another public lands agency), along with managing the nation's subsurface mineral estate of even greater acreage. Yet the administrative change did not come with a clear mandate or mission. As leading authorities Samuel Dana and Sally Fairfax once put it, "the bureau had no coherent mission, no authority, and no statutorily defined existence. It was rather like the lands it managed, a residual category, assigned to administer the loose ends of over 3,500 statutes randomly enacted over the previous 150 years." From this inauspicious beginning, the BLM struggled to figure out how to manage its vast holdings and interact with its main constituents.

BLM land helped support numerous ranchers throughout the American West, as well as diverse mining enterprises, so much so that the agency earned from critics the sobriquet Bureau of Livestock and Minerals. From the 1940s through the 1960s, the politics of these public lands represented a classic version of what political scientists call an "iron triangle" of policymaking and governance: Congress (especially through its committees), an executive branch bureaucracy (the BLM), and an interest group (livestock producers). Iron triangles are known for assisting interest groups, often in a less than open fashion. Grazing advisory boards, still operating from the Taylor Grazing Act, remained central to the management system for BLM lands. These were composed of local ranchers empowered to issue permits and set stocking levels. The boards enjoyed near autonomy, and decisions they made supported their economic interests with few other values (e.g., wildlife or recreation) intervening. Livestock interests reigned supreme. One stark example from 1947 illustrated this power. Congress gutted funds for range management. As a stopgap, advisory boards gave $200,000 to pay for employees. In effect, the groups supposed to be regulated paid the salaries of those who were supposed to regulate.

However, even this light touch sparked resistance, a resistance directed at the BLM as the governing body. In the mid-1940s, some ranchers and their political advocates floated the idea that BLM lands ought to be privatized or at least given to states, a reprise of the ideas from the Hoover Commission. The movement in the 1940s found a staunch opponent in *Harper's* columnist and western historian Bernard DeVoto, who wrote scathing articles in the national press highlighting the heretofore hushed efforts at the "land grab." DeVoto's prose roused conservationists to successfully oppose these plans, but the movement for state control or privatization echoed long after this moment.

The politics of reorganization and the privatization efforts overshadowed the work being done in the agencies to improve rangelands. Overgrazing often led to erosion increasing, a concern by itself but also a problem for streams and what lived in them and for the irrigation projects developed often within or just downstream from public lands. During the Depression, CCC workers built check dams on national forests and worked elsewhere to promote range rehabilitation to stave off erosion or to limit its damage. Efforts also went into reseeding the range, a measure that appealed to managers because, if successful, it would allow ranchers to continue grazing their herds without reduction. By mid-century, a debate had developed about how to approach this problem at the nexus of ecology and management. Should agencies continue to accept Clementsian succession and remove domestic animals, which, according to that ecological view, would allow the range to recover? This was known as *natural improvement*. Or should agencies reject—silently or as a de facto state—such an ideal and intensively manipulate the range? This was known as *artificial improvement*. World War II and the resulting technological innovation and unwarranted confidence that emerged with it pushed managers toward intensive artificial efforts. The geographer Nathan F. Sayre explained in his history of rangeland science the decision and its wide-ranging impulses and implications:

> Despite fifty years of mostly discouraging results, federal agencies doubled down on artificial improvement, taking advantage of post–World War II prosperity, cultivars from overseas, new chemicals and

equipment, and political support for technological solutions. Heavy machinery was developed for clearing, cultivating, and seeding rangelands, and methods of aerial seed and chemical application were perfected. Millions of pounds of grass seed—mostly of nonnative species—were produced, collected, distributed, and planted.

Such intervention captured the zeitgeist in management circles: more, more, more. Managers aimed to make over the living world into a model of modern agricultural efficiency and engineering aligned with economic metrics, not ecological ones.

The four decades following World War I found federal managers addressing the ongoing consequences of overstocked rangelands in ecological distress. They asserted their power and expertise with new legislation, such as the Taylor Grazing Act, and agencies, including first the U.S. Grazing Service and then the Bureau of Land Management. Meanwhile, the Forest Service continued its importance. In the face of degraded environments and evolving scientific understandings, these public lands agencies attempted to intervene on the land. However, the political power of livestock interests shaded the possibilities available to managers attempting to rehabilitate damaged land. Although the public lands agencies fended off efforts to remove ranges from the public estate, the seats at the table remained limited, narrowing the available options. A more intensive management regime had evolved out of a managerial perspective, an engineering mindset, and a capitalist ethos, rather than one that respected an ecological worldview. Forestry followed similar trajectories.

INDUSTRIALIZING FORESTS

From its start, the Forest Service aimed to protect forests from exploitation. In time, the agency refined its methods and goals, always intensifying its managerial hand. From the 1920s to the 1950s, foresters had to figure out how to manage their holdings, which grew over this same period. They planned harvests and devised conservation measures, using a series of assumptions about the agency's purpose, how forests grew, and what served local communities. Those ideas did not always prove to be accurate, and sometimes Congress demanded reforms that pushed the Forest

Service onto different tracks. During this period, though, any observer would have seen a steady stream of increasing control in managerial prerogatives.

In the Forest Service's first years, Chief Gifford Pinchot decided to focus on using the forests for their "most productive use for the permanent good of the whole people." This approach certainly improved on short-term timber mining as many businesses practiced, but it did little to expand the purposes of forests to anything beyond producing commodities. Grazing on public lands, including national forests, produced beef and wool, but the national forests were destined to make timber. Yet in its earliest years, the Forest Service acted mostly as a custodian of wood. In 1910, the nation's highest timber harvest to date of 40 billion board feet included only 480 million board feet from forest reserves, a smidge over 1 percent. Such a small output meant public land timber played an insignificant economic role initially, but the Forest Service's influence extended beyond the economy. Its methods and expertise were influential beyond forest boundaries.

Within the agency, silviculturists dominated the Forest Service's decision-making hierarchy. They devised a sustained-yield approach, which meant at the start not removing more timber than was growing. This method broke with and improved on the cut-and-run practices so common in the nineteenth century that led to calls for stronger regulation and eventually to the rise of the Forest Service. To get the national forests on a sustained-yield schedule, these pioneering foresters believed they had to remake the forests so that they were efficient—a key watchword for conservationists in the early twentieth century. One forester in northeastern Oregon explained in 1913 that "the general riot of the natural forests" took "many thousands of acres" to grow trees that might be managed more efficiently on a smaller acreage. In other words, large forests were less efficient than smaller plots managed as timber plantations. Such a sentiment permeated forestry and moved the field toward remaking natural forests into something more human and manageable.

These foresters relied on a view of ecology much like that of their range scientist colleagues based on Clementsian ideas of succession and disturbance. They believed that if protected from disturbances—such as fire or pest outbreaks—forests would move predictably through a succession of species from grasses to shrubs to trees, depending primarily on soil and especially climate. Competition over sources of light, water, and space shaped the forest's pattern. Armed with these ideas, foresters believed they understood the forests well enough to manipulate them. By adjusting factors for competition, for example, they could change the growth of merchantable timber. For instance, since pines preferred sun, foresters could remove shade trees by logging to open space for pines to grow faster. The results of the theories, however, did not always create the forests silviculturists anticipated. Environmental historian Nancy Langston studied how this process developed in the forests of northeastern Oregon: "Refusing to change meant they were, by default, managing millions of acres of pine lands with logging techniques that were not producing the desired effects. Yet foresters were afraid that if they changed things now, those changes might produce worse effects." Such a stalled experience was common well outside of Oregon and spoke to the difficulty of changing course once an agency committed to a course of action.

Early foresters had failed to recognize the essential role disturbances made to forest functioning. Many systems relied on disturbance, and many western forests depended on fire as an inseparable part of their health. Yet fire control was as central to American forestry as was growing trees, so the federal rangers sought to extinguish fires from the land. This practice produced uneven, unpredictable results, as not all fires were the same. Because some harmed trees or soil, and especially slowed reproduction by killing seedlings, fires became the bête noire of western forestry. But keeping fires from their ecological function generated indirect effects, and the resulting forest often created its own "general riot" of unintended consequences. No fire meant more young trees and greater competition that would create stronger forests, or so ecological theory predicted. Instead, thick forests stagnated and became prone to insect attacks and harsher fires. And to a forester, dead trees were inefficient on multiple accounts—not producing timber, attracting insects, and fueling fires. Later, ecologists recognized that simplified, even-aged young forests—the very qualities foresters had believed were preconditions for vibrancy—made forests more vulnerable. Nature's evolution worked with complexity and diversity; the Forest Service worked for simplicity.

While foresters aimed to promote sustained-yield forestry based on flawed ecological theories, they found other flaws when incorporating the market. Since its founding, the Forest Service defined part of its role as supporting local communities. But local mills sometimes needed different things than foresters offered. Initially, mills wanted only big trees and only certain species. When "liquidating" the old-growth forests to make room to manage younger forests, federal foresters wanted to eliminate most standing timber. To accommodate this difference in needs, the agency adjusted the prices for the timber to make it more attractive to local mills. Soon some managers reinterpreted sustained-yield forestry to mean sustaining communities, not forests, and sometimes that meant cutting more federal timber to keep local mills chugging than the land could handle. Building the roads to get at the trees also was expensive, so the Forest Service lowered prices even more, subsidizing the timber industry in yet another way. Within this loose system, many opportunities for political pressures existed. This knot of silviculture, market economics, and political favoritism made forestry something other than scientific, just like range management had become.

Although the Forest Service always played lip service to serving local communities, complicated market realities and the agency's mission of efficiency collided to undermine this ideal. Again, the northeastern Oregon forests that Langston studied furnished a representative example. In Enterprise, Oregon, a local mill—actually owned by a corporation headquartered in Kansas City—opened in 1915 and rapidly processed all the company's private holdings and then turned to federal logs. By 1928, it was bankrupt in a pattern of cut-and-run no different from the previous century even though the Forest Service promoted itself as something different. The agency coordinated with the timber industry and found it easier to cooperate with larger companies, squeezing out small operators deemed less efficient. Big companies working in concert with Forest Service planners began to clear the old forests to make room for vigorous and faster growing trees that would, theoretically, consistently provide lumber for local mills. Langston captured the tortured logic: "The Forest Service soon held to a perverse-sounding formula: we must cut the forests in order to save them. The faster we cut the forests, the faster they will become regulated, and only then will we have a continuous crop of timber that can support local businesses forever. But this formula never worked. Mills closed, towns collapsed." The intensive agricultural model that the initial Forest Service invested in mostly failed.

But bureaucracies are often slow to change course. The Forest Service moved through the 1920s intending to perfect its planning processes, focusing on reducing old-growth forests—which were no longer adding wood annually—and maximizing wood production. To deploy this strategy, the Forest Service used working circles, an area defined by markets, and envisioned a 180-year rotation where three cuts would complete a cycle. In planning such rotations, foresters relied on estimates based on partial timber cruises and inadequate assumptions about annual growth rates where the chances for error were significant and the opportunities to accept best-case scenarios were irresistible. Compounding those potential problems were political and economic considerations. In one instance, local foresters estimated an annual growth rate of half a percent. The USFS Regional Office based in Portland, Oregon, desiring greater production, quadrupled that estimate, and the Washington Office compromised in the middle at one percent. Clearly, administrators decided policy based on information and values beyond biological evidence, showing how easy it was to manipulate plans for short-term purposes. Variations on this theme plagued the Forest Service wherever it operated.

Timber harvests could dominate foresters' thinking so much that the physical forests shrank out of view. And once the Forest Service started managing the forests by liquidating old-growth trees, the economic results further complicated future planning and sustainability. Timber sales on accelerated cutting schedules encouraged new mills. With more mills and more sales came more pressure to cut federal forests lest mill workers lose their jobs, creating complicity with the Forest Service and leading to sales for reasons other than forestry. Agency policies added to the industry's overproduction that plagued timber companies (and many other industries) in the 1920s and helped to plunge the West into a depression ahead of much of the rest of the nation. For those paying attention, signs of long-term economic and ecological problems already were appearing.

One of the approaches to natural resources that the conservation movement prided itself on was long-term planning, a way to think beyond short-term gains to protect long-term productivity. Agencies like the Forest Service did not always meet such goals, but federal conservation relied on public lands that did not demand immediate profits for shareholders and so could push for longer time scales. Federal conservation also responded to shifting political tides. The combination of these factors led to many reports, assessments of current conditions, and plans for improved conditions in the future. Much as *The Western Range* focused attention on reforming grazing, the Forest Service in 1933 produced *A National Plan for American Forestry*, often called the Copeland Report after the New York senator, Royal Copeland, who requested it.

Foresters began working on the Copeland Report in 1932 and published it the following year. It was a product of the Depression and a blueprint for the New Deal. Although the political question that launched it focused narrowly on whether reforestation efforts might aid the economy, Earle Clapp, who headed the Forest Service's research division, took charge of coordinating the report and saw it as an opportunity to advance a *national* forestry program across jurisdictions.

The massive and ambitious thousand-page report gathered data and indicted private timber programs while arguing for more public forests. Lack of planning, in the authors' words, failed to give American forestry a strong foundation. Truly developing a long-term, stable industry would require greater national planning across public-private boundaries. The vision being offered married scientific and social planning and furnished a multiple-use perspective, including chapters on everything from recreation to fire and regeneration. Indeed, the Copeland Report was the first time the agency articulated a modern concept of multiple use as its *raison d'etre*.

The Copeland Report chastised private forestry for slapdash practices that left communities, human and natural, in tatters. Clapp thought that private foresters accepted little responsibility for effective forestry. To counter that problem, he aimed to both acquire new land to supplement national forests and regulate private cutting in exchange for continued federal assistance and fire protection. This approach did not endear the agency to commercial timber interests, which helped ensure that many of the report's reforms found little support in Congress. Yet for more than two decades, strong advocates within American forestry called for this massive extension of federal authority over the continent's forests. But the economic emergency prompted smaller actions that nonetheless left significant impacts on the landscape.

The actual reforms instituted in the 1930s and after focused on economic elements, trying to support mills and their workers. The National

Industrial Recovery Act (1933), one of the New Deal's central programs, laid the foundation for developing an industry-wide code for working conditions and logging standards. Such a program favored larger timber companies and also extended government influence and authority across public and private forests. The Forest Service promoted itself as the responsible party, emphasizing sustained-yield practices as the standard to be used and required on its land. In 1944, Congress passed the Sustained Yield Forest Management Act to solidify this approach. It was designed to develop long-standing and noncompetitive contracts between the Forest Service and local lumber mills. Because private owners tended to cut faster than trees regenerated, this law provided them with low-cost logs as long as the company regulated the flow of timber to stabilize a rollicking industry and prevent booms and busts. Only a half-dozen units ever used this legislation, and they were not rousing successes. The stability it supposedly offered smacked of favoritism to local mills, not in the contracts. More important, though, sustained yield had morphed from a biological principle to an economic one that could be fit to the goal of maximization, a betrayal of conservation ideals rooted in the environment's long-term health.

The World War II emergency transformed national forests. Timber sales increased almost 250 percent between 1939 and 1945, and national forest timber doubled as a proportion of the nation's timber economy. These trends accelerated after the war, transforming the agency from a custodian of the nation's woods to a significant provider of lumber. Throughout its early history, the USFS sought to develop itself as a counterweight to private forestry, which the agency had always seen as too focused on the short term. Yet by the war and immediate aftermath, both the timber industry and the Forest Service viewed timber production as the main goal. To return to the table metaphor, a new stakeholder took a seat, or at least leaned in close to whisper in the ears of the federal foresters sitting there, when private companies looked to increase what they took from public forests. This approach resembled the ways large-scale livestock operations influenced the Bureau of Land Management. In each case, production goals for industry strongly influenced the federal conservation agency priorities, marginalizing all other activities.

Trends converged within this swirling moment. Demand for wood increased after more than a decade of depression and war. Meanwhile, private forest stocks were dwindling. Both factors pushed the American timber industry toward the national forests. Priorities focused on maximizing production—both in terms of getting forests to grow faster (the long plan of foresters to control their forests) and in getting more trees to the market. The logic stemming from that focus moved toward clearcutting. Up to the 1950s, the Forest Service pitched selective cutting as a preferred method to keep younger trees still standing and seeding the forest. But the new imperatives after World War II shifted, and clearcutting became the preferred method.

Clearcutting was efficient, by some measures. It took down all the trees, which helped facilitate replanting and, foresters forecast, would help create a quick-growing younger forest that would be even easier to harvest in the future when foresters imagined a uniform even-aged stand. It also got logs to market fast. Earlier, the Forest Service had criticized these expedient qualities when practiced by private foresters. But the postwar era, as in other areas of public land management, was an era of intensifying management. Clearcutting offered timber companies a quick way to get a lot of logs and offered the USFS a quick way to start growing its new, efficient forest. The method also devastated the forest's ecology. Although proponents often said clearcuts mimicked natural disturbances like fires or windstorms, the evidence was sketchy and the analogy strained. A controversy around clearcutting emerged later as a strong rallying point for a public that lost confidence. But in the early 1950s, it merely marked one more strategy toward intensifying management and maximizing profits from public resources.

This rapidly expanding timber production posed a dilemma for the Forest Service. On the one hand, it provided a clear focus, what the agency routinely referred to as "getting out the cut." But the Copeland Report had articulated that national forests were guided by diverse priorities—recreation and grazing, wildlife and watershed protection, for instance—and those multiple uses did not always sit well beside clearcuts. The agency in this period often ignored this tension, adopting instead what historian Paul Hirt aptly called a "conspiracy of optimism," the idea that everything would be fine. These were not ignorant foresters but believers in their mission and the capability of technological interventions and best-case scenarios. Furthermore, increased lumber production pleased politicians who increased agency budgets accordingly, and incentives soon were in place to encourage ever more timber cutting, which undermined virtually any other purpose for the national forests. During these decades in the mid-twentieth century, seeds were planted that would lead to conflict within the Forest Service and with the public.

REFUGES

During the mid-twentieth century, the public land system expanded into a national system with new national forests and parks populating the East, and the agencies refined their missions toward a stronger managerial presence and more intensive management. The system also sought to provide some coherence to all the wildlife refuges that had proliferated across the nation. National wildlife refuges are the only federal lands that originated specifically to protect wildlife, although national forests, parks, and rangelands obviously have also played roles by providing habitat and sometimes restrictions on activities that harm wildlife. So the refuges fit uniquely within the public land system, and yet their history is one of the most circuitous in practice and in the institutions developed to promote that protection. At the same time, wildlife refuges demonstrate the same focus on intervention in the environment by public land managers to produce specific ecological outcomes, with mixed results.

In 1956, Congress passed the Fish and Wildlife Act formally establishing the U.S. Fish and Wildlife Service (FWS). However, in 1940, President Franklin D. Roosevelt had reorganized the executive branch and created the Fish and Wildlife Service (without the "U.S.") by combining the Bureau of Fisheries, which had been housed in the Department of Commerce, with the Bureau of Biological Survey, which had been administered through the Department of Agriculture. The U.S. Fish Commission, created in 1871, is the true progenitor of these bureaucratic cogs. Even without a dedicated agency, in the period leading to the bona fide establishment of the FWS, many wildlife refuges were created.

Wildlife preservation as part of public land system existed outside those federal agencies. Origin dates vary by source. Some cite the first federal action for wildlife as the creation in 1868 of a reserve for the Pribilof Islands in Alaska to protect a seal rookery there. Others point to an 1892 order to protect Afognak Island, also in Alaska, as the first, although it was created under the General Revision Act under the authority to protect forests. A law in 1894 prohibited hunting in Yellowstone National Park, which effectively made it a wildlife preserve. Others suggest the 1901 protection of the Wichita Forest Reserve as the origin, because it transformed eventually into a wildlife refuge. But most cite President Theodore Roosevelt, who in 1903 protected Pelican Island as a "preserve and breeding ground for native birds," as taking the first step toward the national system now in place.

The initial impulse to protect animals came from extinctions (e.g., passenger pigeons) and near-extinctions (e.g., bison) that riled up the public, and that impulse emerged from the rather simplistic explanation most believed: that excessive hunting threatened these species. Women's fashion—namely, feathery hats—also devastated many bird species, connecting depletion to consumer choices. Elite hunters organized groups like the Boone and Crockett Club and the American Bison Society to conserve favored wildlife species, while elite women through organizations like the Audubon Society worked politically to stop the plume trade. These private efforts did much to raise awareness and establish new ways of thinking about animals.

These private efforts mobilized policymakers. Pelican Island in Florida was a mere five and a half acres, but Roosevelt aimed to provide a safe haven for the brown pelican and more than a dozen other species who had lost their other rookeries along the East Coast. Perhaps troublingly, Roosevelt possessed no explicit authority to establish such a reserve, but when his aides could not identify any law that prevented him from acting, the president went ahead. By the time he left office in early 1909, Roosevelt left a legacy of fifty-two bird reserves and four big game preserves, the seeds that grew into the wildlife refuge system expanded by other presidents and legislators. Most often these refuges were meant to protect species (or habitat) from hunting or other human depredations.

Although the enthusiastic growth during Roosevelt's presidency may have rested on nonexistent statutory ground, other legal foundations existed. Wildlife refuges face an especially difficult challenge, because they are meant to contain and protect nature that is inherently mobile. This mobility is a key reason why the federal government is involved in wildlife refuges. Derived from common-law traditions, wildlife is classified outside private property systems. That is, I may own land, but

I do not own the bears and ducks that live on it. The Supreme Court confirmed this public trust doctrine in 1842 in *Mater v. Waddell* with regard to water. The Court indicated that some resources—most notably rivers and wildlife, which are both mobile—needed to remain public as the property of the state. In 1896, another Supreme Court decision, *Greer v. Connecticut,* affirmed the federal government's role in regulating wildlife as a public resource. In 1900, Congress passed the Lacey Act and established a federal law against moving killed wildlife across state lines, a reform that slowed the taking of species. In less than two decades, policymakers recognized an international component of the problem and passed the Migratory Bird Treaty Act of 1918 to protect hundreds of migratory species. The treaty established an impetus to protect lands, too, for those migrating birds required places to roost with a great deal of subsequent refuges created to support these birds. When Missouri challenged this federal authority, arguing that it eroded state power, the Supreme Court frankly disagreed and declared it was "insufficient to rely upon the States" to accomplish the stated conservation aims. Another Court decision in 1928, *Hunt v. United States*, confirmed federal authority over game on federal lands, in this case a national forest. In just a few years, then, the legal and political foundations were in place to grow the refuge system with full federal authority.

Meanwhile, losses and problems for wildlife continued. Why? Habitat destruction ranked highest, outpacing the long-held idea of overhunting. Migratory waterfowl populations continued to decline. Starting in 1920, the Bureau of Biological Survey had begun bird-banding studies, which allowed scientists to track birds' routes and led to the recognition that they followed four major flyways—Pacific, Central, Mississippi, Atlantic—a new way of conceptualizing migration and the needs of birds on the ground. Along these flyways, ducks and geese and many other birds relied on rivers, lakes, and other wetlands in an interconnected way. But farmers and urban developers had long seen wetlands as difficult landscapes for economic development, so they pursued drainage as a form of improvement. By the 1930s, more 90 percent of the wetlands of California along the Pacific Flyway were gone, the worst of any state, but Oregon had lost 38 percent and Washington 31 percent. One farmer draining one marsh may not have seemed like a crisis, but each wetland was tied to the others from the perspective of wintering birds. The cumulative impact proved disastrous with vital links severed across the continent. One consequence was the birds crowded on the ever-shrinking remaining lands. The waterfowl became, in effect, collateral damage to development. By 1934 that damage put waterfowl at their all-time low number of 27 million and some species hovered near extinction, such as whooping cranes at 14 and egrets about 150. Once the scientific understanding of these costs became clearer, legislators and parts of the public advocated for solutions.

Adding new refuges to the existing ones obviously could boost the effort to protect waterfowl or other endangered wildlife. But new land acquisitions stuttered forward due to the complicated nature of private property and broader political and economic trends. In 1924, a number of years after the height of conservation achievements, Congress created the Upper Mississippi Wildlife and Fish Refuge, which covered nearly two hundred thousand acres along almost three hundred miles of the river. Five years later, another Migratory Bird Act passed Congress designed to create a commission that would advise and acquire land for new refuges. Bad timing, with the stock market crash also coming in 1929, sidelined this initiative. Franklin Roosevelt's administration revived the dead momentum and relaunched the federal program.

The 1930s ended up being a pivot for wildlife management as it became for many public land issues, and like much in that decade, results were mixed and incomplete. One of President Roosevelt's first acts was to appoint a Committee on Wildlife Restoration, which included Thomas Beck (a journalist), Jay "Ding" Darling (a cartoonist and conservationist), and Aldo Leopold (a forester, professor of game management, and conservationist). This august committee studied available evidence, unequivocally condemned the excessive drainage projects occurring, and recommended $25 million to be used immediately to purchase marginal land for the purpose of refuges. Marginal land buybacks were popular during the drought and depression of the 1930s that saw families forced off land on which many could not make a living. Many of these marginal home places became part of wildlife refuges and national forests where they might be rehabilitated for habitat and forests instead of subpar farms. The committee set a long-term goal of adding another 12.5 million acres to the refuge system, but given where wildlife fell on government priority lists, the committee had to settle for less. Roosevelt found

$1 million, and even that much smaller share got sidelined for a time. He also appointed Darling to head the Biological Survey. Steps now moved in, or at least pointed toward, the right direction.

Congress kept at work. In 1934, it passed the Wildlife Coordination Act that asked other federal agencies to consider wildlife in its construction projects, a request that was without any enforcement mechanisms and thus ineffective. This failure constituted a major problem, because New Deal programs continued working on drainage projects all over the country, as well as building large dams, that far outweighed any improvement produced by the requested coordination. Dams and irrigation projects drastically rearranged habitats. Reversing the development tide of government and industry always faced multiple and often compounding obstacles.

More important than the Coordination Act, which had a minor effect at best, was the Duck Stamp Act (formally the Migratory Bird Hunting Stamp Act), also enacted in 1934. This innovative law tackled the ubiquitous funding shortfall for financing new refuges and became a way to bolster the system. Hunters purchased stamps—including artwork by Darling—to be affixed to their state hunting licenses, and the $1 fee went to fund the purchase (90 percent of the revenues) and improvement (the remaining 10 percent) of wildlife refuges. Darling ably implemented the program as he led the Biological Survey at this critical moment. Still, the funding fell short of the need. A senator from South Dakota, Peter Norbeck, a well-liked politician suffering from terminal cancer, managed to get his colleagues to agree to $6 million earmarked for the refuge system the following year. This financial infusion allowed Darling to extend important rehabilitation work. Nearly forty CCC camps built the infrastructure needed to reflood the wetlands that had been dried by drought and drainage. For example, in eastern Oregon's Malheur National Wildlife Refuge, Ira Gabrielson, Darling's successor, described the process or diverting water back into the marshes as "a moment of tremendous satisfaction to see the water flowing into the channel that led to the thirsty lake bed. . . . Malheur again became a great marsh, teeming and throbbing with life as it had been before its destruction. It was a never-to-be-forgotten lesson of the power of man to destroy, and also of the power of man to restore." Such scenes multiplied across the flyways as federal money purchased new land, often farms that had gone belly up because they had been located in marginal areas, much as the Forest Service acquired eastern forests that had been cut over and abandoned.

Funding remained a challenge in complex ways. Local communities, even if the land was poor and not supporting viable farms, did not always welcome the federal government acquiring land for refuges, because that land, taken out of production—even marginal production—would generate no tax revenue for local counties and municipalities. To help with this problem, in 1935, Congress passed the Refuge Revenue Sharing Act, which gave local counties 25 percent of money received from selling "timber, hay, grass, or other spontaneous products of the soil." The law effectively incentivized locals to pressure refuges to cut timber or make hay, activities not always aligned with wildlife goals.

When wildlife conservation first began as a federal initiative, it seemed simple: provide a refuge space and prohibit hunting within its boundaries. But the needs of wildlife proved far more complicated, and by the 1930s, federal refuge managers were busy intervening in the natural order of things, often in ways that seemed quite similar to the activity that had compromised habitat in the first place. Consider the refuges in the Malheur and Klamath Basins in Oregon and California along the Pacific Flyway. The network of refuges there were the largest bird refuges in the nation before later additions in Alaska. They sat in vast agricultural basins with complex irrigation networks. Although some people, like the Oregon photographer and ornithologist William Finley, opposed the reclamation projects that drained the wetlands and used lakes as reservoirs, federal support meant they proceeded. The region's Bureau of Reclamation projects expanded irrigated farms and meant that wildlife refuges always were the junior partner in the federal landscape. Farmers simply were too powerful a constituency, and their votes added up in ways ducks' votes never could.

Nevertheless, hunters did vote, and the mid-1930s impulse to save waterfowl grew. Armed with some New Deal labor and money, refuge managers used the same type of ecological manipulating that irrigators used to rewater drained lands or to create new wetlands. Using canals and diversions, refuge staff manipulated water levels and pathways. And although all these lands were interconnected, their uses were not necessarily compatible. The lakes and wetlands in wildlife refuges in places like the Klamath Basin in Oregon or the Central Valley near Sacramento attracted thousands of birds, and none of them recognized the difference between a farmer's field and the adjacent refuge. The problematic boundary between public and private, ubiquitous in public land controversies, reared its head.

Farmers demanded a solution to the birds eating their crops. Refuge managers took two strategies, both of which demonstrated the government's intensifying management in mid-century, creating what some environmental historians call hybrid landscapes—places so mixed that boundaries blurred between human-manipulated landscapes and waterways and the wild or autonomous ecological processes carrying on unencumbered by human hands. One, they grew food specifically for ducks and other waterfowl. Two, they sky-herded flocks by airplane to direct birds to the right areas—public commons, rather than private property. Such interventions had traveled a long way from simply creating a refuge boundary and prohibiting hunting.

In fact, hunting by the 1940s had become one of the most important activities that promoted wildlife conservation. Many refuges by then were little more than duck farms whose main purpose was to produce ducks available to be shot. This marked the continuing paradoxical relationship between hunters and wildlife and refuges. Some of the earliest conservationists were hunters who wanted to establish programs to maintain certain type of wildlife—those prized species they wanted to hunt. And one of the key approaches to conserving wildlife was to stop hunting them, but scientists by the 1930s and 1940s understood better the more complicated causes of wildlife decline. But finding a constituency who loved something as amorphous as "habitat" was not possible; tapping into a constituency that loved shooting at ducks was easy. Duck hunting had grown in popularity, and many private clubs were established after World War II. In 1949, Congress amended the Duck Stamp Act, doubling its cost and the resulting revenue. Out of this legislation, a quarter of the refuges were reclassified from "inviolate sanctuary refuges" where no hunting was allowed into "wildlife management areas" where hunting was permitted. The wildlife refuges, then, became an important public hunting ground. More ducks became the single measure of refuge success, but other species did not necessarily benefit from the system. Accordingly, this practice reflected the larger intensification of public land management in this era and included some of the same myopic results that viewed ecosystem health through narrow definitions of increased productivity.

Managing waterfowl was not the only thing the FWS and its predecessors did, although the wildlife refuges overwhelmingly focused on birds. An additional example covering roughly the same years demonstrates again how refuge managers intensified their work on the land.

The National Elk Refuge in Jackson Hole, Wyoming, provides an alternative: a land- and mammal-based management conundrum. Elk once lived across most of North America, but throughout the nineteenth century local extinctions happened regularly, and elk no longer were found in any significant numbers outside the far West. The greatest concentration remained in what is now called the Greater Yellowstone Ecosystem. This relatively wild habitat and Yellowstone National Park, which prohibited hunting beginning in 1894, furnished elk a relatively safe haven. South of the park was Jackson Hole, a high, wide valley in the shadow of the Grand Teton range. For millennia, elk had migrated south through the valley into southwestern Wyoming and northwestern Utah. But in the late nineteenth century, farms and ranches prevented this age-old pattern, blocking elk with new communities, new animals, and new fences. Consequently, elk began wintering in Jackson Hole, where winters could be severe and forage scarce. Two unsatisfactory possibilities followed. Elk broke through ranch fences and raided haystacks, something the livestock interests could not abide for long. Or elk died of starvation, something that horrified the public. During the 1910–1911 winter, about five thousand animals died, and a local rancher, Stephen Leek, toured the country and shared photographs of dead and dying animals, which generated important national interest.

Government officials took note. Wyoming had created a state game preserve already and appropriated $5,000 in 1910 to feed elk in the winter. The following year, Wyoming asked the federal government for money and received $20,000, along with a biologist, Edward A. Preble, who studied the situation. He recognized the economic importance of elk for Wyoming, and he recommended the federal government intervene. In 1912, 1,760 acres were purchased and another 1,000 withdrawn from the public domain to create what is now known as the National Elk Refuge just north of Jackson, Wyoming.

Paradoxes mounted. The region proved to be one of the last major sites where elk could survive, while their numbers thinned across the rest of the continent. But by becoming more concentrated and restricted in their migration patterns, they overwhelmed available habitat, which required the federal government to set aside public land where they could winter without interfering with private farms and ranches. The biologist and later president of the Wilderness Society, Olaus Murie, worked at the refuge for decades beginning in 1927, and envisioned adding more habitat to create what he imagined would be the greatest game paradise in the country. The Depression allowed more properties to be purchased, and soon the National Elk Refuge was part of a large constellation of public lands, including Grand Teton National Park (established in 1929), Grand Teton National Monument (established in 1943 and later incorporated into the park), and various national forests, not to mention Yellowstone National Park not far to the north. Despite all these public lands, problems for the elk continued. Even with the additions, elk concentrated too much for the meager forage in the valley, so refuge managers had to feed elk hay. Although this measure first was introduced as a last resort and meant only to be employed during the worst years, feeding elk at the refuge became a routine activity and even now is incorporated as part of the local economy, in which tourists pay to be out among the elk during feeding time. This is one more example where federal managers intensified their management strategies.

When the U.S. Fish and Wildlife Service finally received its current administrative shape in 1956, more than half a century of history with wildlife refuges was being capped off. Much as had been the case with the earliest national forests, the refuge system started haltingly and had to establish legal precedents and funding to secure a place on the land for mobile creatures who faced threats from hunters and habitat destruction. Built out of both the public domain and purchases of private land, wildlife refuges provided a place where wildlife could rebound in a sanctuary. Yet, to do so, federal managers faced obstacles in politics and on the land. With perennial funding challenges, they needed a mechanism to secure funds, which turned out to be appealing to hunters, paradoxically opening up more refuges to hunting. Meanwhile, to bolster wildlife populations, FWS workers intervened on the land in sometimes dramatic ways to ensure the right species were in the right place and at the right time.

This intensified management turned wildlife refuges by mid-century into highly regulated landscapes meant to produce particular outcomes, just as forests and rangelands were producing two-by-fours and prime rib. The managerial ethos entwined with the hopes that wildlife refuges truly offered refuge.

CONCLUSION

The public land system that was built by the mid-twentieth century had entered a new and important stage characterized by both nationalizing its scope and mission and intensifying its managerial hand in the natural environment and for those who depended on its resources. With the system's pieces in place, the agencies' missions became defined more sharply, managers' confidence and ambition increased, and the public's understanding of these landscapes expanded. Managers grabbed at scientific theories that changed in these years to show a less predictable natural world than before. Figuring out how that world worked had become a high-stakes effort, because the land itself often suffered with deteriorating ecosystems. Rangelands eroded with countless hooves; clearcuts scarred mountainsides; birds flew to the edge of extinction. Meanwhile, corporate powers exerted their influence on the policies being adopted and implemented, while critics in and out of the public lands agencies charted new trails such as wilderness recreation. All told, that meant this era was one of growth and emerging contention. Yet political conflict remained comparatively muted, which can be explained by the near-uniformity of those sitting at the public lands table making decisions. Just around the historical corner, though, lurked bigger challenges when the table enlarged and new laws invited other people with distinct values to assess the landscape, moving this system more toward becoming the public's land.

4

Balancing

INTRODUCTION

IN THE DECADES AFTER WORLD WAR II, the public ventured into the public lands in unprecedented numbers as recreationists, backpacking into isolated backcountry mountains, picnicking outside of metropolitan areas, worshiping at monumental scenic features, or just driving through. They grew alarmed at clearcuts and crowds. They worried about pesticides harming wildlife. They found tamed nature insufficient and wanted something wilder from the heritage of their public lands. And so the public organized, protested, and called on Congress to rewrite the rules to strengthen wilderness and wildlife protections, to include citizens and scientists in decision making, and to identify and enact long-term planning goals. This movement helped motivate wholesale transitions in policies between 1960 and 1980, the second such shift in public lands history along with the arrival of the conservation movement at the century's turn.

Of course, not everything changed; existing trends continued their momentum, but they did so alongside countervailing practices. Timber sales and grazing on public lands persisted. The engineering of wildlife refuges continued. Yet the legacies from agencies intensifying their management produced a public reaction that called for and reinforced the emerging alternatives to rebalancing public land use with restraint and new goals.

The public lands table transformed from the mid-1950s through the 1970s, a process that was born with difficulty but optimism, and the change created a long-lasting legacy that continues to govern both how Americans manage these lands and how they protest those changes.

Using the table metaphor, the biggest change was the number of chairs surrounding the table and who occupied them. Within the agencies, no longer did the engineer or resource specialist occupy all the seats. Now, wildlife biologists and ecologists took up new seats, offering novel criteria to identify management priorities and strategies, as well as redefining what success looked like. In addition, the extractive clients of these agencies—the mining company, the livestock operator, the mill owner—faced a longer gap between themselves and the table. To be sure, they still had the ear of the forest ranger and the grazing inspector, but that ear was not as close as the clients had become accustomed to, a development that many traditional extractive users found frustrating and threatening. Finally, and perhaps most important in a democracy, the public at last had seats at the table. By the end of the era, every agency relied on new processes that required citizen input. New priorities emerged as a result, including wilderness recreation and wildlife conservation. Both had been present for decades, but with citizen pressure applied, they emerged as much stronger priorities that agencies could not easily marginalize. Besides new emphases, citizen input also challenged agency actions. What had heretofore been mostly unquestioned managerial prerogatives became subject to public scrutiny, review, and litigation. By remaking the public lands table, citizens, policymakers, and agencies made things far more complex and slower, but also more inclusive and democratic.

WILDERNESS

American colonists imbued wilderness with great cultural meaning, an obstacle to progress and holder of otherworldly power; postwar activists imbued it with great political meaning, an opportunity for virtuous restraint and repository of natural goodness. Continual efforts to pass the Wilderness Act occupied public land champions for nearly a decade. As a movement, it started over a proposed dam that would alter a national monument, flooding part of the national park system. But the bigger threat lay within the Forest Service, which had a long but checkered history of wilderness preservation but whose authority the public began to challenge. The struggle to get the wilderness bill through Congress entailed a national popular political campaign that demanded engagement with opponents over definitions and compromises, as well as delays and further reforms within public lands agencies that would illuminate the changing values of the times. As well as any political campaign, the fight for wilderness illustrated the democratic promise that lay in the public lands.

Threats to Wilderness

The Great Depression and World War II transformed the West. New Deal spending infused western states with new infrastructure, including roads and massive hydroelectric power dams that spread electricity through rural areas for the first time. When the war arrived, the West depended on these changes to accelerate its industrial capacity, such as new or expanded shipyards and aerospace factories that swelled western cities. The mass expansion of air conditioning for homes also made parts of the desert West more comfortable. To support and encourage more migration and industrial development in the West, boosters in Congress and communities—from small towns to metropolises like Denver or Los Angeles—worked to draw federal resources to massive regional development schemes. One of them, the Colorado River Storage Project (CRSP), galvanized lovers of wildness across the nation.

The Bureau of Reclamation, which was in charge of the CRSP, proposed ten dams in the Upper Colorado River Basin for flood control, hydroelectric power, and storage against drought. Since the 1930s, these large projects had become common—and not only in the West—to massively re-engineer a region's natural resources to support a growing economy and booming population. One dam site in the CRSP plan, Echo Park, sat at the confluence of the Yampa and Green Rivers within Dinosaur National Monument not far from where Utah, Colorado, and Wyoming converge. Dinosaur was a spectacular place where rivers wound through deep canyons amid the surrounding desert. Flooding the riparian area within the national monument seemed sacrilegious, a violation of the park system's sanctity that the public would not abide.

Two leaders of different conservation organizations collaborated on a six-year nationwide campaign to stop the dam. Howard Zahniser, the executive secretary of the Wilderness Society based in Washington, DC, teamed up with David Brower, the executive director of the Sierra Club based in San Francisco. Other groups played notable roles, too, and this campaign presented a new coordinated force in conservation politics. While mild-mannered Zahniser worked hard to build and maintain a grassroots coalition, the brash Brower willingly confronted Bureau of Reclamation officials and supporters of CRSP in Congress. In a famous exchange at a 1954 congressional hearing, Brower pointed out a major error in the calculation of evaporation rates that showed the bureau overestimated the dam project's efficiency and benefits. The error was so large that, arguably, the Echo Park Dam would no longer be needed by adjusting the height of another of the proposed dams outside the national park system. The mistake embarrassed the engineers and infuriated supporters in Congress. Confronting the powerful with math, however, would not be enough.

The centerpiece of the campaign to stop the dam was to get an enthusiastic public behind the cause led by Brower and Zahniser. The Sierra Club organized float trips through the national monument, bringing a couple hundred members in 1953 and nearly a thousand in 1954. Journalists joined, and the awesome beauty of the river coursing through the desert helped some writers change their mind, which they publicized in their newspapers when they returned home. A Sierra Club filmmaker tagged along on one of the float trips, and the documentary he produced captured the scenery for audiences who had never been to Dinosaur, including members of Congress. Finally, the leaders enlisted Wallace Stegner, a writer of novels and histories of the West, to edit a collection of essays celebrating this wild corner of the West. Alfred Knopf published it as *This Is Dinosaur* (1955), and every member of Congress received a copy. A popular movement had coalesced, the first substantially national environmental protest since Hetch Hetchy.

Resolution came in 1956 when Congress removed the controversial dam from the CRSP. However, Brower and Zahniser's strategy contained a weakness. A significant component of their argument rested on the fact that Echo Park was in the national park system, and conservationists drew a line there. The final CRSP stated clearly that "no dam or reservoir constructed under the authorization of this act shall be within any national park or monument." That part of the public land system, they maintained, must remain sacrosanct. The compromise, however, allowed for a larger dam at Glen Canyon—not in the national park system—near the Utah-Arizona border, which flooded a magnificent canyon beneath Lake Powell. Brower agreed to the compromise before spending time at Glen Canyon. When he eventually visited the canyon, he felt instant and deep regret that helped push him toward greater militancy in his activism on behalf of other public lands.

As historians have pointed out, the Echo Park campaign represented an important turning point. That a federal agency—the Bureau of Reclamation—was ready to flood part of the national park system demonstrated that landscapes—places many people considered wild and protected—were vulnerable to despoliation, and not just from corporations seeking profit but from the federal government itself. The Forest Service and the Park Service after World War II seemed willing to allow such desecration, so a citizen movement proved necessary to demand better protection. And so, following the Echo Park victory, Zahniser led the coalition that he helped build to craft new legislation to create stronger and permanent protections for wilderness. If this wilderness bill could be enacted, conservationists thought they would not have to fight repeated battles over places like Echo Park.

Relatedly, the Forest Service fueled conservationists' sense of insecurity with its ongoing reclassification efforts. Just before he died in 1939, forester Bob Marshall had proposed a set of protected wilderness areas within the national forests through the U-Regulations. After World War II, the agency began its reclassification process for wild (5,000 to 100,000 acres) and wilderness areas (greater than 100,000 acres) to clarify boundaries that often were vague. Within these indistinct borders, road building and timber sales were disallowed. But when the Forest Service developed closer ties with the timber industry in the postwar era, conservationists suspected reclassification would strip wild areas of those protections. They were right.

In Oregon, the first big battle over reclassification focused attention on the central Cascade Mountains near the Three Sisters, three peaks amid majestic forests. Three Sisters Primitive Area had been created in 1937, even predating the U-Regulations, and had remained a favorite roadless area for regional backpackers and naturalists who favored its relatively pristine setting. In 1950, the Forest Service informed the public that it planned to reclassify the primitive area and proposed cutting 53,000 acres from the Horse Creek drainage basin to allow timber cutting. In exchange, the agency proposed adding some high-elevation wild areas. The following year, USFS rangers led an automobile tour of the area for interested parties of local climbers and hikers, scientists, and civic organizations. Only two Ruths—Ruth Onthank and Ruth Hopson—voiced strong opposition to reducing the primitive area, so the agency believed it would face few objections when it formally announced its decision in 1954.

Instead, the Forest Service faced stiff opposition. Ruth Onthank and her husband Karl spearheaded a new organization, the Friends of the Three Sisters, to counter the Forest Service proposal. This "Friends of" organization modeled a type of local, grassroots activist community that popped up elsewhere and transformed the wilderness movement, helping to keep public lands from being reduced to just an arm of the extractive economy. The Friends of the Three Sisters emphasized that the trade-off was not equivalent. The group gathered allies from the International Woodworkers of America union, who pushed for better timber management so that the industry would not need to assault public forests and who generally suspected the Forest Service of not serving workers' interests. Others argued for access to recreational lands and for scientific study instead of reducing the wild forests.

At hearings in Eugene, Oregon, in February 1955, the Forest Service heard strong arguments against its proposed reductions. Although most who testified came from Oregon, national leaders in conservation, such as Zahniser, also crossed the continent to express their values, emphasizing that this constituted a *national* issue. Public lands, such as this valley within one national forest, belonged to all Americans. Conservationists argued this point with increasing frequency after the war to counter short-term and local arguments about economic development. Despite the organizing by the Friends of Three Sisters and support from the Sierra Club and the Wilderness Society, activists failed to dissuade the Forest Service and only carved 12,000 acres from the agency's 53,000-acre proposal.

Yet this battle, lost by 1957, ignited important parts of the wilderness movement. It demonstrated that the Forest Service had no compunctions about opening up long-protected areas for timber cutting, and it showed conservationists that the agency saw wilderness almost exclusively as high-elevation areas where timber did not grow in commercial volume. Conservationists derided this as "rock and ice" wilderness. The conflict in the Cascades galvanized the movement by revealing the Forest Service's intent with its reclassification strategy. This campaign proceeded almost simultaneously with the Echo Park effort and pushed conservationists into a new stage of activism that was less defensive—that is, defending each new threat to part of the public lands Americans treasured—and more offensive. Conservationists wanted to create a permanent, safe wilderness system.

The Wilderness Act

The basic idea of the wilderness bill was to strengthen wilderness designation. As the Forest Service showed in Oregon and dozens of other areas in the 1950s, agency administrators could easily change boundaries and reduce levels of protection; although allowed a hearing, the public had few recourses to stymie agency decisions. Zahniser led the way with the Wilderness Society, the organization most focused on promoting wilderness protection. Since the late 1940s, Zahniser had imagined a federal system of wilderness areas but did not turn his full professional attention to this task until the Echo Park controversy concluded. Zahniser drafted the first version of the wilderness bill in January 1956 and worked tirelessly until he died in May 1964. President Lyndon Johnson signed the law on September 3, 1964. This long journey revealed Americans' changing values surrounding public lands generally, making wilderness a useful historical window into broader concerns. In 1956, Senator Hubert Humphrey, a Minnesota Democrat, and Representative John Saylor, an Ohio Republican, introduced the first version of the wilderness bill, launching the eight-year legislative journey. As wilderness allies pushed the wilderness bill forward, Congress gathered information, delayed, and compromised. Such strategies shaped the ultimate Wilderness Act's implementation and the public's understanding of the issues involved and revealed the powerful politics of wilderness.

One of the first fact-finding, delay-inducing measures Congress instituted was the Outdoor Recreation Resources Review Commission (ORRRC). Created in 1958, the ORRRC was directed to recommend to

Congress actions necessary to meet the nation's growing outdoor recreation needs. This commission considered urban recreation options, but its focus centered on public lands. In late 1960, Wallace Stegner, the author who edited *This Is Dinosaur*, penned an especially eloquent appeal to the ORRRC's commissioner in charge of wilderness. Subsequently known simply as "The Wilderness Letter," Stegner articulated feelings about wilderness that many Americans held. At the heart of this idea was wilderness as a place where American character was formed. "I want to speak for the wilderness idea as something that has helped form our character and that has certainly shaped our history as a people," wrote Stegner. This framing, obviously, marginalized the Native people who called "wilderness" home and who, almost without exception, lost land and lives and power in the character-forming episodes that American state and military power exerted in clearing the wilderness. To Stegner and countless other Americans, though, wilderness offered a counterpoint and salve to the urban-industrial civilization that ran riot over land. Closing his letter to the ORRRC, Stegner wrote, "We simply need that wild country available to us, even if we never do more than drive to its edge and look in. For it can be a means of reassuring ourselves of our sanity as creatures, a part of the geography of hope." Many Americans invested their faith in wilderness as a hopeful place, a spiritual place. To Stegner and those who followed him, wilderness was an idea as much as a specific place, a collection of ideals made manifest on the land.

For his part, Zahniser defined wilderness in a way that was not quite so idealized. Having traveled through many wild areas, such as the Gila Wilderness Area—the first one ever created at the behest of Aldo Leopold—Zahniser knew that areas were not pristine in the sense that they were untouched or never used. He saw the damage from overgrazing in the Gila in New Mexico. Using words such as "pristine" or "untouched" would have prevented wilderness designations virtually everywhere, so he sought language that would capture wilderness correctly. Sometime in the mid-1950s, Zahniser was visiting with Northwest activist Polly Dyer, who sang the praises of the wild Pacific coast along a section of Olympic National Park. Dyer described it as "untrammeled," and Zahniser recognized that "untrammeled" fit better than "undisturbed" or "pristine." From his time in places where livestock grazing or mining had damaged the land, he knew places could be damaged.

But untrammeled, meaning unconfined, worked and meant to him that wilderness was "not subjected to human controls and manipulations that hamper the free play of natural forces." Once grazing or prospecting were removed, a landscape could become untrammeled again. The definition Zahniser wrote into the Wilderness Act read, "A wilderness, in contrast with those areas where man and his works dominate the landscape, is hereby recognized as an area where the earth and its community of life are untrammeled by man, where man himself is a visitor who does not remain." This definition remains in effect, an expansive and generous definition that opens the wilderness for the nonhuman world to continue along its evolutionary pathways.

While the ORRRC gathered information from the public and recommended federal investment in outdoor recreation infrastructure, and as Zahniser refined definitions, the Forest Service worried about being sidelined. From the agency's perspective, its long history in conservation was rooted in multiple-use management. National forests from their inception protected forests and watersheds. In addition, their forests and rangelands provided important habitats for both wildlife and livestock. And for decades the agency protected scenic places and developed recreational opportunities. After all, the first protected wilderness was protected by the Forest Service. This history gave the agency confidence in the 1950s that it could continue providing all of these resources to the public without needing the wilderness bill.

Fearing being overrun, the Forest Service wanted some statutory protection for what it saw as its mission and expertise. The agency had easily accommodated increased demands for commodity production beginning in World War II, but the Forest Service recognized that the public's demands for outdoor recreation and the aesthetic value of forests could shrink the agency's freedom to operate as it saw fit. So USFS leaders aimed for new statutory guidance, which became the Multiple Use Sustained Yield Act of 1960 (MUSY). The law stated, "The national forests are established and shall be administered for outdoor recreation, range, timber, watershed, and wildlife and fish purposes." This list of purposes extended what the 1897 Forest Management Act had identified—timber and watershed only—and defined balanced use, deliberately listing outdoor recreation first. However, the brief law—less than a full page—noted that under multiple-use management, "some land will be used for less than all of the resources; and harmonious and coordinated management of the productivity of the land, with consideration being given to the relative values of the various resources, and not necessarily the combination of uses that will give the greatest dollar return or the greatest unit output." This definition weakened the maximization impulse often pursued by the timber industry and its most devoted supporters within the agency and Congress. And MUSY specifically called out wilderness: "The establishment and maintenance of areas of wilderness are consistent with the purposes and provisions of this Act." Notwithstanding these elements that arguably favored reducing commodity production, the definition of sustained yield demanded "the achievement and maintenance in perpetuity of a high-level annual or regular periodic output of the various renewable resources of the national forests without impairment of the productivity of the land." In the context of the time, "high-level" was the key operative word for the agency. Edward Cliff, who was assistant chief of the Forest Service when MUSY passed and chief beginning in 1962, remembered MUSY as defining sustained yield as "sustained production at a high level." In many ways, MUSY gave the Forest Service what it wanted: managerial discretion to keep managing all its resources as it wanted with an eye toward high production. And MUSY *rhetorically* looked balanced, but critics of the agency questioned whether those five uses were equal in practice. In addition, opponents of wilderness adopted multiple-use rhetoric to argue against wilderness, saying that it was single use.

The Forest Service initially opposed the wilderness bill, but with MUSY, it believed it retained its prerogatives and discretion. Once that was assured, the agency supported the bill, albeit with lukewarm enthusiasm. The National Park Service, however, also initially opposed the wilderness bill, which often surprises observers who are unfamiliar with the differences between the agencies. The NPS director at the time was Conrad Wirth, one of the most influential directors in the agency's history. After Zahniser shared a bill draft with Wirth, the director explained the Park Service would not support it because the agency already managed lands so that they remained "unimpaired for the enjoyment of future generations." Nothing could be gained, Wirth thought, for national parks to be included in a national wilderness preservation system. "What we have now," Wirth told Zahniser, "could hardly be improved upon."

Zahniser recognized the importance of getting Park Service support, and he worked hard to convince Wirth. A subsequent draft of the bill, for instance, excluded areas in national parks from inclusion in the system, a way to give the director more flexibility and discretion. Wirth announced support in 1958.

During the same years of the wilderness bill's gestation, the Park Service faced two developments that showed the complexities and paradoxes of the parks and wilderness. First was Mission 66. The national parks had seen better days, as the years of depression and war made up more than a decade of neglect. After Wirth became NPS director in 1951, he sought to address the poor state of parks and expand his agency's influence. In 1955, he acknowledged the dire sanitary situation in some parks, likening campgrounds to "rural slums." Embarrassed by such conditions and tired of congressional cuts, Wirth and allies pushed Mission 66, an ambitious plan that would celebrate the agency's fiftieth anniversary in 1966. With President Dwight Eisenhower's and Congress's support, Wirth remade the national parks over the next decade. That makeover focused almost all of its attention on developing visitor facilities. The program spent more than $1 billion over the decade and tallied an impressive set of statistics: 1,570 miles of improved roads, 1,197 miles of new roads, 936 miles of new or improved trails, 1,502 parking areas, 575 new campgrounds, 221 new administrative buildings, 114 visitor centers, and much more. This new infrastructure attracted more visitors. The year before Mission 66 began, 46 million tourists visited the national parks; during the year of the system's golden jubilee, 133 million visitors spent time in the parks. This full-scale development certainly helped many Americans learn the value of national parks and public lands, but it alarmed wilderness advocates who saw wilderness as a place for undeveloped recreation, for solitude, for an escape from automobiles. The wilderness bill became more urgent for many because the Park Service busied itself making wild places more accommodating to people and less untrammeled.

The other transformation emerged from a specific management challenge at Yellowstone but took on influence far beyond one park and one issue. The Greater Yellowstone Ecosystem offers excellent elk habitat, and by the early twentieth century predators such as wolves had been eliminated and grizzly bears sharply reduced. The elk numbers grew too high for the range to support the herds. As early as the 1930s, NPS biologists decried the ecological consequences of these animals destroying the range: grasses were gone, soil compacted, and willows disappeared (which also reduced beaver populations). With the Yellowstone elk herd numbering ten thousand, managers determined it was twice as large as the range could support. Five thousand animals needed to be killed, according to this plan. Abundant elk had plagued Yellowstone for years. Sometimes, a so-called firing line appeared on the edge of the park where hunters awaited the elk crossing the border and poured lead into them. Director Wirth suggested opening some of the park to public hunting, an idea that received massive criticism, and he soon retracted. The result was the Park Service itself slaughtering thousands of animals. The scenes of carnage disturbed the public, regardless of the fact that most everyone recognized there were too many animals for the range to sustain. The Park Service faced a public relations nightmare. In the time-honored manner of government, a committee was convened to study the problem.

Secretary of Interior Stewart Udall appointed an Advisory Board on Wildlife Management to review NPS policies on wildlife management. The committee chair was A. Starker Leopold, Aldo Leopold's son. The subsequent report, known widely as the Leopold Report, was a mere thirteen pages, but it offered a new way of conceiving national parks and, as such, became a revolutionary document.

Leopold explained that the Park Service's history to that point was about *protection:* keeping hunters from harming wildlife, keeping predators from killing the wildlife the public wanted to view (i.e., killing wolves and coyotes), and keeping fire from burning habitat. However, Leopold, who was a wildlife specialist, argued that more was needed now. Further, and more important, he recommended the proper goal of parks should be "that the biotic associations within each park be maintained, or where necessary recreated, as nearly as possible in the condition that prevailed when the area was first visited by the white man. A national park should represent a vignette of primitive America." This passage encapsulated a new vision that did not center on the visitor experience in the park but focused on ecological processes within the park. The Park Service would need fewer concessionaires selling food and souvenirs to touring Americans and more biologists figuring out how to reintroduce banished species or fire to ecosystems that depended on them. This was, as both Leopold and the new NPS director George Hartzog recognized, a "stupendous" change.

As the Park Service demonstrated in the lead up to the Wilderness Act, countervailing and complementary pressures pushed toward compromises. In Congress, the most important agent of compromise was a Democratic representative from western Colorado, Wayne Aspinall. He chaired the House Interior Committee through which any wilderness bill had to pass, and remained a champion of resource users against those who sought protections. Zahniser and his congressional allies had to work with Aspinall to compromise over issues related to grazing and mining before the wilderness bill would get closer to passage. Aspinall was an effective politician for his constituents of western Colorado where natural resource extraction ruled the economy and thus required a strong multiple-use policy governing public lands. He also was politically savvy, understanding that the national political tides were sweeping in with environmental values. Although ignoring the wilderness bill in 1956 when it was first introduced was easy, Aspinall knew he would have to address it. Almost immediately, he began counseling his allies in Congress and his constituents that they needed to delay the legislative process—such as with the ORRRC—to develop amendments and compromises. If the bill was going to be inevitable, as Aspinall understood it to be, it needed to be palatable.

There are too many changes and compromises in the eight-year legislative history to chronicle, but three are especially notable and bear the heavy fingerprints of Aspinall. As a legislator, Aspinall fiercely protected Congress's prerogative. Conservationists banked on the executive branch being a more receptive steward to wilderness, so Zahniser's initial bills placed power to protect wilderness in the executive branch. Aspinall wrestled it back into Congress. This change ultimately benefited wilderness activists, because once a wilderness area was created by Congress, it became much harder to change, thus strengthening the status. Second, a good portion of Aspinall's district was used by ranchers for public land grazing. Sensitive to the problems of coalition building, Zahniser knew he could not alienate those ranchers—and their congressional champion Aspinall—who strongly opposed wilderness designation. Zahniser reluctantly added to the bill that grazing would be tolerated in wilderness "where these practices have already become well established." Knowing as he did the damage overgrazing caused, this change was hard to stomach, and yet, in the long run, wilderness advocates hoped that grazing would be reduced; besides, the compromise was necessary to get the bill through Congress's Interior committees. Finally, potential wilderness areas held valuable minerals, and mining companies made sure their ability to locate new caches of them remained intact. Zahniser reworked the law again to allow mining to continue within the boundaries of wilderness areas indefinitely and for prospecting to occur within wilderness areas through December 31, 1983. If prospectors located a valuable mineral, they could claim it and develop the mine and necessary reasonable facilities to support extraction. On top of that, the president had the prerogative to withdraw from wilderness designation an area if minerals there could "better serve the interests of the United States." Even with these measures assured, many commodity interests—logging, livestock, and mining companies—still opposed the bill. But Aspinall had secured sufficient legal compromises to move the bill forward. In 1961, the Senate had passed a version of the law with only eight dissenting votes. After public hearings across the West and more compromises, a version finally passed both the House (with one no vote) and the Senate (with twelve no votes) in 1964 that President Johnson signed on September 3.

The Wilderness Act presented something profoundly new in public lands history. Most powerfully, it created the most restrictive category of land protection. The act immediately turned 9.1 million acres of national forest land into the National Wilderness Preservation System. Within these designated areas, commercial activities generally were prohibited, no permanent roads or structures were permitted, and no motorized or mechanical transport was allowed. A handful of exceptions, like grazing and backcountry airstrips, allowed for preexisting uses to continue. Importantly, to modify any of the wilderness areas or create new ones, public hearings were mandatory. This procedure proved a critically important element, for it ensured new avenues for citizen input on public land management, an extension of democratic access to decision-making. Over the course of nearly a decade, the campaign for the Wilderness Act forced agencies to refine their missions and respond to a public clamoring for stronger conservation measures. The law nudged federal conservation onto different tracks.

Additional Wilderness Legislation

But Congress was not done in 1964, or with wilderness. First, on the same day President Johnson signed the Wilderness Act, he signed the Land and Water Conservation Fund (LWCF). Originally recommended as part of the ORRRC work, the LWCF provided a trust fund used "to assist in preserving, developing, and assuring accessibility" for outdoor recreation "for individual active participation . . . and to strengthen the health and vitality" of Americans and visitors from elsewhere. When Congress debated the law in the early 1960s, NPS Director Conrad Wirth urged senators to support it so that unborn generations could develop "their God-given right to understand, enjoy, and obtain inspiration and healthful benefits from the very land, water, and air from whence all have sprung." Such heady rhetoric suggests the import public land advocates put into outdoor recreation and park spaces at this historical moment. The fund furnished money to purchase new lands, such as inholdings within existing federal parks or wilderness areas, and matched state grants to bolster local public parks, including those in urban neighborhoods. Only a single representative and a lone senator voted against the LWCF. Initially, Congress funded the law through a variety of fees and taxes, but since 1968 it switched to being primarily funded through a share of offshore drilling royalties. The LWCF has been overwhelmingly popular because it costs taxpayers nothing and provides tangible benefits both close to home (e.g., local park playgrounds) and in wildernesses and national parks.

Aspinall also managed to get the Public Land Law Review Commission passed by Congress and then secured the chair of the commission from 1964 to 1970. The PLLRC was the fourth public lands commission in the nation's history. Like the previous iterations, the PLLRC assessed existing laws and recommended new ones. Aspinall aimed to make sure that preservation did not overwhelm multiple use on the public lands and that Congress reasserted its power against what he saw as growing executive strength. The PLLRC's work and recommendations as cataloged in the final report, *One-Third of a Nation* (1970), were the most thorough of the public lands commissions. But like the others, many of the reform ideas—such as prioritizing economic returns and replacing multiple use with a dominant use paradigm—withered on the report's pages, never generating legislative interest or momentum. Its real impact came later because it recommended a massive overhaul of BLM policies and practices that Congress implemented in 1976. Before Congress turned to additional reform of its public lands agencies around questions of multiple use, still more about wilderness drew public attention.

Although the wilderness movement rested in western landscapes, mainly forested areas and high mountains, recall that the threat to a river first galvanized the national wilderness movement. The next step for the National Wilderness Preservation System focused on protecting wild rivers from development, especially dams. The postwar frenzy to plug streams for irrigation or flood control or navigation or hydroelectricity changed their ecological functioning, such as ruining salmon runs in the Northwest, and altered their character for recreation. After World War II, surplus rafts helped expand float trips along undeveloped stretches of remote rivers like the Salmon in Idaho or the Rogue in Oregon, both surrounded by public land. Senator Frank Church, a Democrat from Idaho who had been a floor leader in the Wilderness Act legislative campaign, now took up the Wild and Scenic Rivers Act, which passed and was signed by President Johnson in October 1968, four years after the Wilderness Act. The law declared it national policy for "certain selected rivers" that "possess outstandingly remarkable scenic, recreational, geological, fish and wildlife, historic, cultural or other similar values, shall be preserved in a free-flowing condition, and that they and their immediate environments shall be protected for the benefit and enjoyment of present and future generations." It established three categories—recreational, scenic, and wild—that allowed increasingly strict restrictions concerning development and included them in the National Wilderness Preservation System. Like the Wilderness Act, the Wild and Scenic Rivers Act immediately included a handful of rivers (eight) but grew so that now it now protects more than 13,000 miles of 226 rivers in nearly every state. These numbers are remarkable, but they constitute less than half a percent of the nation's rivers that count 75,000 large dams altering more than 600,000 river miles. Many of these rivers flow through protected public lands, and, to a degree, their status can influence management decisions on those lands.

The same day that President Johnson signed the protective river legislation, he signed the National Trails System Act. This latter law resembled the river law in that they each designated immediately some areas and left others for future study, seeds that grew into a much larger system. The NTSA established recreational, historic, and scenic trails. The scenic trails initially designated—still likely the most iconic—the Appalachian Trail (AT) and the Pacific Crest Trail (PCT). Each of these scenic trails crossed, north-south, virtually the entire country along ridgelines. Because trails, like rivers, move across the landscape through multiple jurisdictions, trail advocates and managers have had to become excellent civic partners to gain access to private land, to create conservation easements, or to encourage selling private land (often funded through the Land and Water Conservation Fund) to make these trails function. At times and in particular places on the trails, the federal government led; at other times, local citizens did. These trails' history reveals how conservation has grown from what historian Sarah Mittlefehldt characterized as "tangled roots" where public and private power worked for the land. Public land conservation has always necessarily included private land and citizens. It has been the interaction of citizens with public land that makes conservation a revealing manifestation of democracy.

National Wilderness Preservation System: Tests and New Parks

While rivers and trails enlarged and filled out the public landscape, the nascent National Wilderness Preservation System faced a series of tests. Industry pushed its priorities. Federal agencies struggled to define their authority and strategy. Conservationists sought to further expand their influence. Within this context, the public demanded Congress enact more protection in other public landscapes and made the mid- to late 1960s a moment for solidifying gains and influence.

The Forest Service furnished the best examples of an agency facing public tests over wilderness. After Congress passes a law like the Wilderness Act, administrative agencies like the Forest Service have to figure out how to put sometimes vague terms—like "untrammeled"—into practice. The agency's initial task force defined wilderness in the national forests only as places that were "pure" or pristine. When they started to conduct the mandatory review of roadless areas, the Forest Service applied these purity standards, which typically meant the agency excluded any area where human activity had occurred, and that meant vastly reducing their recommended acreage for wilderness compared with what conservationists wanted. For instance, in one of the first cases, in the proposed San Rafael wilderness just north of Santa Barbara, California, a 70,000-acre fire in 1966 saw the Forest Service bring in equipment to create firebreaks. This happened to be a habitat for the endangered California condor, which requires large wild areas to survive. Because of the firebreaks' presence, the Forest Service struck that critical habitat from its wilderness proposal. The eventual wilderness area Congress established was large, but it excluded some of the areas with the firefighting impact.

Some in the Forest Service and some wilderness advocates believed that wilderness protection required this sort of purity politics. They thought it was the only logically defensible approach. In addition, some argued this strict standard prevented too many visitors from overrunning wild areas. However, more cynically, many wilderness opponents adopted the purity standard to exclude areas that might include potentially valuable resources, such as commercial timber. The debate held special resonance in eastern national forests, virtually all of which had been logged and therefore could hardly be considered "pure." Partisans battled it out until the Eastern Wilderness Area Act passed in 1975, a little more than a decade after the initial Wilderness Act. This law included sixteen new wilderness areas and explicitly rejected the Forest Service's stringent wilderness definition. Advocates, especially those in the Wilderness Society who favored this inclusive approach, relied on a pragmatic reading of the Wilderness Act. Far from being idealists interested in some putative pure wilderness, most activists understood the practicality of wilderness politics.

Other tests besides purity played out in the early years after the Wilderness Act. One of the most significant concerned the mining exception written into the law. Mining company executives no doubt breathed easier knowing that the Wilderness Act maintained their rights to prospect in wild places, but they wished to be certain they could exercise those stated rights. For their part, conservationists aimed to make it politically unfeasible for corporations to desecrate wilderness with mines. Meanwhile, federal authorities struggled to know how to respond. All of this came to a head in a test case in Washington State's Glacier Peak Wilderness in the North Cascade Mountains.

In 1966, Kennecott Copper Corporation publicly announced its plans to develop an open-pit copper mine within the boundaries of the wilderness area on claims it had held for a decade. This announcement set off a furious countereffort. Local conservationists used grassroots organizations, such as the North Cascades Conservation Council and the Mountaineers, and coordinated with the Sierra Club for a stronger national voice to get out a message about the spectacular scenic spot Kennecott planned to carve up. The corporation asserted its legal right to establish the mine and insisted the nation needed the copper for its war in Vietnam. The volatility of the copper market belied these claims eventually, but the real story here was how the opposition gathered. The secretary of agriculture spoke out at the Sierra Club's biennial wilderness conference, urging conservationists to stop Kennecott. Supreme Court Justice William O. Douglas, who had hiked the region and had been a longtime advocate for wilderness, led a large protest group into the woods nearby where he declared that "just because something's legal doesn't necessarily mean it's right." A local doctor bought three shares of Kennecott stock and then crossed the country so he could speak at Kennecott's shareholders meeting, where he argued that if Kennecott developed its mine, the company's public image would be so badly damaged that his stock's value would drop. USFS officials repeatedly insisted that an open-pit mine was "incompatible" with wilderness, but the law explicitly prevented them from stopping the mine. This did not, however, stop some foresters from speaking out. Throughout the campaign to stop Kennecott, attention grew and stories in national magazines and newspapers regularly presented the situation and clearly preferred wilderness protection. Eventually, Kennecott sold its claim in 1986 without having opened the mine. The company never said the opposition mattered to its decision-making, but the vocal and visible activism ensured that the company could not operate without pushback. And similar companies took note; the mining exemption never was applied.

The Forest Service was not alone in facing challenges at the time; the Park Service in the late 1960s had to both withstand threats to its parks and marshal the support needed to add new ones with stronger wilderness protections. Grand Canyon National Park was threatened with partial inundation when the Bureau of Reclamation proposed two dams that would have flooded parts of the park, an outrage to many conservationists and large parts of the American public. The Sierra Club succeeded in publicizing the issue with full-page ads in the *New York Times* reading, "Should we also flood the Sistine Chapel so tourists can get nearer the ceiling?" Not everyone agreed. Tribal groups, the Hualapai especially, favored one of the proposed dams and accused environmentalists of "denying us, the first Americans, our right to help ourselves and condemning our families to lifelong poverty by forcing us to keep our homeland a wilderness." Most environmental and political leaders in 1968, though, simply ignored Indigenous claims and preferences. The symbolic cultural power of the Grand Canyon made it comparatively easy for conservationists to keep dams from altering the national park.

As the 1960s moved forward and Grand Canyon National Park seemed safe for the present, the Sierra Club prioritized two other areas for national park protection. In the North Cascades, just north of where Kennecott had proposed constructing its open-pit mine, lay millions of acres of rugged mountain scenery. Much of it had remained protected by the Forest Service for decades. Many wilderness advocates hoped the Forest Service would protect the North Cascades as formal wilderness, but by this point they distrusted the Forest Service's willingness to say no to timber companies. The agency's inability to stop Kennecott helped create an image of a weak agency, so conservationists turned to the Park Service, even though its development ethos surrounding Mission 66 was anathema to wilderness. After studying the region, public lands administrators recommended a national park and a host of other changes. After the usual debates and compromises, North Cascades National Park Complex was signed into existence in 1968, the same day President Johnson approved the Wild and Scenic Rivers Act and the National Trails System Act. North Cascades included a national park that was nearly all wilderness—a single road traverses it. The complex also included two national recreation areas and protected some wilderness on national forest land. Often called the "American Alps," the North Cascades now put nearly 700,000 acres into the national park system, subtracting it from national forests. For conservationists, this campaign demonstrated how their power could wrest a swath of land from one agency and get it transferred to another.

A more complicated situation lay in northern California's redwood region. Conservationists had been trying to save redwood forests from timber companies for most of the twentieth century. In 1918, the Save the Redwoods League was founded and raised enough money to purchase land and donate it to the state's park system. By mid-century, industrial logging threatened remaining redwoods. To counter this threat, conservationists, including the Save the Redwoods League and the Sierra Club, set their eyes on another national park. The Save the Redwoods League, a milder organization, aimed to protect the most majestic trees, while the increasingly militant Sierra Club eyed entire ecosystems for protection. While the two conservation organizations butted heads over strategy, timber companies started clearcutting, showing how, in the words of historian Darren Speece, "North Coast companies were hell-bent on derailing any discussion of creating a national redwood park." The logging assault helped bring compromise not only between the league and the club but also between the House, where Aspinall put forth a park of 28,000 acres (and received record hate mail for it), and the Senate, with a 61,000-acre proposal. The final result was 58,000 acres with more added later.

When President Johnson signed it into law—on that same momentous day as North Cascades and the rivers and trails legislation—he said, "For once we have spared what is enduring and ennobling from the hungry and hasty and selfish act of destruction." This remark framed a lot of the experience around public lands at the time from the side of public conservationists. They believed they were fighting against a ticking clock, and any delay meant desecration and loss forever. The Sierra Club's David Brower once put it like this: "All a conservation group can do is to defer something. There's no such thing as a permanent victory. After we win a battle, the wilderness is still there, and still vulnerable. When a conservation group *loses* a battle, the wilderness is dead." This pressure to protect wilderness in the public lands expanded beyond just wilderness as the 1960s moved into the 1970s, but the spirit unleashed in wilderness campaigns continued as other policies transformed. That spirit showed a distrust in the extractive industries that used and exploited public lands. But it also manifested in a fear that the federal agencies were not strong enough guardians, either. In the laws passed in the 1970s, Congress strengthened its prerogative and gave more stringent guidelines to federal agencies, while granting the public more power to influence decisions.

EXTENDING CITIZEN AND SPECIES PROTECTIONS

During many of the campaigns described above, Wayne Aspinall's counterpart in the Senate was Henry "Scoop" Jackson, a Democrat from Washington State. Jackson could be counted on for strong support of conservation measures. For example, more than anyone, he ensured that the North Cascades park received national park status. Then he set his sights on a far more important law, one that offered protection far beyond one park in the western mountains: the National Environmental Policy Act (NEPA).

NEPA revolutionized not only public lands management but also the way the federal government approached any of its projects that touched on environmental matters. The 1960s had brought a wide array of environmental concerns and values to the forefront of policymaking, including pollution control, endangered species legislation, and wilderness. The Cuyahoga River caught on fire (again), and, in January 1969, the largest oil spill in American history to that point just off the coast of Santa Barbara, California, riveted the public's attention. These spectacles of harm encouraged the public and politicians to call for a stronger governmental response. Because many problems crossed jurisdictions and because the reach of the federal government grew more pronounced throughout the twentieth century, a policy to direct all federal agencies was needed. NEPA provided that, creating a Council on Environmental Quality (CEQ) in the executive branch to guide agency decision-making and eventually make rules for standard practices. Besides creating the CEQ, NEPA produced two other key points: a statement of policy and a new procedure, both of which reoriented how the public lands agencies managed their lands.

The statement of policy reflected the confidence of the era. The preamble of the law, which passed with only fifteen total objections in both houses of Congress, stated that the "national policy . . . will encourage productive and enjoyable harmony between man and his environment" as well as promoting "efforts which will prevent or eliminate damage to the environment and biosphere and stimulate the health and welfare of man; to enrich the understanding of the ecological systems and natural resources important to the Nation." Such a policy announced grand ambitions and hinted at no necessary sacrifices among economic growth, environmental protection, and human welfare. NEPA explained that the new national policy would "create and maintain conditions under which man and nature can exist in productive harmony, and fulfill the social, economic, and other requirements of present and future generations of Americans." With NEPA, Congress announced a long-range view, incorporating tomorrow's environmental fate into today's decisions. Moving forward, the law was supposed to provide a guidepost for the type of policy the federal government would follow. However, this statement of policy proved far less revolutionary than its potential because the procedural element of NEPA came to dominate the history of its implementation, and nowhere was that impact greater than on public lands.

A law can proclaim aspirational phrases, but it requires a mechanism to ensure the policy gets carried out. NEPA required that before undertaking "major Federal actions significantly affecting the quality of the human environment," federal agencies and their partners now had to submit "a detailed statement," which has come to be known as an environmental impact statement, or EIS. This requirement applied to all public lands agencies and major projects: timber sales, grazing plans, scenic roads, or water projects affecting waterfowl. A team of scientists and planners needed to study a project's potential to affect the environment and present multiple options, even ones that cost more. This practice significantly transformed normal operating procedures. For one, the EIS process was interdisciplinary, which led to public lands agencies hiring far more biologists and hydrologists to help study issues, whereas before engineers and foresters might have been the only ones consulted—or at least with the greatest power in planning a project. With new experts at the table, new questions were asked about fish or fowl or other noncommercial parts of the land. NEPA thus ignited an institutional cultural change, albeit sometimes a sputtering one, among the Forest Service and other agencies. Besides EIS preparation and attending to new questions, each EIS faced public scrutiny and comment. No more could the Fish and Wildlife Service or the Bureau of Land Management make a decision and do it. Opening up the planning process to public input allowed knowledgeable and engaged citizens to assert their values, priorities, and objections for the public lands that belonged to all Americans, not just the public lands agencies or their primary economic constituents.

The procedures that stemmed from NEPA, especially the public involvement component, presented multiple opportunities for filing lawsuits. More than anything before it, NEPA allowed legal interventions that have become a central part of public land politics. Thus, NEPA complicated federal land-use planning and increased the politicization of public lands. Democracy does that: the more voices involved, the greater the possibility of dissent and conflict and the longer the process. By changing priorities and processes, NEPA allowed public lands agencies to investigate alternatives that faced greater degrees of choice and a franker acknowledgment that timber sales or gas leases might damage habitat or cause other environmental problems. In the end, NEPA did not require agencies to select the alternative most favored by the public or the one with the least anticipated deleterious ecological effects. But for the first time, these costs had to be calculated beforehand and subjected to public scrutiny.

President Richard Nixon signed NEPA on January 1, 1970, effectively inaugurating what is often called the environmental decade. Nixon recognized some of the importance of NEPA, saying that the 1970s would be the time when "America pays its debt to the past by reclaiming the purity of its air, its waters, and our living environment." Tapping into the same urgency Brower and others had expressed, the president added, "It is literally now or never." In truth, Nixon held few deep environmental values and saw NEPA and related legislation he signed to be a way to gain some political advantage. Many, perhaps most, legislators also did not recognize the power NEPA unleashed.

Yet NEPA was not infallible or foolproof. In fact, one of the first examples of its use on public lands revealed its fragility. In Alaska, oil had been discovered on the North Slope. Plans to build an eight-hundred-mile pipeline and an accompanying road to transport petroleum and people had stalled in 1968 when Secretary of the Interior Stewart Udall stopped it amid disputes between Native lands, state lands, and the federal government role. The new Republican administration wanted to finish the project, but to proceed now required an EIS. Walter Hickel, the new interior secretary, presented a short, eight-page EIS, and immediately three environmental groups sued on the grounds that the statement was inadequate. The courts agreed. The second EIS was much longer—nearly 250 pages—but it, too, proved poor. The Interior Department's own solicitor called it "wholly inadequate." In the third EIS attempted, a six-volume statement (and three more volumes of supporting material) was prepared, and the district court lifted the injunction to allow construction to resume. Once again, environmental groups appealed. Meanwhile, the growing oil crisis worried members of Congress, who feared what further court decisions might require or restrict. Consequently, Congress exempted the pipeline from following NEPA requirements. Although Congress took some teeth out of NEPA to ensure that the oil pipeline was completed, this episode demonstrated that courts recognized NEPA required careful attention from federal agencies. Moving forward, NEPA shaped virtually all large-scale activity on national forests, parks, rangelands, and refuges.

NEPA's revolutionary potential probably was only matched by the Endangered Species Act, signed by President Nixon in 1973. Declining wildlife as much as anything sparked the conservation movement at the end of the nineteenth century. As the twentieth century unfolded, conservationists' ideas about wildlife evolved. As he did for so much related to conservation, Aldo Leopold serves as a barometer. One of the great parables in conservation history is Leopold's conversion about predators. As a young hunter, he supported killing predators, believing that would lead to abundant game. Leopold then told the story of being a young forester in the mountains of the Southwest when he and others came across a wolf pack and killed them, seeing a "fierce green fire" die in one wolf's eyes. He connected the demise of predators to damage on the range where too many deer ate themselves out of their habitat, leading Leopold to formulating his concept of "thinking like a mountain," a holistic approach that saved all parts of an ecosystem. Later still, he wrote his classic book, *A Sand County Almanac* (1949), in which he said of ecological communities, "A land ethic of course cannot prevent the alteration, management, and use of these 'resources,' but it does affirm their *right to continued existence*, and, at least in spots, their continued existence in a natural state" (emphasis added). This right to continued existence undergirded endangered species legislation.

Although hunting (or predator control) often caused some species to decline, habitat destruction, such as draining wetlands or cutting down old-growth forests or suburban expansion, decreased the populations of many species. A scientist and award-winning writer who spent a long career with the Fish and Wildlife Service helped enlighten Americans about these threats. Rachel Carson was a popular author already when she published *Silent Spring* in 1962, which introduced a broad audience to the dangers of pesticides, particularly DDT. Especially following World War II, Americans applied pesticides widely to their forests, orchards and fields, and lawns to remove weeds and insects deemed harmful to crops. Yet Carson documented many of the unintended effects of such a broad application of chemicals. For example, she described a cooperative effort between the Montana Fish and Game Department and both the Forest Service and the Fish and Wildlife Service to study almost a million acres treated with DDT in 1957 at a level that was deemed safe. Carson characterized the result: "Always, the pattern of death assumed a characteristic shape: the smell of DDT over the forests, an oil film on the water surface, dead trout along the shoreline." Again and again, these results repeated across the nation's forests and rangelands, regardless of whether they were public or private.

Carson's book, filled with beautiful writing and painstaking research, asked Americans to imagine a silent spring, because the birds had died from their chemical exposure. Although many birds suffered, symbolically the decline of eagles focused public concern. Carson related multiple studies that showed how DDT entered the environment and through food webs reached predators like eagles in concentrated toxic forms. Eggshells formed improperly and endangered the reproduction of the species. Populations dropped sharply. Carson's scientific credentials and accessible prose helped many Americans understand ecological concepts for the first time, ideas such as the web of life that showed how connected the environment was: chemicals sprayed on a forest to kill insects were ingested by fish that were eaten by eagles, helping to endanger raptor populations. As she succinctly put it, "[I]n nature nothing exists alone." These ecological lessons hit at a time when Americans were already thinking about restraint in the natural world, and *Silent Spring* helped bring many to the cause of ecology. And the cause of ecology helped prompt Congress to legislate to protect species like the bald eagle that seemed to be on the verge of extinction.

Previous versions of the ESA had passed but had been inadequate to stem worsening crises. The law that passed in 1973 received only a dozen no votes in the House and passed unanimously in the Senate. The law's stated purpose was "to provide a means whereby the ecosystems upon which endangered species and threatened species depend may be conserved." The intent was clear. Federal agencies had to ensure "that actions authorized, funded, or carried out by them do not jeopardize the continued existence of such endangered species and threatened species or result in the destruction or modification of habitat of such species." The law included little equivocation. In the first test case that reached the Supreme Court, the justices found Congress's intent inarguable. "The plain intent of Congress in enacting this statute was to halt and reverse the trend toward species extinction," read the Court's opinion in *Tennessee Valley Authority v. Hill* (1978), adding for emphasis, "whatever the cost." When concerned about bald eagles or California condors, many members of Congress and the public understood reasons to halt activity to save the species; however, *TVA v. Hill* focused on a not particularly pretty three-inch fish, the snail darter, and stopping a dam project on its behalf showed the ESA's power in a way that most legislators had not reckoned with. (Subsequent legislation in Congress allowed the dam to go forward, not unlike the exemption the Alaska pipeline received from NEPA.)

The ESA did not function automatically. Its mechanism to list species was based on the Department of Interior's Fish and Wildlife Service for most land species and freshwater species (along with a few marine mammals), while the Fisheries Service within the Department of Commerce's National Oceanic and Atmospheric Administration concentrated on marine life and anadromous fish. The FWS was most critical for public lands. The agency determined which species were endangered or threatened, and it defined what constituted the critical habitat necessary to maintain the species. Species could be listed when their habitat was threatened or when commercial or other activities weakened species viability. The FWS or a public petition can start the process. The law directed the agency to use only the best available science and not consider economic elements. After a species was identified as either endangered or threatened, the public could testify at public hearings. Much like with NEPA, this process gave citizens a greater role, something that politicized and often slowed decisions—a fact that irritated many but, again, was part of the discourse of democracy.

Also like NEPA, the ESA applied to all public lands. And because national forests, parks, rangelands, and refuges offered some of the best remaining habitat for threatened species, the federal land agencies have been on the forefront of implementing the ESA—and on the frontlines of battling the law's opponents. Although the ESA focuses on maintaining species' populations, species rely on habitat. Consequently, environmentalists used the ESA to protect ecosystems through endangered species. (The next chapter demonstrates how controversial these political and scientific battles became in subsequent decades.) NEPA and the ESA extended the rights of the public and the moral and political consideration of other species, while also instituting national standards and processes. Both laws undeniably tilted toward protection, but conservation began under the guidance of enlightened use, and agencies worked at the same time to rebalance their multiple-use missions.

REFORMING MULTIPLE USE

MUSY started the 1960s and NEPA launched the 1970s. Each law stated policies and established procedures to transform resource management in existing agencies. And the Wilderness Act and the Endangered Species Act announced radical reorientations, suggesting that land left alone deserved standing and that species enjoyed a right to continued existence. In the mid-1970s, amid these political upheavals, both the Forest Service and the Bureau of Land Management received new charters. The National Forest Management Act (NFMA) and the Federal Land Policy and Management Act (FLMPA) both passed in 1976 and reflected an unwillingness on the part of the public and its representatives in Congress to allow forests and rangelands to continue to be managed as they had been. For the Forest Service, this reform push largely resulted from crises related to clearcutting and resulting lawsuits. For the Bureau of Land Management, for which Congress had never written an Organic Act—the founding directive for an agency—FLPMA formally established for the first time the BLM's charge.

When the Forest Service intensified its management practices in the middle of the twentieth century, those changes played out heavily on the land. Institutional pressures encouraged heavy hands on the national forests. Congress tied budget allocations to high timber output. USFS administrators were rewarded for high harvest levels and wished always to maintain their discretion. Meanwhile, the timber industry desired the "efficiency" of clearcutting and easy access to public trees. All of these factors encouraged clearcutting. But that ran headlong into changing public values, stoked by a growing awareness of ecology. Many in the public grew unwilling to watch how intensive management transformed and seemingly devastated public forests.

Two controversies have come to be associated with outrage directed at the Forest Service and led to reform in the 1970s. The first occurred in West Virginia in the Monongahela National Forest. In 1964, just as Congress finalized the Wilderness Act, large clearcuts appeared in the Monongahela. This bothered local hikers and, especially, turkey hunters who saw the so-called even-aged management practice as harmful to hunting. When a group of hunters gained an audience with USFS Chief Edward Cliff, they heard an indifferent response. Cliff saw the hunters as "a very self-centered protest from a very small segment of the population who wanted the national forest to be managed just for their own personal pleasure." This dismissal badly underestimated the grassroots strength behind those turkey hunters. The Izaak Walton League, a longstanding conservation organization of hunters and anglers, initiated a lawsuit, which was not how the organization tended to operate. The League persuaded the courts that clearcutting on national forests violated the 1897 Organic Act, which specified selling only "dead, matured, or large growth of trees" that had been "marked and designated" by federal foresters. Clearcutting did not satisfy these requirements, something that the Fourth Circuit court in *Izaak Walton League v. Butz* confirmed in 1975. In its decision, the court chronicled the transformation of the Forest Service, noting that it had gone from being a custodian of forests to a producer of timber. The decision recognized that in 1975, the 1897 law might be "an anachronism which no longer serves the public interest," and if that was the case, Congress needed to resolve this incompatibility. This decision effectively ended clearcutting within the Monongahela and forced Congress's collective hand.

Brewing along the same time frame across the continent was a controversy in the Bitterroot National Forest. In this national forest in western Montana, an intensive program to clearcut lodgepole pine, terrace the steep hillsides with heavy equipment, and replace them with more commercially valuable ponderosa pine created an ecological disaster for the forest and a public relations disaster for the Forest Service. Photographs showed a devastated landscape, and Guy Brandborg, a local forester who had retired a decade before these clearcuts began, ensured that the press and important politicians saw it. The Bitterroot forest lay deep in the rural West where extraction—of trees and of minerals—was accepted as the basis of the economy. But the clearcutting and terracing pushed too far. Montana Senator Lee Metcalf asked the dean of the forestry school at the University of Montana, Arnold Bolle, to investigate. The resulting report—officially "A University View of the Forest Service" but commonly known as the Bolle Report—shocked the forestry community when it was released in 1970. It stated baldly that "Multiple use management, in fact, does not exist as the governing principle on the Bitterroot National Forest." Of course, multiple use was the guiding precept for USFS management, but what was happening at Bitterroot was "timber mining," an extraction of resources that was nonrenewable and unsustainable. In other words, the Forest Service was not only violating its legislative directives but also likely ruining the land for future forests. The Bolle Report did not blame the agency solely, recognizing that Congress and others within the federal government created the system in which the local forest operated. Still, that meant that the "overriding concern for sawtimber production" suppressed any other values, whether ecological, economic, or democratic. The culture of the Forest Service (and its timber company clients) clearly stood apart from emerging public values.

The general changes in law and values as reflected in the Wilderness Act, NEPA, and the ESA combined with these clearcutting controversies and forced congressional action. The result, the National Forest Management Act of 1976, included a number of compromises and has not always lived up to reformers' expectations. Nonetheless, the NFMA reoriented Forest Service practices. The law explicitly repealed the 1897 Organic Act and effectively became a new Organic Act. The NFMA allowed clearcutting under certain circumstances. But Idaho senator Frank Church established a series of rules that prevented clearcutting on land with poor soil, exceptionally scenic land, and areas where reforestation was unlikely to work or be economically feasible. It stipulated that cutting could not endanger the "diversity of plant and animal communities," eventually establishing that the agency must "maintain viable populations of existing native and desired non-native vertebrate species" as part of its planning. However, according to historian Paul Hirt, the law included "loopholes large enough to drive logging trucks through."

The NFMA also instituted a planning process for each national forest, to be renewed every fifteen years. This planning reiterated the sort of process NEPA had implemented—study, propose alternatives, gain public feedback—before acting on the land. Just like NEPA, the NFMA demanded the Forest Service look at its activities and lands through a multidisciplinary lens and thus continued the change in diversifying the expertise of employees. The law also incorporated ESA requirements to ensure animal and plant species continued to exist. This new planning process, as with NEPA, generated ample opportunities for lawsuits because the many steps provided opportunities for mistakes or cutting administrative corners. Additionally, public trust in the Forest Service had declined, which increased public opposition and challenges to forest plans. The first seventy-five forest plans, in fact, led to six hundred lawsuits. In all, this new organic act changed some of requirements under which the Forest Service operated, and yet it still pushed intensive management and high timber output. Policy scholar James Skillen has explained that this era challenged public lands agencies, because they "continued their traditional programs while struggling to add science, public participation, and species protection to their decision making." They added to their duties rather than fundamentally rethought them. In an optimistic approach, agencies expected that they could still please all the masters they tried to serve.

The BLM traveled along similar pathways, but distinct issues made its history somewhat different. Often derided as the "Bureau of Livestock and Mining," the BLM administered the most public land, but it had no statutory authority, no congressional organic act, and no stated mission. The number of employees lagged far behind that of the Forest Service. Although mining and energy development came to occupy a significant portion of the BLM's management, the agency primarily served ranchers. As the agency entered the 1960s and 1970s amid the upheaval created by new environmental public values and consequent legislation, the Taylor Grazing Act from 1934 still provided a main legislative touchstone. This, obviously, would need updating for the modern era.

The BLM got started in the 1960s by explicitly adopting multiple-use management with the Classification and Multiple Use Management

Act. The bureau attempted to remake its image into that of the Forest Service. The CMUA directed the BLM to identify which lands it would manage for multiple-use outcomes and which would be sold off. Analyzing the lands was supposed to lead to classifying parcels for their highest use, such as grazing, mining, wildlife habitat, and the like. The effort was the bureau's first experience consulting broadly with the public, a process that revealed quickening and unsettling changes. Wildlife and outdoor recreation values had become incorporated into the new multiple-use direction of the BLM, which ranchers felt marginalized them, a feeling that kept growing. In the second half of the 1960s, the BLM surveyed more than 150 million acres, and the process helped modernize the bureau and develop its administrative structure.

During the same years the BLM developed its classification system, the Public Land Law Review Commission completed its work. In 1970, its report, *One Third of the Nation's Land*, focused significant attention on the land and resources the BLM managed. This shifted the arena where reform occurred. The CMUA pushed the BLM to make *administrative* changes; the PLLRC pushed Congress to make *legislative* changes. The commission's chair, the ubiquitous Wayne Aspinall, ensured that environmental values did not overwhelm a traditional emphasis on resource extraction, which he characterized as "the maximum good for the maximum number." By 1970, though, Aspinall's influence was waning—in fact, he lost his Democratic primary in 1972—and public land reform would curtail even the BLM's long history of catering solely to extractive resource users. But reform took time to develop. The bureau needed clear direction from Congress—an organic act that defined the BLM's mission—and legislators spent half the 1970s arguing with resource users working to tamp down any measure meant to hamper their access to public resources, while environmental groups aimed to strengthen recreation and wildlife values and to make miners and ranchers pay a greater share for the use of public resources.

The congressional controversies and compromises sorted themselves eventually to produce the Federal Land Policy and Management Act (FLPMA), signed by President Gerald Ford in late October 1976. In the main, the legislation confirmed how the BLM had been managing its lands for some time, but some changes felt downright oppressive to traditional users. It affirmed multiple-use management, initiated a wilderness review process, asserted the need to obtain a fair financial value for land uses, and established that the land would be retained by the federal government—that is, the law closed homesteading, privatization, and transfer to the states. Consistent with both NEPA and the NFMA, the BLM would also now engage in long-term, multiple-use planning that incorporated more scientific data and analysis, along with allowing the public to weigh in. One method supporting this new direction was advisory boards. In the past under the Taylor Grazing Act, ranchers had formed grazing advisory boards that established rules. FLPMA expanded those bodies and renamed them multiple-use advisory boards (now called resource advisory boards), which put more voices around the table to serve a wider array of interests. This expansion, along with potentially including BLM lands within the National Wilderness Preservation System, produced immediate backlash and resistance that would grow significantly in the coming decades among traditional public lands users.

In some ways, though, the BLM continued to serve its traditional users. During the debate over legislation, some in Congress aimed to radically reform the General Mining Law of 1872 that still largely governed public lands mining and was highly favorable to mining corporations. The severe regulations never made it into law. Ranchers worried even more. Between 1970 and 1976, grazing fees had increased from $0.32 to $1.50 per animal unit month. This bump, which amounted to a fivefold increase in ranchers' expenses, preconditioned the ranchers to oppose any more changes to grazing fees, long the most controversial part of public lands livestock management within both the BLM and the Forest Service. The issue of establishing a new formula to determine fees was kicked to the future pending a study that would investigate whether grazing fees were "equitable to the United States and to the holders of grazing permits and leases." Most ranchers understood their fees were set well below market value, so any reassessment likely would reduce their slim profit margins. Despite their concerns, ranchers received some security from FLPMA as well. Grazing permits were extended to ten years with existing permittees given priority for renewal, an arrangement that gave them power. Also, if a permit was not renewed because the land was no longer satisfactory for grazing, the rancher would receive compensation for improvements made. These changes established ranchers as firmly as ever on the public's lands.

Overall, much like the vast lands the BLM oversees, FLPMA was a diverse document that was both mundane and transformative. In most ways, it affirmed what the bureau had been doing for a decade, and it linked the BLM with other federal agencies in updating its planning process and aligning it more with NEPA and the new democratic and environmental values that ascended in the 1960s. It introduced few immediate changes for its main resource users, although ranchers and miners remained nervous about the addition of wilderness studies now looming and the expanding multiple-use advisory boards. Who knew how radically environmental such things might become? The BLM had long been understood as a "captured" agency, controlled by the very interests it was meant to police, but the agency received diminishing support from those interests. The reform underway seemed unlikely to amount to much because the BLM remained understaffed. Two years after FLPMA passed, the BLM managed 480 million acres (compared with the Forest Service's 189 million) with 7,000 employees (compared with 44,000) and a budget of $440 million (compared with $1.19 billion). Nevertheless, FLPMA lit a fire of opposition that, in many ways, still burns.

ALASKA NATIONAL INTEREST LANDS CONSERVATION ACT

Alaska was both the exception to and the epitome of the flurry of public lands politics in the 1960s and 1970s. The last large territory added to the United States in 1867, Alaska became a state in 1959. Its long experience as a territory far from the U.S. capital made its residents and politicians prone to feeling neglected, which shaped Alaskans' response to conservation measures. Although the state included national forests, parks, and wildlife refuges since the nineteenth century, Alaska's conservation history seemed to travel along a separate historical track. That changed in the 1970s.

When Alaska entered the United States, the federal government did not address Indigenous land claims. As the territory sought admission as a state, this situation no longer was tolerated. Part of statehood required addressing these claims. The Alaska Native Claims Settlement Act (1971) aimed to secure Indigenous land rights, and it simultaneously introduced new uncertainty for public lands in Alaska.

The situation ANCSA helped resolve was complicated, as would be the solution. The Alaska Statehood Act from 1959 gave the state the right to select 103.5 million acres of federal lands for transfer into state control, although Alaska could not take Native territory. So what constituted Native territory had to be established. ANCSA led to the creation of a number of regional Native corporations meant to manage tribal lands, which amounted to 44 million acres selected in the three years after the act, along with $1 billion. If this was all ANCSA did, it would not belong in a book on public lands history.

Yet another part of ANCSA empowered the interior secretary to reserve up to 80 million acres of Alaska as part of the national park and wildlife refuge systems. (Alaska contains well over 400 million acres.) Congress imposed a five-year time limit to act on Interior's recommendations. President Nixon's appointee, Interior Secretary Rogers C. B. Morton, sent recommendations to Congress in 1973, and Congress mostly ignored them at first. However, local politicians reacted harshly. Then Jimmy Carter was elected president in 1976 with support of the conservation community. About the same time, environmentalists lost their effort to stop the Trans-Alaska Pipeline. These two events pushed environmentalists toward an aggressive stance in settling Alaska's public lands question.

In 1977, environmentalists organized into the Alaska Coalition to lead this campaign. This group represented national organizations, such as the Wilderness Society and the Sierra Club, better than Alaska's own environmental community, which was represented by the Alaska Conservation Society. Celia Hunter had led the ACS for years, and between 1976 and 1978, she served as the executive director of the Wilderness Society, showing a tangible way the local and national groups tried to weave their interests tighter together. Hunter proved crucial to holding the Alaska Coalition together in its determination to nationalize the issue. But most Alaskans—those who favored development or those who favored preservation—felt Alaska's exceptionalism deeply, and the fit was never perfect.

As the five-year time limit approached, Congress picked up the recommendations. Conservationists saw Alaska as their last chance to accomplish conservation the right way. Here, they thought, intact ecosystems could be preserved, rather than the piecemeal protection achieved throughout the continental United States. The message from the Alaska

Coalition was that "Alaska is the last chance to do it right the first time." This idea reflected a variety of things, including the scale of landscapes in Alaska, the strength (current but waning) of conservation politics, and the recognition that preservation for ecosystems rather than just scenery merited the highest priorities. The coalition's allies in Congress hoped to pass a strong bill. The House version championed by Morris Udall (former Secretary of the Interior Stewart Udall's brother) was strong and included 27.1 million acres of national parks, 15.6 million acres of national preserves (parks that allowed hunting), and 76.8 million acres of new wildlife refuges. Scattered among these acreages and others already protected were 65.5 million acres of newly designated wilderness. The Senate proved less welcoming, not least because Alaska senator Mike Gravel filibustered the bill. When Congress adjourned, it did so without an Alaska lands bill.

With the initial withdrawals expiring because of the five-year limit, President Carter chose executive action, mostly using the Antiquities Act (1906) as had most presidents before him to initially protect places like Grand Canyon, Arches, and Joshua Tree, all of which eventually became national parks. He declared 56 million acres as national monuments; most of these had been proposed as national parks, but not acted on by Congress. Another 40 million acres were temporarily withdrawn by Cecil Andrus's Interior Department for wildlife refuges. But because only Congress could designate wilderness, there was not a single acre for wilderness. Carter's action was so bold, he asked Andrus whether he was sure a president could do it. Carter's decision prompted Congress to get back to work.

The political tides were turning toward conservatism and away from the conservation measures that had marked the 1960s and 1970s. And in Alaska, locals greeted federal agents with hostility and violence: windows were shot out, equipment gas tanks were filled with sugar, and federal employees were refused service. Conservationists worked to get the best possible bill out of Congress. Again, the House produced a stronger bill than the Senate could muster, but the election in November 1980 shifted the presidency and the Senate to Republicans. Rather than get nothing, the House agreed to the Senate version, and Carter signed the Alaska National Interest Lands Conservation Act in December, barely a month before he returned to Georgia.

By any measure, ANILCA was a compromise bill. Still, it offered a good deal for conservation in the public land system. The law protected more than 100 million acres in national parks, refuges, and forests, and it added 56.4 million acres to the National Wilderness Preservation System. New national parks included Glacier Bay National Park and Preserve, Kenai Fjords National Park, and Wrangell–St. Elias National Park and Preserve. It added acreage to preexisting protected lands like Denali National Park and Tongass National Forest. Never had, or has, any government protected that much wilderness with a single stroke of a pen.

Yet, for all the law's accomplishments, the concessions in it also were telling. Two of the biggest concerned the Tongass National Forest and the Alaska National Wildlife Refuge. The Tongass in the southeastern part of the state was the nation's largest national forest, and conservationists hoped to strengthen wilderness protections. Instead, the Tongass would continue to see some of the highest logging levels in the national forest system. Although much of ANWR's 18 million acres in the northeast corner of Alaska was protected as wilderness, a 1.5-million-acre slice next to the Prudhoe Bay oil field remained open to study for oil development, a frequently contentious political football for the future.

There were other concessions, too, that bore on the future. Because President Carter's audacious use of the Antiquities Act angered Alaskans, ANILCA included a provision that restricted further uses of the law. Any executive withdrawal greater than five thousand acres in Alaska would now require explicit congressional approval—a strong brake on a president's ability to act in the state. Last, protected land, including parks, allowed access for traditional subsistence activities such as hunting, trapping, and fishing. In some wilderness areas, too, access with snowmobiles was permitted. These exceptions to the typical rules opened the door to further exceptions elsewhere; however, they also recognized the importance of rural subsistence in Alaska. In that, ANILCA showed its paradoxical and compromised achievement. Conservationists celebrated it and also bemoaned the compromises necessary to get it passed, while local politicians such as Senator Ted Stevens saw it as his greatest disappointment in a forty-year Senate career. ANILCA, like Alaska, was big enough to contain contradictory multitudes.

CONCLUSION

In the campaign to create North Cascades National Park, Senator Scoop Jackson explained to activists, "I can't *give* you a park.... But if you get up a big enough parade, I'll step out front and lead it on in." Crediting Congress with the remarkable changes in public lands between 1960 and 1980 is necessary but insufficient. Advocates for a new public land regime generated sufficient political power to have politicians like Jackson willing to step in front of the parade. This newfound political power marked a new age.

The conservationists who pushed public lands agencies and politicians to rewrite the rules came from predominantly white, middle-class, professional families. The rising affluence for many—although by no means all—Americans after World War II led to concerns about quality of life, especially outdoor recreation, which was seen as part of an amorphous thing called the "good life." In a search to find rivers to raft and mountains to climb and scenic vistas where families could set up tents, Americans not only increased protections on public lands but also challenged the power of federal agencies and traditional public land users who benefited from public resources. These efforts made this moment both an extension of the power of the white middle class (which had never lacked power or access to it) and a check on the power of government and resource corporations.

The metaphorical table by 1980 looked profoundly different. The table itself changed shape. What once appeared to be land available to be remade into property and later a set of resources to be managed carefully for use now took on different purposes, including corners dedicated only to wildness. Those wild pockets grew dramatically from 9.1 million acres in 1964 to more than 80 million acres in 1980. Eighty million acres sounds like a lot, but it only amounted to about 12 percent of the entire public land apparatus (and 3 percent of the nation). On the rest, well over half a billion acres, grazing and logging and road building continued. Yet business as usual changed at the table, around which sat new groups of people. The requirements of NEPA, the NFMA, and FLPMA especially meant that agencies employed far more specialists in science. Fish and wildlife biologists sat next to silviculturists, while hydrologists shared the table with road engineers. When public lands were managed as ecosystems—the direction they were heading by 1980—the staff necessarily shifted from managing land as a crop of trees or forage. The shifts led to different questions asked, and it presented answers—such as no timber sale here or no grazing there or fewer tourists now—that would have been unthinkable during the age of intensified management that preceded this one.

Besides new specialists at the table were new seats for the public. The BLM's grazing advisory boards that became multiple use advisory boards were the most obvious embodiment of this institutional change. But the planning processes imposed by Congress and implemented by the agencies gave citizens and organizations new power to ask questions, share ideas, and make objections. In real ways, these reforms firmly put the *public* into public lands unlike ever before. In this way, although conservation in this period seldom is considered in the same breath as the simultaneous civil rights movement, these reforms helped extend democratic access to managing these places, a process that continues and often still falls short.

However, not everyone felt that way. No one was kept away from the public lands table, but by sharing the space, many people saw their influence diminished. Ranchers no longer controlled the BLM; timber companies no longer got their way with the USFS; tourists did not call the shots at the NPS; and hunters did not rule the roost with the FWS. All of these interests still enjoyed power and often overwhelmed the public and the agencies. But for many of these interests, the shift in law that required them to share power seemed intolerable. The next chapter of public lands history, the chapter we are still living in, is characterized by the conflict emerging out of this new order of power and purpose for the public lands. Conservationists became adept at using the new tools to enact change on the land and in agencies to protect wilderness and wildlife and nonextractive uses of the public's resources. In reaction, those who favored economic development organized to reject this new order. Conflict was common; big victories for either side were rare; extremes became more extreme. At the heart of these conflicts were debates over the fundamental purpose of public lands, whom they were for, and who counted for the public.

5

Polarizing

INTRODUCTION

NEVADA SITS CENTRALLY in the western United States, and Twin Spring Ranch rests a little south of the state's center point in an isolated spot about seventy miles east of Tonopah, the nearest town today. The Fallini family moved onto this land in the 1870s, acquiring water rights and using the public domain to graze cattle. As the family built their livestock operation, they bumped into federal policies that kept changing. The Taylor Grazing Act of 1934, which organized most of the remaining public domain, threatened the Fallinis' slim profit margins, but they received a rare exemption and delayed placing their district under the law. Then came World War II, and a bombing range required some of the lands they traditionally used. And then came the Cold War, during which the Atomic Energy Commission moved onto the range for its atomic testing program. By 1971, the Wild Free-Roaming Horses and Burros Act introduced yet another purpose and priority for these public lands. When the Federal Land Policy and Management Act passed in 1976, the Fallinis and many other Nevadans and westerners felt overwhelmed, confused, and frustrated. In the face of these competing and growing complications on the land, the Bureau of Land Management organized the range and regulated the Fallinis' activities to an unprecedented degree. When Helen Fallini sat for an oral history in the late 1980s, she frankly and simply explained what the experience felt like: "The BLM has been nothing but a pain in the butt." Fallini desired some certainty and stability in policy, rather than what seemed like frequent shifts in policies that ate into the family's customary range and their ability to profit from a livestock operation in an American outback. She was not alone in her frustration.

Farther south in the state, nearly in Arizona, a town called Bunkerville sat in the Mojave Desert with the Virgin River running through it, drenching the place in symbolism. This was the habitat for the desert tortoise and a few hardscrabble ranchers—both endangered species, although what threatened them differed. In the 1980s, Las Vegas grew into the surrounding desert, bumping into federal lands. Clark County finagled land swaps to allow the metropolitan area to continue expanding in exchange for more public land farther away in the Mojave. Then, in 1991, the desert tortoise, at home in these hinterlands, was listed by the Fish and Wildlife Service as an endangered species. Cattle grazing and tortoise habitat did not mix well, so in 1993 the BLM modified the grazing permits of a rancher named Cliven Bundy. Limiting the number of livestock in fragile desert ecosystems seemed like one intrusion too far. Bundy released nearly nine times his permitted animals on the range and then stopped paying his grazing fees. By 2014, the fees and penalties he owed the federal government exceeded $1 million. When federal agents failed to obtain the past due payments, they informed Bundy that they would confiscate his cattle. Bundy called for support, and militia members came from around the country to support him and to intimidate federal law enforcement agents. A widely seen photo from the ensuing standoff showed one militia member from an overpass aiming a weapon at a federal agent. The citizen effort to stymie the government worked, as agents left without the cattle or payment. To be sure, Bundy held extreme views, once proclaiming, "I don't recognize the federal government as even existing." Such a position, so far outside the mainstream and beyond the reach of reason or law, proved attractive only to fringe groups, but by 2014 extreme views found ready audiences through social media.

These two snapshots share similarities: Nevada ranchers frustrated with the new public lands regime established in the wake of a political and legal shifts of the 1960s and 1970s. Suddenly, it seemed to them, the public land on which they and many other resources users depended had been closed or restricted. Their livelihoods hung in the balance, and their sense of identity, rooted in the land, was threatened. Meanwhile, environmentalists seemed to be only interested in wildlife and plants and disdained hardworking Americans. They came from cities and did not understand rural America or rural Americans. And somehow, this group—a small minority—had captured the Democratic Party and the levers of power in government. At least, this was how it might have seemed to the Fallinis, the Bundys, or their neighbors and similarly situated westerners in ranching communities and timber towns. This description largely caricatured environmentalists and distorted causes and consequences; however, its symbolic power was real.

These snapshots also might suggest that federal initiatives through public land agencies consistently protected ecosystems and the flora and fauna that depended on them. Yet in this era, from 1980 to the present, environmentalists and scientists routinely believed conservation measures were too meager to protect biodiversity and too often favored resource extraction over more benign land uses such as backpacking or tourism. The dissatisfaction that seemed ubiquitous spelled polarization, a theme consistent with broader cultural and political trends of the period. The table no longer seemed a place around which Americans gathered to work out a public lands agenda that valued—or even tolerated—multiple perspectives. Instead, it was like a long picnic table with two benches farther and farther apart, and those seated could see only an opponent across a widening gap and not even hear those on the same side. On a few occasions, small groups worked out collaborations and compromises against this larger backdrop of polarization. Additionally, new scientific understandings about ecosystems called into question many certainties conservationists long believed. As always, public lands history reflected national trends. This new age proved politically and ecologically complex and uncertain.

THE SAGEBRUSH REBELLION AND ITS WISE USE AFTERMATH

That the Fallinis and the Bundys hailed from Nevada was unsurprising. The Silver State counted nearly 85 percent of its lands as federal, and after the revolution in conservation legislation in the 1960s and 1970s, Nevadans pushed back. In 1979, the state passed Assembly Bill 413, a remarkable law that asserted Nevada's moral and legal claim to all Bureau of Land Management lands in Nevada. When Nevada Territory entered the United States as a state, it—like virtually all the western states—disclaimed "all right and title to the unappropriated public lands lying within said territory." But in 1979, Nevada asserted that Congress never possessed the power to demand this concession and thus it was void. This novel—and erroneous—legal interpretation grew out of an emerging political movement and helped inspire a radical reading of public lands history.

Earlier in the 1970s, new conservative organizations had formed and dedicated their work toward reversing environmental legislation and increasing state, as opposed to federal, power. From these organizations, such as Mountain States Legal Foundation and the League for the Advancement of States' Equal Rights (LASER), rationales and legal strategies were devised for divesting the federal estate. As the state with the highest percentage of federal land, Nevada made sense as the birthplace for what soon was called the Sagebrush Rebellion. Hearings about the Nevada bill revealed widespread and often enthusiastic support. One state senator complained that federal agencies "dry gulched the cowboy, bushwhacked the miner, and ambushed the sheepherder." Not content with his own folksy language, the senator also claimed state law enforcement would "arrest all the BLM" to prompt court action. The rebellion was off and running.

Despite this enthusiasm, complications arose. First, not everyone supported this Nevada scheme to take over federal lands on practical grounds. One state senator pointed out that taking over the public lands might bankrupt the state. Federal grazing fees always were far below market value, and if ranchers had to pay higher fees, their operations would falter. The state would probably have to sell the land, he said, which inevitably would deny public access and likely degrade land and water quality. In response, a woman rose at the hearing, pointed her crutch at him, and threatened him: "Either let's shoot the son of a bitch, or we ought to hang the son of a bitch." The state senator's thoughts squared with market conditions and past treatment of state lands, while the reactive vehemence suggested the seething anger of many Nevadans—and westerners more broadly.

Second, Nevada's legislative plan was not thought through, despite its rapid spread. Many westerners welcomed Nevada's statement of rebellion; it resonated with their own dissatisfaction with the new public lands status quo that raised wilderness and endangered species protection as priorities. In the year after Nevada passed its law, New Mexico, Utah, and Arizona followed the same route. Wyoming did not stop with claiming BLM land but also grabbed at the national forests. Other states passed similar legislation only to have it vetoed by governors, or they passed simpler resolutions in support of the widening rebellion. But what, precisely, would divestment of public lands look like, and how would it proceed? No one quite knew. The *Nevada State Journal* mocked the movement with a headline, "Nevada, Rebel without a Plan."

A sense of common cause swelled gatherings of rebels, such as a major LASER conference in November 1980. The meeting was presided over by influential western senators and produced a long list of resolutions. Senator Orrin Hatch of Utah, a proud rebel and keynote speaker, disdained environmentalists as "dandelion worshippers" and those in government as "land embalming park managers." But in the aftermath of this event and the new statements coming out of legislatures, divisions appeared and the common cause withered. Would states maintain ownership? If so, how would they afford them? Would grazing fees increase to pay for them? How would states pay firefighting costs? Would the states sell the lands? If they did, how could ranchers, who almost universally operated close to financial margins, afford to buy large tracts of grazing lands and pay property taxes on them? Going by the history of state lands, most observers assumed states would sell off these lands and believed that corporate entities would benefit most. In addition, most state lands were required by law to maximize the economic return, which meant more logging, mining, and grazing and less recreating and fewer biodiversity protections. Expressing anger over federal management united western critics of the public lands; developing realistic solutions fractured them.

Third, the legal foundation on which "Sagebrush Rebels" claimed states were sovereign over federal lands was shaky at best. Mostly, they were simply wrong. The Constitution's Property Clause (Article 4, Section 3, Clause 2) stated, "The Congress shall have power to dispose of and make all needful rules and regulations respecting the territory or other property belonging to the United States." Yet Sagebrush Rebels often pointed to the so-called Enclave Clause (Article 1, Section 8, Clause

17) as limiting the federal government to power only over the District of Columbia and military forts and similar installations. Their interpretation has not been found credible by courts, but it continues to succor supporters.

The movement also relied on arguments referencing the Equal Footing Doctrine. The Land Ordinance of 1784 required that each new territory joining the union would be welcomed on an "equal footing with the ... original states." Sagebrush Rebels posited that not controlling the lands within their borders rendered western states as unequal. The Supreme Court in 1900, though, pointed out that the Equal Footing Doctrine concerned political equality, not social or economic equality. Western states sent two senators to the capital just like Massachusetts and Virginia. The legal case that the rebels marshaled did not pass muster in courts.

Nevertheless, the Sagebrush Rebellion fired the imagination of American politics. Running for president, Ronald Reagan declared, "Count me in as a rebel." His victory along with a Republican-controlled Senate put powerful allies of the movement in power. These developments signaled a swing toward the values of decentralized, small government that rose with what is sometimes called the New Right. Conservatives filled Reagan's administration, and no one was more symbolic of the Sagebrush Rebellion than the new interior secretary James Watt.

Watt had worked in government before but most recently had been president of the Mountain States Legal Foundation. The organization, bankrolled by the Coors family, aimed to promote commercial development on public lands. Watt identified with the Sagebrush Rebellion, a link that mobilized widespread opposition to his nomination and subsequent time as interior secretary. Watt focused on reducing what he and his allies saw as unnecessary and burdensome regulations on resource users and what ranch families like the Fallinis experienced as dictatorial. He also adopted what he called a "good neighbor" policy, which translated to cooperative arrangements between ranchers and the BLM that significantly reduced both oversight and the management of the range for ecological values. Watt also maintained grazing fees despite these being well below market value. Being a good neighbor—that is, making it easier for resource users to use the lands—deprived the Sagebrush Rebellion fire of its oxygen. Watt's Department of the Interior also pursued more aggressive oil and gas development on the public lands as a reaction to the oil crises of the previous decade. One of his proposals would have opened drilling across two hundred million acres. In the mix of all of these policy changes, Watt also de-emphasized scientific work, such as the ecological inventories mandated by FLPMA or assessments required by NEPA. Instead, he deferred to the experience and so-called common sense of ranchers and other extractive users. This orientation made Watt popular across much of the rural West.

Reducing regulations or enforcement on land where resource extraction ruled was one thing, but when Watt undermined the National Park Service, he attracted critics who charged him with extremism. After a decade of expanding park units, often using the Land and Water Conservation Fund, the Park Service now had a hostile boss. For example, Watt appointed a committee to investigate what divesting the federal government of some of those new additions would require, an action that sparked outrage among the public and in Congress. Watt seemed to relish his role as a lightning rod, and as much as any single figure, he helped polarize the public debate and galvanized opposition. Led by the Sierra Club, environmentalists gathered a million signatures under the slogan "What's Wrong? Watt's Wrong!" The Wilderness Society meanwhile developed a "Watt Book," a two-volume tome that gathered his industry connections and showed how he undermined environmental protection. The backlash against Watt benefited such organizations: Wilderness Society membership grew from 48,000 in 1979 to 100,000 in 1983 and the Sierra Club jumped from 181,000 to 346,000. Watt lasted less than two full years, resigning in December 1983 after uttering offensive comments, although in truth the opposition he attracted made him a political hindrance to the Reagan administration. Watt helped make public lands a central part of the larger partisan debate, a key front in a national political struggle.

Curiously, while Watt made changes in Interior that riled environmentalists, he undermined some of the Sagebrush Rebellion's ideological warriors. Watt's good neighbor strategy eased tensions, which made it harder for free-market advocates who sought the transfer of lands to the states or their privatization. Free marketers wanted government out of the land business entirely. This group, whether represented by libertarian intellectuals committed to an ideology or large corporations committed to the idea that this would increase their bottom line, felt that the moves by Watt and the Reagan administration left them out and behind.

Indeed, the Sagebrush Rebellion fizzled out as a movement. It had attracted supporters who coalesced around a shared set of grievances against the newly robust environmental administrative state. But a political movement against something can be hard to maintain as a program when holding governing power. It also became clear that not everyone who called themselves a rebel had the same idea for a solution. A ranch family might resent an eastern-educated range scientist telling them how to change their grazing practices, but they were in no position to buy hundreds of thousands of acres to support their herds or were unable to pay grazing fees not subsidized by the federal government. A libertarian corporate executive might be able to afford a large purchase of land and wanted no interference or regulation on pumping oil from the ground. Rebel politicians might care only for gaining votes and reveal their commitment to be rhetorical more than anything. In that way, the Sagebrush Rebellion's power rested in its symbolic might as much as any policy achievement.

Early in the movement, a protest revealed this strategy of spectacle. On the Fourth of July in 1980, a group of citizens gathered outside Moab in Utah's red rock country. The chair of the Grand County Commission, Harvey Merrell, climbed up into a bulldozer bearing a "Sagebrush Rebel" sticker and addressed the crowd. The federal bureaucracy was the enemy, its growth "cancerous." "We will take control of our destiny in Southeastern Utah and not delegate it to a bureaucracy," Merrell argued. Fellow commissioners agreed, explaining that the FLPMA was devastating the nation. Then, after the speeches concluded, the bulldozer started up and scratched a road into the soil following an old mining pathway, pushing into a BLM wilderness study area and violating FLPMA. Nothing symbolized a wilderness threat more than a road. One counterprotester stood in the way but stepped aside when asked by law enforcement, but not before tossing a rock at the machine. A second protester sat farther away and was surprised the bulldozer never reached him, because he was sure he sat at the wilderness study site boundary. When the BLM later pointed out to the county commissioners that they had misread the map, they sent out a county road grader to finish carving the road all the way into the study site. The BLM demanded restoration within ten days, and if the county failed to do that, the federal agency would do it and charge the county. In the end, the wilderness study continued. Symbolic stunts and standoffs like this one brought attention to political fault lines, but they ultimately changed little.

After a flurry of activities like the Moab road protest and controversies like Watt's resignation, the Sagebrush Rebellion moved into dormancy, only to revive a decade later in slightly different form. The opposition from rural westerners that emerged in the 1990s was often known as the Wise Use Movement. The WUM arose out of the ashes of the Sagebrush Rebellion and picked up many of its same objections, but the political environment had evolved in the intervening decade and the character of the movement changed, too. Scholar James R. Skillen likened the political contests emerging from this movement as the "war for the west," which suggested how the reaction moved toward a more radical response. Although some people in the Wise Use Movement emphasized economic and political arguments, others moved well beyond ideological arguments.

One of the most prominent leaders of the WUM was Ron Arnold, who articulated an ideology of the movement. Although Arnold had once believed environmentalists had legitimate concerns, he grew disillusioned and believed that their worldview threatened the nation. In 1996, he published the following list as a summary of the movement's beliefs as an explicit contrast to how he saw environmentalist values:

1. Humans, like all organisms, must use natural resources to survive.
2. The earth and its life are tough and resilient, not fragile and delicate.
3. We only learn about the world through trial and error.
4. Our limitless imaginations can break through natural limits to make earthly goods and carrying capacity virtually infinite.
5. People's reworking of the earth is revolutionary, problematic, and ultimately benevolent.

Collectively, these principles might be restated as human use of natural resources through technology does not harm the environment, because trying things out will lead to the best solution for society. This worldview was well suited for an extractive economy that prioritized market exchanges ahead of ecological networks. By contrast, Arnold believed environmentalists were using their power to interfere with property rights and economic markets, to produce an ecological welfare state, and to eliminate industrial civilization. Arnold once declared, "Now they're Goliath and we're David, and we intend to put a stone in their head." Such rhetoric fueled conflict over public lands.

The nation's politics had become more conservative, so the West's Sagebrush Rebellion–turned–Wise Use Movement took on national hues. The rebellion of the 1980s built up from the grassroots, but this WUM received support from national conservative politicians, organizations, and media personalities. This influence pushed ranchers' frustration with BLM regulations or loggers' impatience with USFS planning processes toward the margins of typical protests—like the Nevada Assembly's law or the Moab road grader—at a time when the region was shedding jobs in its rural areas.

In this context, the rhetorical extremism of Arnold and others made it difficult to work on solutions for the land and easier to move to extremism. Meanwhile, militias in the 1990s attacked environmentalists, one of whom shrugged it off by saying death threats "come with the territory these days." In 1994 and 1995, bombs were detonated at BLM and USFS offices in Nevada. Militias used Wise Use gatherings to recruit. In the 1990s and after, the concerns expressed by the Wise Use Movement, militias, the County Supremacy movement, and other causes on the far right became hard to disentangle. And the violent context made it even more worrisome. The day after the Alfred P. Murrah Federal Building in Oklahoma City was bombed, a rancher in New Mexico informed Forest Service employees who were reducing his grazing permit because his practices had overgrazed the range: "If you come out and try to move my cattle off, there will be one hundred people out there with guns to meet you." Such threats against federal employees increased, turning federal agency employees into targets and igniting an ongoing contest over the legitimacy of environmental management of public lands.

For decades, the public lands supported key segments of the western economy, but the environmental revolution of the 1960s and 1970s changed the rules to respond to new public values and deteriorating ecologies in forests and rangelands. Accustomed to privileges on the land, many westerners argued against the new laws and asserted an economic and political vision meant to erode environmentalist support or cast it as illegitimate. What began in political protests and symbolic acts moved into more ideological and even violent expressions, as opposing sides hardened their views and made discussing issues—much less compromising over them—far more difficult.

DEVELOPING A RADICAL ENVIRONMENTALISM

It can be tempting to paint the reactionary forces on the right as the only side that was radicalizing. But environmentalists fractured, too, and a new radical wing achieved prominence in these same years. This development helped form a chasm on public lands issues. As with many parts of public lands history, wilderness provided the impetus.

The 1964 Wilderness Act required the Forest Service and the Park Service to inventory their roadless lands to judge whether to include them in the National Wilderness Preservation System. The Forest Service was reluctant. Although the agency did not mind putting high areas, often called "rock and ice," into wilderness designations, millions of roadless acres included commercial timberlands, and the agency hoped to keep those tracts available for cutting trees. The first Roadless Area Review Evaluation (RARE) launched in 1971 and identified nearly 1,500 roadless areas including more than 56 million acres that would need to be evaluated. The USFS promised to complete the process in two years, a pace many wilderness advocates believed to be rushed. Its recommendations contained fewer areas for wilderness than activists believed was warranted. The agency, timber interests, and environmentalists all mobilized for public hearings to express their positions. In 1972, disappointed in the initial recommendations, the Sierra Club filed a lawsuit arguing that RARE did not satisfy the National Environmental Policy Act's requirements for adequate information or time for public input. A federal court issued a temporary injunction against all timber sales in roadless areas. Eventually, the conservation organization and the Forest Service settled out of court in an arrangement that promised no new logging in roadless areas without an environmental review. NEPA provided the legal leverage, and the Sierra Club used it to get stronger wilderness reviews that ensured public input.

The immediate response was a second round of reviews, RARE II, begun in 1977. This time the process covered nearly 3,000 roadless areas and 62 million acres and broadened the Forest Service's earlier criteria. In many ways, it was a more thorough and satisfying approach to conservationists (even though it sparked the animosity of local resource users and contributed to the environment that launched the Sagebrush Rebellion). But some in the conservation community became frustrated.

By this time, a solid group of conservation organizations operated in the mainstream of American politics. The Sierra Club and the Wilderness Society had become mainstays, and their organizations had grown in size and sophistication with large staffs. As they became more bureaucratic, they became more moderate, willing to compromise, and comfortable litigating. Amid the slow reviews, these moderates threatened lawsuits and also angled with Congress to protect roadless areas. In 1978, they succeeded in passing the Endangered American Wilderness Act, legislation that protected 1.3 million acres of roadless tracts across the West. At the time, it seemed to be an important achievement, but looking back, some activists who turned more radical saw the law as the beginning of too many compromises.

The political process that emerged out of RARE II demanded compromises. Across the country, public hearings in local communities revealed the public's ideas, and the majority of voices favored multiple-use management. Wilderness organizations knew that they could not achieve wilderness protection over all the remaining roadless areas, so they put forward proposals that favored wilderness for 63 percent of those places. The Carter administration proposed a disappointing 25 percent. This was the difficult political context in which legislative compromise occurred.

The timber industry and wilderness advocates parried through their congressional representatives. The focus came down to not only issues of where boundaries would be drawn but also whether there would be potential for future wilderness designations. This was called hard or soft release language. The timber industry wanted assurances for the future, so they demanded that if any wilderness was designated after the roadless review, the legislation explicitly stated that all of the rest of the area would be open for resource development. This was known as "hard release." Wilderness advocates pushed for "soft release" language that reserved the possibility for reviewing roadless areas' potential for wilderness during future rounds of revising the forest plans mandated by the National Forest Management Act of 1976.

All of this might seem like reasonable terms for compromises in a democratic political process. Yet within the wilderness contingent, it became more complicated and controversial. Local or state groups threatened to sue, which might have upset the balance the big organizations had achieved with legislators. If the leaders demanded too many more wilderness designations, it might jeopardize the soft release measures being worked out legislatively. Keeping soft release language was the priority, so the national leaders often settled for less wilderness at the time, to the frustration of others.

This drift toward compromise produced a backlash within the environmental community best represented by the founding of Earth First!, a radical group that grew out of disaffected wilderness proponents. One of the cofounders of Earth First!, Dave Foreman, had worked for the Wilderness Society through the 1970s and symbolized this transition best. The group formed in 1980, taking inspiration from the writer Edward Abbey's iconoclastic novel, *The Monkey Wrench Gang* (1975), which told of a group of people rollicking through the West sabotaging machinery set to wreak havoc on the earth. The group's coming-of-age announcement came at Glen Canyon Dam in March 1981 when activists hopped a fence and unfurled a 300-foot black plastic roll that looked like a crack in the dam. The arrival of Earth First! on the scene announced a new phase in public lands history, one marked by direct action and spectacle that attracted a new generation to the cause and people ready to transcend old conservation strategies.

Although it found its first fifteen minutes of fame on a dam in a desert, Earth First! spent most of its early years in forests. Inspired by the civil rights movement, Earth First! put people on the line to force confrontations. They first deployed these strategies in the Siskiyou Mountains at the Oregon-California border in the early 1980s, a place of high biodiversity. Within the mountains, the Kalmiopsis Wilderness already existed, surrounded by roadless acres gradually being eaten away by logging roads and timber sales. Old-growth forests north of the designated Kalmiopsis attracted the covetous eyes of timber companies and the determined might of environmentalists. A Forest Service road directed toward Bald Mountain brought this issue to a head because it effectively would cut off any possibility for an enlarged wilderness area. There, in spring 1983, Earth First! members brought their direct tactics to the forests. They blocked roads by linking arms to stop bulldozers. Soon, they chained themselves to equipment. Their presence tried the patience of construction crews. One day, a bulldozer pushed dirt into a group of activists and reportedly called them a "bunch of communist bastards"; two days later, some of the crew drove a pickup into Dave Foreman and dragged him along for a while. As with the civil rights movement, direct action often worked when the opposition grew violent against the protesters. By June, Earth First! coordinated with the Oregon Natural Resources Council to file a lawsuit that succeeded in stopping construction. Since the Sierra Club Legal Defense Fund failed in its lawsuit a year before, the lesson many drew was that direct action worked. One activist, Molly Campbell, remembered, "I no longer have doubts about my commitment to action NOW for the wilderness. If we wait and go through 'proper channels' one more time, there will be no forest left. . . . The strength of my beliefs and convictions grew after facing the angered bulldozer driver." The comment reflected the immediacy activists felt and how their actions confirmed their beliefs.

While blockades were perhaps most common, other direct actions gained more notoriety. Some activists not only blocked roads by linking arms but also buried their feet in concrete in an effort to delay even longer. Others climbed trees marked for logging for a tree sit that could last weeks, months, or even years. More controversial were ecotage methods. Activists tampered with equipment, removing sparkplugs or filling filters with dirt and otherwise making road-building and other industrial equipment inoperable. Tree spiking caused the most controversy, and although it did occur, its *specter* caused more alarm than the frequency of the practice. A spike in a tree could harm a chainsaw or saw in a mill—and those operating them—so it significantly raised stakes. However, the ecotage did not intend to harm people. Tree spikers told logging companies where such a campaign had occurred. In many cases, activists even marked the trees with paint or survey tape. According to Mike Roselle, one of the founders and most active members of Earth First!, the point was to disrupt and slow logging: "All they had to do was locate and remove the nails. The big deal is that it's a very marginal business, harvesting on public land, and spiking threatens its economic viability."

Despite this benign explanation, spiking trees proved controversial. Opponents called it terrorism, and even environmental allies struggled with whether to support it publicly. In 1987, when a spike (not connected to Earth First! but another radical) hit a saw in a mill in Cloverdale, California, that then shattered and hit a man and put him in the hospital with a broken jaw, tree spiking brought greater objections and drew more opponents. Still, Earth First! and other radical activists raised attention and directly confronted the violence of extraction on public lands.

Two elements—one philosophical, one scientific—formed the foundation for Earth First!. Biocentrism (sometimes ecocentrism) was the philosophy its members adopted. Basically, a biocentric worldview posited a moral equivalency among all life, whereas an anthropocentric one placed humans at the top of some sort of hierarchy. The Norwegian philosopher Arne Naess inspired biocentrism by developing what he called deep ecology. Traces of these ideas could be found earlier in some of the writings of Henry David Thoreau, John Muir, and Aldo Leopold. In 1985, academics Bill Devall and George Sessions packaged the ideas for Americans in a book, *Deep Ecology: Living as if Nature Mattered*. Shallow ecology was professional and anthropocentric, while deep ecology was grassroots and biocentric. The terms suggested both organizational and philosophical traits. Biocentrism put a philosophical foundation beneath legislation such as the Endangered Species Act, demanding that all life deserved to continue to exist. Even more important, its moral clarity inspired activists, even reinvigorating organizations that found in it something new and inspiring, a way of rethinking conservation that did not depend on compromises with economic and political interests.

While the philosophical debates attracted Earth First! activists, so did a transformation in ecological science that set the stage for changes in conservation practices and strengthened the case for new policies and practices on the public lands. For most of the twentieth century, the ecology used in public lands administration relied on concepts developed early in the century that relied on the idea of balance and climax, which depicted rather predictable ecosystems. Prediction helped managers do their jobs. But by the 1960s, ecologists had developed new ideas. One of the most important was the theory of island biogeography developed by Robert MacArthur and E. O. Wilson. Their idea was simple and intuitive: the smaller the area of an island, the less diverse the species. The scientific theory was quickly adapted as an advocacy position and applied to public lands and wilderness, easily imagined as island-like. If a larger area produced more diversity of species, then the agenda for conservation seemed obvious: protect more and larger areas. These scientific breakthroughs pushed biodiversity to the forefront of conservation debates.

With island biogeography and other advances in ecology, scientists recognized their work had important perspectives necessary for better conservation management. Although scientists typically idealized objectivity, some ecologists recognized a need to enter activism and policy realms. In 1986, biologists who worked on conservation issues formed the Society for Conservation Biology. One of the founders and perhaps most articulate acolytes was Michael Soulé. He defined conservation biology as "the application of science to conservation problems, [addressing] the biology of species, communities, and ecosystems that are perturbed, either directly or indirectly, by human activities or other agents. Its goal is to provide principles and tools for preserving biological diversity." Thus, conservation biology pulled together research that had been revolutionizing ecology for a generation and was directed toward explicit new goals.

Traditional conservation on the public lands had emphasized rational resource extraction—at least theoretically—and preservation of monumental landscapes and charismatic wildlife. By emphasizing the goal of biodiversity, conservation biologists exposed how shallow and scientifically uninformed that tradition was, and it developed an agenda for a new direction. The incremental changes and political compromises that characterized most political reform failed to address the biodiversity crisis that at its heart was about shrinking and disconnected habitats. While the extinction crisis helped motivate and, in some cases, radicalize activists to protect wilderness, in some cases it directly challenged economic livelihoods and further polarized the politics surrounding public lands.

SPOTTED OWLS AND PUBLIC TIMBER

All of these trends converged in a decades-long battle over the northern spotted owl and old-growth forests in the Pacific Northwest: radical activists, application of novel philosophical and biological ideas, and a complicated political economy. After World War II, harvesting timber on national forest lands increased dramatically, and nowhere more so than the Pacific Northwest. Between 1946 and 1950, timber receipts tripled; then, over the next six years, they tripled again. Before the war, national forests sold 1 billion board feet annually; by 1966, a record high of 12.1 billion board feet was counted. Washington and Oregon provided almost 45 percent of all national forest harvests. During the 1980s, the region averaged 4.5 billion board feet annually. To round out the statistics, in 1989, 15.6 billion board feet was cut on public and private timberlands. Long a timber economy, the Pacific Northwest jumped significantly after the war, driven by technological changes—chainsaws and logging trucks—and an extensive and growing road network. Such magnification pleased rural timber communities and their political sponsors, but the toll on the land could not be masked forever.

Activists had already pushed against these trends. Wilderness advocates, of course, worked to preserve some of the remaining roadless areas to good effect, and other laws strengthened forest protection. Nonetheless, the highest timber harvests occurred decades *after* the slew of protective legislation that Congress passed in the 1960s and 1970s. In other words, the immediate aftermath of the legislative revolution did nothing to slow down timber extraction on public lands.

The Northwest forests that drew the most attention in this period were old growth. A longtime prejudice against old-growth forests prevailed among foresters who viewed them as mostly decadent. Forest planners saw even-aged stands growing vigorously as efficient forests, while old-growth forests included decaying trees. Timber companies, however, saw these forests as standing treasure. Douglas firs, the most dominant species in the region, could be a thousand years old and three hundred feet tall. A single tree might yield 2,000 board feet; seven trees were sufficient to build a house. From the traditional perspective of managers and timber executives, old-growth forests needed to be removed for profit and to make way for a faster-growing young forest.

Scientists reassessed old-growth forests in these same years and came to different conclusions about their value. One of the most consequential discoveries came from Eric Forsman, a graduate student in the 1970s at Oregon State University studying northern spotted owls. The growing clearcuts in the region consumed old-growth forests, leaving only about 15 percent in the region. The fragmented, shrinking forest provided inferior habitat for the owls. A mating pair of owls required something like 3,000–5,000 acres to survive, and by the 1980s, only 3,000–4,000 pairs remained. Although the subsequent attention in public debate focused on the northern spotted owl, the species served as an indicator species, which meant that it represented the fate of other species that depended on similar habitat, such as anadromous fish like the region's totemic salmon species, other birds like the marbled murrelet, and mammals like the pine marten and lynx. As old-growth forests fell, habitat needed for these animals to survive disappeared and were not replaceable.

When the Forest Service heard of Forsman's research findings, its response lacked urgency and seriousness, which compounded the subsequent debate. Its initial response was to protect four hundred mating pairs with 300-acre set-asides, a paltry response by any measure and one that betrayed the public's trust. Environmentalists appealed this plan, driving the agency back to work on drafting a marginally improved plan that increased the set-asides where no logging would be allowed to 1,000 acres, but that still was inadequate for biological necessities. Another successful administrative appeal by environmentalists required the agency to justify its timber management scientifically.

Litigation continued because the federal agencies—namely, the Forest Service and the Fish and Wildlife Service, along with the Bureau of Land Management—spent much of the 1980s and early 1990s not following the law. When Congress passed NEPA, the ESA, and the NFMA in the 1970s, it spoke clearly about the need to protect species and include public input in land-use decision-making. The emerging spotted owl crisis tested these laws for the agencies, and when their response was lacking, courts stepped in. The broad litigation strategy environmentalists deployed aimed to protect the owls and their habitat using the ESA, to force the Forest Service to revise its timber harvest plans, and to do the same for the BLM, although it required a slightly different strategy since FLPMA and the NFMA were not perfectly compatible.

The Fish and Wildlife Service's record at the outset was one of delay and ignorance. An environmental organization petitioned the agency to list the northern spotted owl as an endangered species, but the FWS in 1987 refused, stating it was "unwarranted at this time" despite clear contrary evidence. A federal court ruled that the agency violated the law by disregarding "all the expert opinion . . . including its own expert, that the owl is facing extinction." In 1990, the FWS reversed its action and listed the owl as threatened. Doing so put the FWS into the position of having to review USFS timber sale plans to ensure they did not harm critical habitat for the owl. Yet the FWS refused, saying that it was unable to determine critical habitat for the owl, and the same judge pointed out that the agency was ignoring its statutory requirements and ordered a report due six weeks later. It took two years for the FWS to identify the critical habitat for the owl, nearly seven million acres that blocked most commercial activities.

Meanwhile, environmentalists sought to ensure that the Forest Service respected and followed NEPA and NFMA requirements. A critical part of the NFMA required the Forest Service to maintain viable populations of vertebrate species on the forests. Along with the ESA, this promoted biodiversity as a policy. Congress implemented a temporary workaround by passing riders to necessary appropriation bills that established higher timber harvest levels, overturning court orders and preventing further judicial review. But when the riders expired, federal courts again judged the agencies negligent, in one decision stating, "the most recent violation of the NFMA exemplifies a deliberate and systematic refusal by the Forest Service and the FWS to comply with the laws protecting wildlife . . . [which] reflects decisions made by higher authorities in the executive branch of government." Subsequent developments in this ongoing litigation found the Forest Service relying on dated and inadequate scientific information with courts forcing the agency to produce better management plans, specifically designed to protect biodiversity. Finally, in June 1992, USFS Chief Dale Robertson announced a new management approach—ecosystem management—and reduced clearcutting. It was a last-ditch effort, a way to assert agency prerogatives after being outmatched in courtrooms.

Meanwhile, in southern Oregon and northern California, the BLM managed public timberlands. Its history followed a slightly different trajectory, because FLPMA did not contain the same requirement to maintain viable species populations. Nevertheless, like the Forest Service had initially, the BLM ignored the latest scientific findings in planning its timber program. Courts, again, forced the agency to consult the FWS. Not wanting to change its managing philosophy because of the owl, the BLM asked for the Endangered Species Committee (often called the

God Squad) to exempt it from having to protect the bird. The committee allowed thirteen of forty-four planned timber sales go forward, a decision that environmentalists appealed. Political change, though, allowed for a respite.

Throughout the 1980s and early 1990s, a clear pattern emerged of the executive branch repeatedly violating the law. Perhaps the only thing more "American" than suing someone is complaining about the litigious nature of Americans. However, in the case of the spotted owl the suits might have been minimized, had agencies followed the law in the first place. One should not have to sue to force federal agencies to follow the law.

While all this litigation, bureaucratic delay, and political finagling unfolded, an Interagency Scientific Committee (ISC) was convened in 1989, by authority of Congress, to create a permanent solution to protect owls. Headed by Jack Ward Thomas, an elk habitat specialist, the ISC comprised scientists, along with advisors, dedicated to determining what would sustain biodiversity. Forsman, who had sounded the initial alarm for the northern spotted owl, said, "I don't think the higher-ups in the agencies had any idea what they were doing." Forsman's reflection indicated how powerful the science had become. The ISC traveled to old-growth sites, pored over scientific literature, and soon recognized that the forest "islands" necessary to sustain the owl would be large. The final recommendation reduced logging on national forests by 25 percent and on BLM-administered lands by 40 percent. This sharp reduction surprised agency leaders and policymakers who assumed small adjustments that did not fundamentally alter the status quo would be sufficient. Secretary of the Interior Manuel Lujan let the public know, "No bunch of biologists are [sic] going to determine policy for the United States government." The ISC infused authoritative science into the debate, even if agencies and administrators wished to ignore it. Thomas's reputation and the committee's careful work could not be challenged on its scientific merits.

A crisis for Pacific salmon also emerged at this same time, complicating things further. Conservation biologists and activists had discovered that old-growth forests provided essential ecological functions for anadromous fish. To protect them, verging on their own listing on the threatened or endangered species list, more of the West Coast forests would need protection from logging. As scientific evidence built on more scientific evidence, and as judges continued to force agencies to follow the law, tensions mounted.

More protection spelled potential conflicts in the communities between environmentalists and local workers, especially in the Pacific Northwest. Timber communities felt keenly the threat to their livelihoods that ESA requirements demanded. Temporary injunctions closed work, and any future where spotted owls or salmon took sizable chunks of public lands outside production loomed as a major obstacle. These communities and the timber companies that fueled them had benefited from boom times since the 1950s when the Forest Service redefined sustained-yield forestry in a way that divorced the concept from ecology. Meanwhile, technological changes in mills and exporting logs greatly reduced workforces. Occasionally, timber workers identified corporate practices as threatening their way of life, but more often, the corporations succeeded in framing the conflict as a battle between jobs or owls.

Besides drawing the line between employment and endangered species, timber communities often framed the conflict in terms of outsiders and insiders. Community members believed *they* were the rightful beneficiaries of public timber. Not only should they continue to profit from the forest's use, but they also improved the forests. One worker's comments at a public hearing in Oregon painted a picture of loggers working with nature harmoniously: "Ask any logger who daily shares his lunch with a raccoon, a chipmunk, a raven, or even a doe and her fawn if he is destroying habitat or enhancing it. The timber industry has done more to perpetuate our natural resources than any other group I can think of." The clearcuts that increasingly dominated public forests after World War II told a different story. Nevertheless, the worker knew the forests of Oregon closely based on his work, his daily life, while most activists who took up the opposing position knew the forest not by work but through their recreation. These differences divided the groups.

If backpackers and activists could not speak to their personal economic stake in the forest, they could and did articulate a question about more fundamental rights and relationships. At the same hearing mentioned above, another citizen said, "I don't feel that any one species has the right to condemn any other species to extinction." Earth First! agreed and extended the concept of rights, as Dave Foreman explained: "When we fully identify with a wild place, then, monkeywrenching becomes self-defense, which is a fundamental right." Activists genuinely felt connected to these ancient forests, as they characterized them, and believed they were theirs to protect, part of the public estate. Others might not develop a philosophical argument around self-defense to justify their activism. Instead, they simply wanted laws followed and perhaps some reform in forestry practices.

While local workers and activists justified their respective positions, some foresters recognized that traditional forestry methods no longer worked and advocated new approaches to management that incorporated broader ecological views than simply growing more trees faster. Jerry Franklin best represented this approach, called simply New Forestry. Franklin had worked for the Forest Service for most of his career before leaving to be a professor at the University of Washington. He dispelled the idea that clearcuts mimicked natural disturbances and advocated more random and smaller cuts as better for habitat, regeneration, and evolution of the forests. For a century, professional forestry sought to simplify forests to make them more efficient. Now, Franklin's New Forestry favored diversity and complexity in a challenge to the commodity-driven management favored by timber companies. But Franklin allowed for cutting, making environmentalists at times uncomfortable too. Cutting plans under New Forestry, though, included fewer roads, leaving snags, and true mimicking of natural disturbances. Franklin and other scientists and foresters like him helped move the agency toward officially adopting ecosystem management in 1992.

What ecosystem management actually constituted is a tricky question. As the leading scholar of ecosystem management, James Skillen, has explained, everyone in the 1990s seemed to favor it as a new way that might integrate management across federal boundaries and jurisdictions, could promote both economic development and biodiversity protection, and would generate more collaboration and less hierarchy. It seemed like all things to all people, so good in fact that eighteen federal agencies adopted it. One reason it proved so popular and malleable was that some observers emphasized *ecosystem* and others prioritized *management*. Skillen summarized the differences this way: "Some scholars described ecosystem management as a substantive paradigm that prioritized ecological protection; some described it as a procedural paradigm that resolved tensions between ecological protection and resource development through inclusive deliberation." Scientific advances like the emergence of conservation biology and legislative changes like NEPA paved the way for adopting ecosystem management. The spotted owl controversy became the crucible that forced the change to be adopted.

President Bill Clinton took office amid this swirl of conflict and change. While campaigning, he promised to convene a "timber summit" to listen to all sides and help forge a compromise. Clinton was joined in Portland, Oregon, by not only Vice President Al Gore, who had environmentalist bona fides as the author of a best-selling book called *Earth in the Balance* (1992), but also several cabinet members. They listened for more than eight hours to a range of opinions. Clinton maintained, "A healthy economy and a healthy environment are not at odds with each other." And the timber industry and the environmentalists and everyone scattered in between seemed to think that some sort of ecosystem management would produce a solution. Through these initial stages, Clinton aimed to recognize the importance of both owls and jobs, but he signaled that ecosystem management in some form might prevail when he appointed Jack Ward Thomas to head the Forest Service. Thomas became the first chief with a biology background, not forestry or engineering. He brought a new perspective, but Thomas suggested ecosystem management might well be too challenging, noting once that perhaps "not more than a hundred or so people in the entire world . . . are geared up to really think about what ecosystem management means." Thomas knew it would be complicated and constrain actions for all actors.

In 1994, the Forest Ecosystem Management Assessment Team created a long-term plan that became known as the Northwest Forest Plan (NWFP). And proving Thomas prescient, the plan angered some on every side. It opened 20 percent of the old growth to full-scale logging, when some activists had argued for a zero-cut option and felt betrayed by the compromises. This amounted to roughly 1.2 billion board feet annually, a 75 percent reduction from the boom years of the 1980s. To compensate for the reduction in the region's cut, the plan accelerated timber harvesting in inland forests. Still, timber companies saw the reduction as destructive to their bottom lines and were angered. Overall, it seemed to many that federal timberlands on the West Coast now emphasized restoration and protection of old-growth forests over production of sawlogs or traditional multiple-use management. As might have been anticipated, a solution designed to please every interested party did not find universal acceptance.

Besides establishing a broad-scale ecosystem management plan, the NWFP also introduced the adaptive management approach to public land management. In earlier eras, the public lands agencies relied on the best scientific information and assumptions, gathered as much information as possible, and then made what seemed to be a rational decision for management. Adaptive management proposed something different, something akin to a scientific experiment. Scientists and managers developed a plan as a hypothesis, and its management activities were like experiments that were carefully observed, with adjustments made once results were tallied. The process was iterative and accounted for changing information in a quicker manner than older regimes allowed. For complicated ecosystems, especially those where information changed quickly, this adaptability appealed to scientists. Yet, after a decade in effect, the results were mixed. An exemplar of adaptive ecosystem management, the NWFP promised jobs and owls but had failed in meeting those goals. However, it succeeded in establishing new priorities for managing forests in the Northwest and a new agenda: to restore and repair past abuses on the land. Corrective measures increasingly became central to public land management, informed by new scientific approaches and implementing new laws at the insistence of environmentalists.

REINTRODUCING WOLVES AND FLAMES

The political movements of the Sagebrush Rebels and Earth First! continued to polarize public land management. Meanwhile, conservation biology and other factors led to new management priorities to reintroduce both predators and fire to landscapes where they had been reduced or eliminated. Early conservation practices removed predators like wolves from the public domain and worked to squelch flames as part of conservation's managerial ethos: control the land and make it produce only what is desirable. Unanticipated problems arose out of this policy regime, but shifting agency priorities and values occurred slowly. The impulse to reintroduce wolves and fire drew from a common set of concerns and hopes: the idea that a functioning ecosystem required all its pieces, and predators and fires were necessary on many public lands. This impulse had been articulated in the Leopold Report in 1963, but, because of long-standing antipathy toward wolves and fires, both reintroductions took time and generated challenges and opposition. Although it was not the sole site of such practices, Yellowstone National Park symbolized many of them.

The Yellowstone region's odd geology inspired (and bemused) the earliest American preservationists, but its wildlife proved no less an attraction to a public that traveled to see some of the last remaining bison and other creatures that had become uncommon across the continent. Predators generally were detested across the nation, and no predator raised ire like the wolf. Citizens and government agents trapped, shot, and poisoned wolves across the continent. The last wolf had been trapped in Yellowstone in 1926 during a time when the value of predators remained low in the public mind. Between the world wars, however, ecologists began to recognize the ways predators helped regulate ecosystems. Yellowstone's elk population helped drive home the point.

Elk had declined throughout the continent but remained viable in the high elevation of the Northern Rockies. Two changes on the land, however, produced problems. First, their traditional migration patterns had been pinched off by ranches, especially to the south of the national park. Pressed into a smaller range, elk herds quickly ate themselves out of forage, prompting the federal government to create the National Elk Refuge in Jackson Hole, Wyoming. Federal and state officials fed the elk hay to keep them from starving to death, a practice that was meant to be temporary but has become an annual occurrence.

The second issue concerned the lack of predators. By killing most of the predators in the larger Yellowstone region, the government produced conditions that increased the Yellowstone herd's population to unsustainable levels. In the national park, too many elk crowded on the range and overgrazed it. George Wright, a biologist working for the National Park Service in the 1930s, visited Yellowstone and concluded that noninterference should guide management. However, without predators, the system already was in trouble. The rangelands in the park bore clear signs of overgrazing by the elk—"deplorable," according to Wright. Outside the park's northern boundary, ranching and hunting discouraged northward migration and penned in the animals, which exacerbated the problem.

The herd was twice the size the range could support, and to compensate, the Park Service killed thousands of animals per year. By the early 1960s, the public learned of the practice and objected. It was this crisis that precipitated the Leopold Report. Following its prescription of ecological restoration meant Yellowstone needed to bring back its long-displaced wolves.

Purposefully reintroducing wolves to Yellowstone National Park, though, struck most of the public in the 1960s as a wild idea, even if attitudes were changing. The Endangered Species Act became another tool when in 1974 wolves were listed as an endangered species, and in 1982 they became an experimental population, which include less stringent protections to allow for unique trials. The Reagan administration had no interest in wolf reintroduction, though, and delayed the required recovery plan. Amid the ongoing Sagebrush Rebellion, ranchers opposed the idea, worried about not only predation of their animals but also any interference with their grazing practices. Regional politicians generally aligned with the extractive users and lacked enthusiasm for wolves. Environmentalists and the national public, though, favored reintroducing wolves to revitalize the region's suite of species and improve ecosystem functioning. By 1991, politicians' delaying tactics had run out and real work began.

Wolves were released in Yellowstone (and in central Idaho) in 1995. By the end of the decade, around 360 wolves lived in the Greater Yellowstone Ecosystem and the central Idaho wilderness. To blunt ranchers' criticism, the Defenders of Wildlife created a fund to compensate those who lost livestock to wolf predation. From 1987 to 2009, 3,832 domestic animals had been killed, and ranchers were compensated with almost $1.4 million. States, which normally manage wildlife, and western ranchers remained angry about the restoration, feeling their rights were overrun and their values ignored. This reality shaped future efforts at restoring other species.

Despite those frustrations, the effect on the land was remarkable. The elk population dropped. Fewer elk meant less pressure on riparian plant life, which increased songbirds and beavers; this in turn changed how streams functioned. Aspens increased. The face of the landscape transformed. The number of tourists who started to visit the region just for the wolves was not insubstantial, either. Despite the grumbling of local ranchers and some state officials, most observers counted wolf reintroduction as a success. So effectively did wolves spread out that the Fish and Wildlife Service began the process of de-listing the gray wolf from endangered species protection in 2007, which was completed in some states in the 2010s when a few states permitted hunters to kill wolves. The history of wolves demonstrated the possible success of larger conservation plans.

In the years leading up to the wolf reintroduction, conservation biologists helped develop the idea of the Greater Yellowstone Ecosystem, a concept that embodied many of the new ecological insights and policy needs. They discussed the need for cores, buffers, and corridors. Yellowstone National Park represented a good core for biodiversity purposes, and its surrounding areas, which included the national forests surrounding it and Grand Teton National Park to the south, allowed for a good buffer zone, too. Defining an area beyond just the park or national forest boundaries implicitly recognized that public land management was failing to prevent biodiversity disasters. Solving biodiversity dilemmas required thinking beyond borders and traditional conservation measures.

Returning a key predator to the Greater Yellowstone Ecosystem set the stage for greater ambitions. Conservation biologists joined with activists to dream bigger. Dave Foreman, one of Earth First!'s key cofounders, founded a new initiative, the Wildlands Project, which included Michael Soulé, perhaps the most evangelistic conservation biologist. The Wildlands Project predated wolf reintroduction and focused on getting the public to rethink the necessary scale of conservation beyond public land boundaries. To protect biodiversity, the Wildlands Project proposed half the nation's land be put in core reserves and corridors connecting them. While mainstream wilderness activists thought in terms of protecting one or two million acres of wilderness, these rewilding proponents aimed at fifteen million. The proposed Northern Rockies Ecosystem Protection Act offered one vision that would knit the continent together through an initiative known as Yellowstone to Yukon. Only by scaling up could a biodiversity crisis be stopped, they argued. Public lands would be central to such an endeavor, but it would require more and would involve more than adding predators back to the landscape.

Fire proved to be even more of a problem and opportunity than wolves for public land managers. In many ways, the history of public lands can be told through fire. The earliest focus of the Forest Service was to stop forests from incinerating, and the agency set the precedent for all the public land agencies, with minor variations. The attempt to manage fire followed a common trajectory across federal and state agencies and through the twentieth century. First, agencies aimed to stop fire to protect the land's key economic and aesthetic resources. Then they used new technology and personnel to intensify the efforts to manage fire. Later, managers and the public reconsidered the values that had guided those practices, based on new ecological insights and a growing wilderness ethic. Because putting out fires had provided a clear moral imperative, reconsidering those values proved difficult to explain to many Americans and agency personnel who had come to rely on that certainty. Meanwhile, not only had values changed, but nearly a century of fire suppression had also deeply transformed the forests and rangelands, creating a significantly different environment when, in the 1960s and 1970s, the agencies began trying new things. By the twenty-first century, fire had become one of the most complicated and intransigent problems facing the public lands, especially where they intersected with human settlements.

The idea of lighting fires, or letting them burn where they did not threaten human life or property, had always had adherents. Institutionally, though, they remained a small, dissenting voice and typically outside the public lands agencies. Harold Biswell offered a useful example. Trained in botany and forest ecology, Biswell worked for the Forest Service in both California and North Carolina. The southern experience mattered, because in the South broadcast burning had never been entirely suppressed. By the 1950s, Biswell, going against USFS wishes and traditions, began experiments with fire in ponderosa pine forests and found that fire improved some ecological functions. Then the Leopold Report provided a policy direction in which such experiments might fit.

Saying that parks ought to be managed to create a "reasonable illusion of primitive America," the Leopold Report called for reintroducing not just animals but also processes to the landscape. Fire was the most obvious tool to use, the "easiest and cheapest to apply," said the report. Not coincidentally, Biswell and Leopold were acquainted, working across the street from each other at the University of California, Berkeley, teaching jointly, and advising students who investigated what became known eventually as restoration ecology. Fire, in this new world, was natural and necessary to many ecosystems, not something to be suppressed no matter the cost.

By 1968, the Park Service took the policy lead by issuing a new guideline. When a fire started within a place and under conditions already determined, it would be allowed to continue burning. That same year, park personnel purposefully set a fire in Sequoia-Kings Canyon National Park. The new policy and experiment did not signal a complete reversal, because parks were administratively and ecologically complicated. Some who focused on ecology saw fire as a welcome return; some who had gone up the ranks putting fires out were reluctant; and those who marveled at all the new visitors and new buildings built with Mission 66 funds worried. Budgets divided among these parts were not equal, and, not surprisingly, the experimental prescribed burn budget was minuscule compared with suppression. Nevertheless, a once-standard bulwark against free-burning flames had been breached.

For the Forest Service, the Wilderness Act rather than the Leopold Report provided the biggest impetus. As far back as the 1930s, a forest ranger named Elers Koch in the Selway area of Idaho and Montana questioned the wisdom of fighting fires in the deep backcountry. Now, his idea's time had come, but it became institutionalized slowly. The agency incorporated new scientific insights along the way that argued for the importance of fire, but it did not issue an agency-wide directive until 1978, when it replaced the 10:00 a.m. policy of total suppression. In some cases, in some places, fires would be suppressed. In some cases, under the predetermined circumstances, they would be allowed to burn as prescribed natural fires. In still other cases, agency personnel would light the fires as prescribed burns. It was a complicated, layered approach.

For any agency, allowing natural fires to burn or applying fire deliberately were attempts to rebalance fire regimes that suppression policies had knocked off-kilter. With wilderness as a new ideal, allowing fire—which was natural—seemed like the right thing to do. And repairing landscapes proved to be a popular idea in theory. Yet forests across the nation, especially in the West, had changed in the absence of flames, making big fires more common and likely, as well as often more dangerous and damaging. Getting control of the uncontrollable situation has proved difficult, and the ideals that undergird it are often difficult to implement.

While the agencies slowly were changing their practices and recognizing the need for fire in some landscapes, they faced a test. In 1988, the massive fires at Yellowstone marked an important point in public lands history. Because the fires occurred at the first national park and because of their scale, their symbolism became outsized. Fire managers at Yellowstone had become interested in what a fire might reveal about the workings of the ecosystem. Their predictions, though, wildly underestimated the impact and extent. Throughout the summer, many separate fires grew and grew and eventually threatened some of the park's most iconic sites, like Old Faithful Inn. When the fires began, discussions praising natural fire were common—one ecologist even was quoted widely as saying, "Burn, baby, burn"—but as things worsened, the nuances of fire ecology and policy became obscured beneath the smoke. One observer, in the aftermath, concluded, "The Yellowstone fires seared away any notion that man could leave nature alone and still run a park around her—a park full of people, a park surrounded by summer homes, tourist businesses, and commercial forests." After thousands of firefighters and more than $120 million spent, the fires were growing to eight hundred thousand acres, beyond any human control. Ecosystem management, just then emerging, tried to find a place for fire in the landscape, but Yellowstone provided an illustration of how complicated this would be ecologically and politically.

A mountainside of burning or charred trees—of which there were many examples—might appear dramatic, but the greatest drama and costliest risks occurred when fire hit buildings. No scene stirred the American public more than when the Yellowstone fires threatened to engulf the Old Faithful Inn. This kind of threat became increasingly common on what fire professionals dubbed the wildland-urban interface, or WUI. The historian Lincoln Bramwell has investigated this phenomena's unique form in what he has called "wilderburbs." In recent decades, private homes have edged into forest environments, often right at the line where public land and private property meet. Homeowners enjoy the natural setting and its distance from cities, although they are close enough to still be connected. These homes frequently rest on literal fire lines, at high risk and attracting a lot of attention and resources. Recent years have seen tragic story after tragic story of communities overrun by fires that keep growing annually amid the climate crisis.

The public lands had transformed ecologically and politically after nearly a century of management by various federal agencies. The new values and laws established in the 1960s and 1970s prompted the agencies to make amends, as it were, on the land by restoring eliminated species and processes. Activists and scientists helped push these agencies in new directions and achieved halting progress. Yet the changes raised objections among traditional resource users and managers and proved unpredictable on the land after so many environmental transformations across the decades. The obstacles mounted as ecological and economic conditions tied public lands users in a knot of seemingly unresolvable problems.

COSTS AND STALLED REFORMS ON THE RANGE

At times, the public lands produced wealth for ranchers and timber companies who relied on the public range and forests. However, extractive activities frequently deteriorated ecosystems and accrued costs for their management. The major laws and reforms implemented in the 1960s and 1970s failed to solve all these problems, so efforts to account for environmental change and economic responsibility continued. Traditional commercial users of USFS and BLM land enjoyed political power, though, and often effectively forestalled needed changes and demonstrated another way that polarization and stalemate were becoming key themes in public lands history.

Recent reforms focused on substantive goals such as protecting endangered species, and on procedures such as requiring public input to management decision-making. Those changes produced opponents. But when environmentalists or economists challenged the various subsidies that benefited commercial activities on the public lands, opposition powered up further. Westerners who relied on federal resources and the favorable arrangements set in place for them wanted to ensure they continued to enjoy what writer Donald Snow called "the West's commodity favoritism." These loggers and ranchers and miners saw themselves as living dignified lives passed down through generations where they settled, improved, and reclaimed the land from waste. But these activities depended on a history of federal largesse going back to killing and removing Indian nations from the land to offering free land for homesteaders to investing in dams and irrigation projects. In other words, federal gifts to private property holders were a long tradition.

Grazing fees had been controversial from the moment the Forest Service first issued them in 1906. Stockgrowers opposed them as unconstitutional then and continued throughout the twentieth century to work to ensure that they remained low, normally well below market value for similar private rangelands. Every so often, Congress raised the fees during eras when the Forest Service and Bureau of Land Management intensified their management. Typically, those increases were nominal. In the 1960s, the Bureau of the Budget pushed hard toward setting fees at fair market value, but it spaced the increases over a decade to reduce the immediate effects. The fees remained comparatively low, but the political power of livestock interests was so great that when Congress passed FLPMA, it had to cut any new measure related to grazing fees. In 1978, Congress added the Public Rangelands Improvement Act (PRIA) that established a new grazing fee formula to go into effect temporarily for the next seven years. It was a moderate increase and pushed more fundamental reform to a later date.

In the mid-1980s, then, grazing fees remained unresolved, and the next decade produced insistent calls for reform and persistent opposition. As the cliche goes, politics sometimes makes for strange bedfellows. A group of environmentalists, budget hawks in the Reagan administration, and agency officials called for significantly changing grazing fees. Worried about overgrazing's deleterious ecological effects, environmentalists wanted to increase fees in the belief that this would reduce the number of cattle and sheep on public lands and even remove them from the most marginal tracts. The cost-conscious accountants in the administration saw the low grazing fees as an unwarranted subsidy, especially problematic in a time of big budget deficits. Agency officials believed that higher fees would help them manage the lands better and to reach a degree of political independence from livestock interests who had long pressured management decisions. It seemed everyone except ranchers and their political allies understood the necessity of reform. (A similar concern arose about timber sales in national forests, the vast majority of which lost money and sometimes resulted in investing thirty times the amount paid out. Accounting tricks and the few regions with profitable sales offset the losses.)

Several factors complicated public lands grazing fees. In 1985, the federal fee on BLM land was $1.37 per animal unit month (AUM, which equaled a cow-calf combination or five sheep), while comparable private land cost $6.00 per AUM or more, and state lands were several times higher than what the BLM charged. The shortfall between costs and revenues in BLM's grazing program stood between $30 and $50 million annually. Yet ranchers resisted rectifying the gap for a variety of reasons. Obviously, increased fees cut into their profits, but they argued that grazing permits attached to their ranches held a financial value (they could use it as collateral for bank loans, for instance, and their ranches' property values were higher because of the permits). To ranchers, raising fees seemed to be double charging. It not only cost more out of pocket but also reduced the value of their operation. To them, this practice violated constitutional protections against takings in the Fifth Amendment. This was a contested legal principle, but it drove much of the resistance ranchers expressed. Public rangelands also included additional management expenses that private ranches did not have to pay for. Thus, it was appropriate that those fees were lower. In such an economic context, political solutions were difficult to devise. Yet the political context made it harder, because western politicians, often from both parties, worked to protect livestock operators from significant changes. Having no appetite for antagonizing the ranchers, the Reagan administration merely signed an executive order extending the grazing fee schedule implemented in PRIA. A long-lasting solution remained distant.

By the time the Clinton administration took over, the situation had hardened further. Environmentalists had become more aggressive; western economic powers had become more resistant; rangelands had not improved sufficiently, with a sizeable percentage of BLM lands in poor ecological conditions. Clinton appointed Bruce Babbitt to head the Interior Department and Jim Baca to run the BLM. When Babbitt took over, the fees were $1.86 per AUM compared with about $8.00 on private lands; the administration proposed a $5.00 fee, which scared even western Democrats. Babbitt was committed to ecosystem management, which the Clinton administration saw as a way to modernize public land management and put it on a scientific footing, as well as encouraging more public/private collaborations. Babbitt proposed a rule change that would have increased the fees from $1.86 to $4.28 over three years, in addition to changing grazing advisory boards into resource advisory councils with broader representation and other measures to reduce ranchers' proprietary control over the federal range. The proposal was dead on arrival, with public land ranchers and their political supporters united against it. When Babbitt revised his proposal, he dropped the fee to force Congress to decide, which it did by raising the fees to $3.45. Opponents in the Senate filibustered the bill, as Senator Alan Simpson from Wyoming declared, "We are defending a Western life style in this administration's war on the West." The fees were dropped; BLM Director Baca resigned. These efforts to rein in the power of livestock operators failed, and a significant public subsidy for ranchers stayed in place.

Meanwhile, the range itself remained unhealthy. These lands tended to be fragile almost by nature—in dry regions often with thin and poor soil. Homesteaders had passed over most of this landscape for good reasons. Grazing these arid plains and foothills disturbed soils and invited invasive species. In the 1930s, government agents found them neglected and deteriorating. The BLM did not always show strong interest in changing practices. A 1974 federal court decision, *Natural Resources Defense Council v. Morton*, forced action because it required the BLM to follow NEPA guidelines for its individual grazing permits. A blanket statement covering all BLM allotments was insufficient. The court recited a series of reports from the bureau and other government agencies that documented environmental deterioration without the BLM taking sufficient corrective action. Nevada alone, according to the bureau, was being degraded by "uncontrolled, unregulated or unplanned livestock use" across the state's public rangelands. The court allowed using the land for economic production, but environmental quality mattered, too. Just as the court issued its opinion, which would require the BLM to do more conservation work, the agency released its own figures that tallied 17 percent of the range in excellent or good condition, 50 percent in fair, and one-third as poor or bad. By the early 1980s, the BLM established an Ecological Site Inventory system meant to assess the range's health. By 2000, it had only inventoried about half its lands but concluded that roughly 40 percent was in excellent or good condition, 42 percent fair, and a little more than 17 percent poor. In five states—Arizona, Idaho, Oregon, Utah, and Washington—poor conditions prevailed across more than 20 percent of its land. Improvement had occurred, but there was room for more.

The efforts to continue progress had to navigate complicated terrain. In 1994, the BLM and USFS worked together to develop a draft environmental impact statement titled *Rangeland Reform '94* to move forward on stronger ground. Conditions had improved on the range recently, the report acknowledged, but concerns centered especially on riparian areas which faced arguably the worst conditions ever recorded. Most of the ranges were steady or improving, but more than twenty million acres were not functioning as they should ecologically. This was the context in which Secretary of the Interior Babbitt made strong calls for change in grazing fees and practices. Not long before, some environmentalists took up the slogan "cattle free by '93" to eliminate public lands grazing. Add in wolf reintroduction, and it is not difficult to understand why ranchers felt besieged.

Some ranchers recognized their vulnerable position and sought new collaborative models, but others rejected the environmental values now inscribed in law and adopted radical alternatives instead. Western ranchers were responding to what seemed like a world upturned. Federal policy largely had been written to support their economic pursuits. But as the Fallini example that opens this chapter showed, ranch life that depended on public ranges was far from stable. The Fallinis had grown tired of the shifting policies that made it difficult to make long-term plans. However, some of the more radical opponents to the conservation laws implemented in the 1960s and 1970s started to deny the very legitimacy of these federal agencies and the laws that guided them, and some started asserting novel—and unsuccessful—legal theories.

A contemporary of the Fallinis was Wayne Hage, another Nevada rancher. Hage advanced an argument about property rights that mostly failed in courts but highlighted a common set of ideas and frustrations. In 1978, Hage bought a ranch in central Nevada, not far from the Fallinis. The ranch included seven thousand acres and a number of water rights. To run cattle, he used grazing permits on nearly three-quarters of a million acres of USFS and BLM land. Almost immediately, he challenged the Forest Service, which had found a series of violations to his grazing practices. Hage was annoyed that Nevada's wildlife department released elk, which competed with his cattle, onto the range toward which he had developed a proprietary sense. He thought the Forest Service's practice of fencing in the head of springs kept his cattle from getting access to water and violated his property rights. Frustrated, he wrote *Storm over Rangelands: Private Rights in Federal Lands* in 1989, which was published by a Wise Use Movement press. He had come to believe, and many western ranchers before and since concurred, that grazing allotments were "personal, private property." Despite this idea being popular, it was not true. Hage continued undermining the Forest Service by arguing that it and all the scientific management approaches the federal government used were merely political levers designed to acquire private ranch lands. In court, he developed a more subtle argument: his water rights functioned like his private property, and agency actions and regulations that changed his access (e.g., fences) were a takings prohibited by the Constitution. The subsequent litigation, part of which was led by the Mountain States Legal Foundation (which James Watt had headed), dragged on for decades—after Hage's death, in fact—and resulted in a decision that mostly affirmed the Forest Service's right to manage its lands as it had been doing. Hage's son, Wayne Hage Jr., said the decision disappointed him and might "swell the ranks of the militias."

The Hage case pulls together a great deal of the last few decades in public lands history. Hage was part of and well connected in the Sagebrush Rebellion and its Wise Use Movement aftermath. His assumption of property rights over land he did not own proved to be an attractive idea that spread. Just as common was the idea that federal agencies' actions limited the ranchers' activities because of conservation purposes. This put ranchers and federal land agencies at loggerheads. The increase in conservation activity in these years produced many instances of conflict that were rooted in declining material conditions on the land but were shaped by intellectual, political, and legal ideologies. Hage refused to accept legitimate management actions or what he judged illegitimate ones. This refusal to follow the law inevitably launched his journey that landed him in federal courtrooms. The fact that his son's immediate reaction to an adverse court decision was to suggest it would swell militia numbers demonstrated just how closely anti-conservation ranchers were to threatening violence when they did not get their way. This would produce more tragic results in the twenty-first century.

PERILS AND PROMISE IN COLLABORATION

Threats of violence continued and could be counted on in some quarters connected to public land use. However, so could collaboration. As the twentieth century wound down and the twenty-first took off, experiments in collaboration and coalition-building across the public landscape demonstrated opportunities and difficulties at a time when American politics became broadly polarized, making any coming together a fraught project.

Biodiversity and endangered species drove the need to collaborate. Reintroducing wolves to Yellowstone and the Idaho wilderness symbolized to its critics how the federal government and environmentalists neither understood nor cared about rural westerners and their livelihoods. But wolves were only one missing predator in the Northern Rockies. As progress on wolf reintroduction occurred, activists turned to the grizzly bear. The story of grizzlies in the Bitterroot Mountains along the Idaho-Montana border reveals that lessons were learned from the Yellowstone wolves experience and that cultural and political currents churned with new dynamics. Both proponents of grizzly reintroduction and its opponents sought a better plan than Yellowstone, which they criticized as slow and heavy-handed. By most measures, those who had opposed wolves lost. This time, with bears, they wanted to keep their seat at the table. The Resource Organization on Timber Supply (ROOTS), a timber industry citizen group, approached the grizzly issue with the idea that cooperation might produce a stronger position for them.

Instead of opposing grizzly reintroduction, ROOTS collaborated with Defenders of Wildlife and other environmental groups in a coalition to develop an approach that would allow grizzlies to be reintroduced in the Selway-Bitterroot Wilderness. As an experimental population allowed under the ESA with greater flexibility, the collaborative plan contained a citizen management element that gave local populations a greater voice than most species recovery programs permitted. By the mid-1990s, just as wolf reintroduction to Yellowstone National Park boiled in controversy, this unusual coalition from basically the same region with essentially the same political divisions managed to devise an encouraging plan through a willingness to forgo winner-take-all approaches. The result was an environmental impact statement released in 2000 that supported grizzly reintroduction.

Unfortunately, this high point crumbled amid increasingly ideological objections to the plan from constituencies on both sides, although often outside the process. That is, the increasingly ideological battle, stoked throughout the 1990s culture war, overwhelmed local cooperation. Political support was polarized by outsiders who deployed caricatures and invoked symbols rather than doing the work of building coalitions and compromises. Amid this, grizzly reintroduction died. As frequently became the case in these years and those that followed, specific local questions turned into national referendums on ideological and political issues. In this way, someone's political values over abortion or gun control ended up driving their view on wildlife in a local national forest. The rise of the cooperative grizzly plan demonstrates the strength of sitting at shared tables, and its fall proves the vulnerabilities of leaving them behind or arranging the seats in parallel, opposing positions.

Sometimes, the collaborations that emerged did so because of threats that hung over the parties involved. The success of environmental groups in pursuing litigation frequently motivated more traditional extractive users of public lands to find ways to compromise. Federal officials in both the executive and the legislative branches also knew how to hold out the promise of action to bring recalcitrant interests together. At other times, a different antagonist appeared and showed environmentalists and ranchers, for instance, that they shared some values against a different interest. Some of all these elements were at play in southeastern Oregon at Steens Mountain, which became a site of creative, collaborative activity in the late 1990s.

Consider the threat from Interior Secretary Babbitt against the backdrop of California interests moving into eastern Oregon. The Clinton administration sought to strengthen conservation along riparian areas to protect redband trout, a native species that had suffered major declines in its range. More conservation measures, though, alarmed local ranchers who worried their operations' value would drop. Babbitt visited Steens Mountain in late summer 1999 and announced that the mountain was going to be protected, but he told the various interest groups to search for a solution or it would be imposed on them. Ranchers sat down, repeatedly, with others to whom they had long been hostile—outfitters, environmentalists, tribal members. These meetings eventually brought forth a compromise that added some wilderness with no grazing allowed, retired some grazing allotments along vulnerable riparian areas, and provided some long-term grazing permits elsewhere to provide financial stability and predictability. Babbitt's threat of unilateral federal action offered one incentive, but the secretary reminded all involved that Californians and others eyed the region for real estate development. So the compromise also prohibited subdividing private land for second-home development. The economic and political threats that hung over Steens Mountain like a summer storm cloud forced a compromise that upheld continued ranching. Although it had not been easy, the example showed that compromises and solutions could happen when politics, law, and other threats brought people together with shared attention to a problem.

The Southwest has produced a number of interesting collaborations, too. In 1997, the Quivira Coalition, based in Santa Fe, began gathering interested parties to build the so-called radical center for rangelands. Acknowledging that traditional ranching practices had produced bad ecological outcomes, the Quivira Coalition aimed to develop what it called the New Ranch, which could support wildlife habitat, biodiversity, a good watershed, and domestic grazing. The coalition it aimed to bring together included private ranchers, federal land managers, and scientists, all working to restore the landscape and the communities that relied on it to a healthier and more resilient state without legislation or litigation. The New Ranch campaign required planned grazing (which included changes to timing, intensity, and location), monitoring results, and lots of education and public outreach, all of which meant the numbers involved remained small but growing.

The Quivira Coalition developed and deployed unique initiatives. One was a grass bank, an idea that had originated with the Malpai Borderlands Group of southern New Mexico and Arizona. Grass banks serve as an alternative range for livestock while ranchers work on restoration or other conservation projects. For instance, the Valle Grande Grassbank started in 1997 on a 36,000-acre Forest Service grazing allotment; nearby ranchers could run their cattle there for two or three years while conservation work—such as forest thinning or prescribed fires—was accomplished on their normal range. That grass bank ended after a decade, primarily because of drought and lack of funding, both from grants and within the Forest Service whose staff and budget were stretched too thin. This fate demonstrated the economic challenges of ranching within different constraints and incentives besides federal subsidies and market-based principles. In fact, the Quivira Coalition faced setbacks in other parts of its collaborative conservation activities when government budget cuts hit the Carson National Forest, where they had been working on riparian restoration projects to protect the Rio Grande cutthroat trout, a species facing serious threats. The Quivira Coalition experience has demonstrated how building coalitions with partners like public lands agencies and ranchers has become nearly as difficult as rebuilding resilience into the land after more than a century of overuse.

The idea of a "radical center," a term that helped inspire and shape the Quivira Coalition, emerged out of the work of the Malpai Borderlands Group. The group formed in 1991, officially incorporating as a nonprofit in 1994, after a fire started near the U.S.-Mexico border. Ranchers wanted the fire to continue, but the Forest Service extinguished it. In the aftermath, ranchers worked together to develop a "working wilderness" that reintroduced fire to the grasslands in the region, developed better ranching practices for the land (including the use of grass banks), and used easements to prevent second home and ranchette construction. The Malpai Borderlands Group managed some eight hundred thousand acres split roughly evenly between public and private lands. Since the early 1990s, group members have worked together with other ranchers, the Nature Conservancy, and the Forest Service to apply prescribed fire across hundreds of thousands of acres, consulting with the Fish and Wildlife Service to ensure endangered species protection. Here, as at Steens Mountain, the fear of real estate development and more federal control helped drive collaboration, but the Malpai group also wanted to avoid the gridlock and animosity that characterized the era's relationships among environmentalists, public land managers, and ranchers. Its relative success in community-based collaborative conservation is frequently touted, for it allowed ranching to continue and open space to be preserved while protecting species and reintroducing a key ecological process.

Collaboration, though, has been difficult. According to the legal scholar Robert Keiter, the lesson from local and collaborative groups has been that "often-ignored environmental values must be accounted for, that degraded ecological conditions must be restored, and that equitable solutions sensitive to all affected parties must be devised." Because, for instance, an Earth First! activist, an Arizona rancher, and a BLM biologist all possessed diverse environmental values and have different ideas about equity, building agreement takes time. With unpredictable and shrinking budgets, not to mention a history of hostility among the parties, collaborations come rarely. But cracks in the polarization that has so often characterized public land management have appeared, and within that opening, seeds have grown.

CONCLUSION

Politics in the United States have become increasingly polarized since the rise of the New Right in the Reagan years. Public lands controversies have been mapped onto those larger political dynamics and fueled them. Finding opportunities to slow or break down the polarization has been difficult and rare. One reason has been that stakes are high; the livelihood of timber communities and ranching families were at stake. However, so was the continued existence of species, and a large percentage of Americans believe that humans no longer possess the right to behave in ways that would eliminate species. The protests on each side egged on the other and raised the ire of many. In most ways, this dynamic continues in American political life and on its public lands. At the table where these debates occurred appeared a new configuration. The previous era found new people at the table, which many of the longtime members found threatening. While the public lands remained the object of attention, now those at the table increasingly sat not at a table of common concern, where diverse ideas and perspectives are aimed at the forests, parks, rangelands, and refuges. Instead, sides aligned and opposed each other, more like armies squaring off against each other. The contests over these places once more were revealed to be more about power than the common good.

Conclusion

The Promise of the Public's Land

A SATELLITE IMAGE OF SOUTHEASTERN UTAH shows few roads and a lot of rugged territory. Such a view masks the contentious politics and history that center there in a beautiful region of mountains, rangelands, and canyons. Since time immemorial, Indigenous people have called this area home, and they remain deeply rooted in the fabric of life in what is often known as the Four Corners area (after the place where four states meet). In 2015, five tribal governments—Hopi Tribe, Navajo Nation, Ute Mountain Ute Tribe, Pueblo of Zuni, and Ute Indian Tribe—joined the Bears Ears Inter-Tribal Coalition to collaborate and press for federal protection of nearly two million acres of the region they call in their own languages Hoon'Naqvut, Shash Jáa, Kwiyagatu Nukavachi, Ansh An Lashokdiwe—or, in English, Bears Ears. The land contains not only historical territory but also sacred sites and an abundance of material culture. Worried about further depredations and destruction in the area, the coalition urged a solution.

Consistent with the political tenor of the age, resolution came slowly and with controversy. In the final years of the Barack Obama administration, the Republican-led Congress attempted to craft a solution, although the committee in charge was chaired by a Utah representative hostile to federal conservation efforts. The compromise legislation the committee devised adopted a flexible management framework that favored grazing and energy production, as well as ending presidential authority to use the 1906 Antiquities Act. The Bears Ears Inter-Tribal Coalition, which by this time included support from dozens of allied tribes and conservation organizations (including the Nature Conservancy, which has a long history of flexible collaborations), expressed disappointment and opposed the measure, calling instead for President Obama to create Bears Ears National Monument. In the final days of his presidency, Obama did just that, setting aside more than 1.3 million acres, half a million acres shy of what the coalition wanted. Nevertheless, the monument was a historic one.

Consider the history that culminated in Bears Ears National Monument. Indigenous people shared a continent, holding land and its fruits in common, a gift from the Creator to be used and enjoyed by all. When colonists invaded North America, they brought with them an ideology about private property that transformed Indigenous common lands into parcels controlled by individuals. Even when the U.S. government decided to maintain some areas as common forests, parks, rangelands, and refuges, Native people were excluded. Those public lands were carved from ceded and unceded territories and sometimes from Indian reservations. And these reductions were not consigned long ago in the nineteenth century; federal Indian policy in the 1950s saw hundreds of thousands of acres sold out from Indigenous control and purchased by timber companies or placed in national forests or wildlife refuges. Policies practiced on protected lands routinely violated treaty arrangements. The conservation project has consistently eroded Indigenous sovereignty. Still, despite all these ways public lands had failed tribal people, the Bears Ears Inter-Tribal Coalition turned to federal conservation for support. Bears Ears became the first Native-initiated national monument, a point of pride and, for many, a hopeful signal of change.

When Donald Trump became president, however, the new monument fell victim to an administration hostile to many public land initiatives. Conservative Utah politicians and residents remained angry about President Clinton's creation of Grand Staircase-Escalante National Monument in the waning days of his first term in 1996. Nursing that grievance for decades, with Bears Ears stoking the fires of resentment further, Utahns pressed President Trump to reverse the Democratic presidents' legal use of the Antiquities Act in the state. Trump charged Secretary of the Interior Ryan Zinke with reviewing the use of the law since the Clinton years and soliciting public input. Zinke, who later resigned amid allegations of misusing taxpayer resources, spent a disproportionate amount of time with commodity interests during his review, and the public comments overwhelmingly favored leaving Bears Ears National Monument alone. Yet the Trump administration rescinded Obama's use of the Antiquities Act and created instead a monument of barely two hundred thousand acres—a reduction of 85 percent—and nearly halved the size of Grand Staircase-Escalante National Monument. This move was unprecedented and has ended up, unsurprisingly, in litigation. As of this writing, Deb Haaland, from Laguna Pueblo and President Joe Biden's secretary of the interior, recommended restoring the cuts, which Biden did in 2021.

What happened with Bears Ears quickly became a larger symbol for public lands. Recently, Robin Wall Kimmerer, a botanist, writer, and member of the Citizen Potawatomi Nation, wrote an open letter to "America, Colonists, Allies, and Ancestors-yet-to-be." In it, Kimmerer described the Windigo, a creature that embodies the "nightmare of greed," that "cares more for itself than anything else," while laying "waste to humankind and our more-than-human kin." You can find the Windigo in cultures based on the commons, where the selfishness of one endangered all. In her modern retelling of the Windigo story, Kimmerer cast President Trump as "Windigo-in-Chief" and excoriated him for viewing public lands "as a warehouse of potential commodities to be sold to the highest bidder," specifically citing Bears Ears. Then she reminded us that the public lands are "ancestral lands" first. When colonization blanketed the continent, not only was land privatized, but the commons-focused cultures indigenous to North America also faded in influence. To rethink our public lands as a home, as a source of identity that sustains communities and their history and futures, as places where we belong as one of many communities, human and more-than-human—these are the tasks before us. "What kind of ancestor do you want to be?" Kimmerer asked the colonists. The public lands, she suggested, offered a place where we can choose to forgo Windigo ways and instead be a common ground out of which both Native and newcomers come.

The short, recent history of Bears Ears recalls much of the history of public lands. It reminds us that all public lands were Native lands, and the sovereignty of tribes remains real but constantly threatened, sometimes by conservation and sometimes by conservatism. The shifting outcomes at Bears Ears also demonstrate the ways the executive branch shapes policy and how the legislative branch plays its role, with courts often having the final say. Since the 1990s, Congress has become especially gridlocked on environmental legislation, but political scientists Christopher McGrory Klyza and David J. Sousa have shown that there has been what they call a "green drift" in policy coming through means other than legislative ones, such as executive orders, administrative rule-making, and the budget process. The ways the Bears Ears campaign moved, forward and backward, showed the fundamentally unstable way the public land system is currently built. Finally, it suggests that public lands battles often remain mired in zero-sum thinking while an approach that seeks the public interest falls away.

Perhaps no better example of such conflicted approaches exists than the occupation at Malheur National Wildlife Refuge in eastern Oregon. Ammon Bundy came to the public's awareness first as the son of Cliven Bundy, the Nevada rancher whose standoff with federal law enforcement over his illegal grazing activities in 2014 attracted national attention. Ammon Bundy and his allies seized control of the refuge in January 2016 and held it for more than a month, claiming they wished to "return" the land to the original settlers. Bundy meant white ranchers, though, not the Burns Paiute Tribe on whose land the Malheur refuge sat. In fact, numerous stories circulated about how the occupiers disturbed Indigenous artifacts at the refuge. Frequently in these public lands controversies, opponents of federal lands called for them to be "returned" to the states, but in almost no cases were federal lands ever state land to begin with. Their call merely announced a misunderstanding of history and an allegiance to legal interpretations and principles that enjoyed no standing in courts or history but played well with a sliver of the public. The Bundy family's opposition to federal power and conservation laws attracted all sorts of radicals to the refuge, including militias and county supremacy advocates, few of whom demonstrated accurate historical knowledge about the public land system generally or the Malheur experience specifically. The occupation presented tense moments, and one protestor died at a showdown with Oregon State Police officers on a roadside in rural Oregon as he reached for his handgun. Supporters called it a political assassination; detractors saw it as inevitable given the feverish conspiracies and abundance of firearms circulating there. The takeover lasted a little over a month and subsequent legal proceedings failed to secure guilty verdicts, doing little to quell the rumblings among the Bundys and their supporters.

The occupiers of the refuge ostensibly came to Burns, Oregon, to support local ranchers but hoped they would inspire a wider uprising. The ranchers, Dwight Hammond and his son Steven, faced ongoing conflicts with local federal agencies, including the Fish and Wildlife Service and the Bureau of Land Management, reaching back more than two decades. In the mid-1990s, during the heyday of the Wise Use Movement, the Hammonds interfered with the Malheur refuge staff, tearing down fences and preventing them from being rebuilt. They also threatened violence against federal employees. A refuge manager recalled that one of the Hammonds once said "they would tear my head off and shit down the hole." The period's antigovernment hostility reflected in such threats helped shock the local community into trying to lessen the tensions. Malheur was in the same county as Steens Mountain, where threats from Secretary of the Interior Bruce Babbitt had helped opposing interests find some middle ground. So Harney County continued to collaborate with the High Desert Partnership, doing important work to build relationships across the county, a painstaking process that yielded fragile alliances and improved resilience in local ecological and human communities across public and private boundaries. In this context of hopeful change, the Hammonds were released from prison after a few months after being found guilty of setting a series of unauthorized fires on federal lands, but they were ordered back after a federal judge determined that their mandatory five-year sentence was, in fact, *mandatory*. Ammon Bundy called for supporters to descend on Burns, Oregon, to show support for the Hammonds, expecting the local community to join up in another antigovernment crusade. However, Harney County was not the same place it had been in the 1990s; a commitment to collaboration had weakened polarization and strengthened the community, helping it resist the incendiary rhetoric and activities of Bundy and his followers.

Many lessons might be taken from the Malheur takeover. The geographer Peter Walker spent time in Harney County during the occupation, and he concluded his book, *Sagebrush Collaboration: How Harney County Defeated the Takeover of the Malheur Wildlife Refuge* (2018), with a poignant point: "Instead of glamorous revolution, Harney County returned to the unglamorous, time-consuming, sometimes tedious but often effective work of sitting across the table with people of different viewpoints to find mutually beneficial, practical solutions to shared problems." In a time of political polarization, the choice to walk away is easily made, and yet the choice to stay can reveal common ground. Terry Tempest Williams describes a similar moment in *The Hour of Land: A Personal Topography of America's National Parks* (2016). Representatives of a dozen Southwest communities and organizations sat around a table, gathered there to discuss protecting land in southern Utah. Separate parties drew maps and then shared them. "What we quickly recognized," Williams related, "was that we all wanted the same thing and that the boundaries we had drawn separately were closer together than anyone knew once we gathered around one common table of concern." The stories from Oregon and Utah suggest that tables—real and figurative—work, just as Hannah Arendt theorized.

This point is not meant to suggest that using and governing public lands in the future will be, can be, or should be easy. It never has been. The work of living within environmental constraints is among world history's most complicated—and important—tasks, and the exercise of democracy in a diverse and complicated society like the United States challenges citizens and their elected decision-makers to set aside narrow interests and seek a broader public interest. To make matters even harder, the twenty-first century includes global problems of climate change, biodiversity crashes, and political corruption. Moving toward the future, public lands can and should play a central role in combating these compounding crises. Recall Williams's words quoted in this book's introduction: "The integrity of our public lands depends on the integrity of our public process within the open space of democracy." Promoting and maintaining that integrity demands an honest reckoning with history, a past that includes the exploitation of people and the land as well as the protection of places and democracy. Kimmerer stated, "The very land on which we stand is our foundation and can be a source of shared identity and common cause." The task before us, then, is to ensure that our common forests, parks, rangelands, and refuges, scattered across the nation, function as the *public's* land and not the preserve of one group or another, for that undermines the promise of a democratic and ecological citizenship that might bind the nation together. One way we might begin to repair the earth and our politics is with the public lands.

A Note on Sources

As a work of synthesis, this book relies on myriad scholars. I am indebted to their work far more than these notes can reflect. I have tried to include the most relevant scholarship below. Omissions are my fault, and I apologize in advance for any inadvertent slights. Research in primary documents supplemented the historical literature, and I have cited the main and most accessible versions of those documents.

INTRODUCTION: HUCKLEBERRIES AROUND THE TABLE

The framing devices come from "Huckleberries," in Henry David Thoreau, *Collected Essays and Poems* (New York: Library of America, 2001), 468–501; and Hannah Arendt, *The Human Condition*, 2nd ed. (Chicago: University of Chicago Press, 1998). I first learned of the Arendt metaphor from Marguerite S. Shaffer's "Preface" in Marguerite S. Shaffer, ed., *Public Culture: Diversity, Democracy, and Community in the United States* (Philadelphia: University of Pennsylvania Press, 2008). I adopted this Arendtian framework first in Adam M. Sowards, "Sometimes, It Takes a Table," *Environmental History* 23, no. 1 (January 2018): 143–51.

Terry Tempest Williams provides important and artful perspectives in *The Hour of Land: A Personal Topography of America's National Parks* (New York: Sarah Crichton Books/Farrar, Straus and Giroux, 2016); and *Erosion: Essays of Undoing* (New York: Sarah Crichton Books/Farrar, Straus and Giroux, 2019). The same is true of Gary Snyder, *The Practice of the Wild: Essays* (San Francisco: North Point Press, 1990).

CHAPTER 1: GATHERING

Several sources inform the early history and ideology around land and property. Easily accessible is legal scholar Jedediah Purdy, *After Nature: A Politics for the Anthropocene* (Cambridge, MA: Harvard University Press, 2015); and especially helpful is the economist Daniel W. Bromley's chapter, "Private

Property and the Public Interest: Land in the American Idea," in William G. Robbins and James C. Foster, eds., *Land in the American West: Private Claims and the Common Good* (Seattle: University of Washington Press, 2000), 23–36. Case studies that highlight property and how it shaped colonial history include Virginia DeJohn Anderson, *Creatures of Empire: How Domestic Animals Transformed Early America* (New York: Oxford University Press, 2006); William Cronon, *Changes in the Land: Indians, Colonists, and the Ecology of New England* (New York: Hill and Wang, 1983); Brian Donahue, *The Great Meadow: Farmers and the Land in Colonial Concord* (New Haven, CT: Yale University Press, 2007); and Carolyn Merchant, *Ecological Revolutions: Nature, Gender, and Science in New England* (Chapel Hill: University of North Carolina Press, 1989). Broader, but essential, from Indigenous claims to the continued existence of the public domain, is Louis Warren's "Owning Nature: Toward an Environmental History of Private Property," in Andrew C. Isenberg, *The Oxford Handbook of Environmental History* (New York: Oxford University Press, 2017), 398–424.

Moving out of the colonial era, new topics arise. For context explaining the era of Confederation and the Northwest territories, see Merrill Jensen, *The Articles of Confederation: An Interpretation of the Social-Constitutional History of the American Revolution, 1774–1781* (Madison: University of Wisconsin Press, 1940); Peter S. Onuf, *Statehood and Union: A History of the Northwest Ordinance* (Bloomington: Indiana University Press, 1987); and John D. Leshy, *Debunking Creation Myths about America's Public Lands* (Salt Lake City: University of Utah Press, 2018). The process of creating the grid and the ideology it represented is a critical topic in James C. Scott, *Seeing Like a State: How Certain Schemes to Improve the Human Condition Have Failed* (New Haven, CT: Yale University Press, 2008); and Theodore Steinberg, *Down to Earth: Nature's Role in American History*, 3rd ed. (New York: Oxford University Press, 2013). To capture the movement west in the early republic, including Jeffersonianism and its paradoxes, consult Roger G. Kennedy, *Mr. Jefferson's Lost Cause: Land, Farmers, Slavery, and the Louisiana Purchase* (New York: Oxford University Press, 2004); Steven Stoll, *Larding the Lean Earth: Soil and Society in Nineteenth-Century America* (New York: Hill and Wang, 2003); and Andrea Wulf, *Founding Gardeners: The Revolutionary Generation, Nature, and the Shaping of the American Nation* (New York: Alfred A. Knopf, 2011), as well as the overview in Matthew Dennis, "Cultures of Nature: To ca. 1810," in Douglas Cazaux Sackman, ed., *A Companion to American Environmental History* (Malden, MA: Wiley Blackwell, 2014), 214–45.

The antebellum period and especially free land and labor ideology promulgated by the Republican Party that produced the Homestead Act and similar trends is best captured in the excellent study by Adam Wesley Dean, *An Agrarian Republic: Farming, Antislavery Politics, and Nature Parks in the Civil War Era* (Chapel Hill: University of North Carolina Press, 2015), which also includes a useful treatment of Frederick Law Olmsted. Further studies that elaborate on these themes include the following: Lynne Feeley, "The Elevationists: Gerrit Smith, Black Agrarianism, and Land Reform in 1840s New York," *Environmental History* 24, no. 2 (April 2019): 307–26; Mark Fiege, *The Republic of Nature: An Environmental History of the United States* (Seattle: University of Washington Press, 2014); James Willard Hurst, *Law and the Conditions of Freedom in the Nineteenth-Century United States* (Madison: University of Wisconsin Press, 1956); Stoll, *Larding the Lean Earth*; Heather Cox Richardson, *The Greatest Nation of the Earth: Republican Economic Policies during the Civil War* (Cambridge, MA: Harvard University Press, 1997). A new history of homesteading contrasts conventional wisdom; see Richard Edwards, Jacob K. Friefeld, and Rebecca S. Wingo, *Homesteading the Plains: Toward a New History* (Lincoln: University of Nebraska Press, 2017). For the social and heteronormative context of land laws, see Peter Boag, "Thinking Like Mount Rushmore: Sexuality and Gender in the Republican Landscape," in Virginia Scharff, ed., *Seeing Nature through Gender* (Lawrence: University Press of Kansas, 2003), 40–59.

For Indigenous environmental justice, see Dina Gilio-Whitaker, *As Long as Grass Grows: The Indigenous Fight for Environmental Justice from Colonization to Standing Rock* (Boston: Beacon Press, 2019). For genocide in the California context, see Benjamin Madley, *An American Genocide: The United States and the California Indian Catastrophe, 1846–1873* (New Haven, CT: Yale University Press, 2017). For dispossession in the Great Basin, see Ned Blackhawk, *Violence over the Land: Indians and Empires in the Early American West* (Cambridge, MA: Harvard University Press, 2006). The Nez Perce example and broader context of the Pacific Northwest comes from Elliott West, *The Last Indian War: The Nez Perce Story* (New York: Oxford University Press, 2009).

Several studies provide thorough statistical data that can be relied on for laws, acreages, and similar details: Samuel Trask Dana and Sally K. Fairfax, *Forest and Range Policy: Its Development in the United States*, 2nd ed. (New York: McGraw-Hill, 1980); Michael P. Dombeck, Christopher A. Wood, and Jack Edward Williams, *From Conquest to Conservation: Our Public Lands Legacy* (Washington, DC: Island Press, 2003); and Paul Wallace

Gates, *History of Public Land Law Development* (Washington, DC: Government Printing Office, 1968). On John Wesley Powell's vision of the West, consult Wallace Stegner, *Beyond the Hundredth Meridian: John Wesley Powell and the Second Opening of the West* (New York: Penguin, 1992).

Many of the primary sources consulted for this chapter can be found in multiple formats and locations, including online. Listed here are full and accessible versions: John Locke, *Second Treatise of Government*, 1690, Project Gutenberg, https://www.gutenberg.org/files/7370/7370-h/7370-h.htm; Thomas Jefferson, *Notes on the State of Virginia*, 1787, Avalon Project, https://avalon.law.yale.edu/18th_century/jeffvir.asp; James Madison, "Address to the Agricultural Society of Albemarle," 1818, Founders Online, https://founders.archives.gov/documents/Madison/04-01-02-0244; George Perkins Marsh, *Man and Nature; or, Physical Geography as Modified by Human Action* (London: Samson Low, Son and Marston, 1864), https://www.biodiversitylibrary.org/item/272449; John Wesley Powell, *Report on the Lands of the Arid Region of the United States: With a More Detailed Account of the Lands of Utah, with Maps* (Washington, DC: Government Printing Office, 1879), https://archive.org/details/reportonlandsaro2drumgoog/mode/2up; and *Report of the Public Lands Commission* (Washington, DC: Government Printing Office, 1880), http://archive.org/details/reportofpubliclaoounit.

CHAPTER 2: FORMING

The topics explained in this chapter are some of the most-covered episodes in public lands history, and a complete set of sources would be impossible. The clearest and most complete overviews of the origins of these public lands systems are Christopher McGrory Klyza, *Who Controls Public Lands? Mining, Forestry, and Grazing Policies, 1870–1990* (Chapel Hill: University of North Carolina Press, 1996); and Charles F. Wilkinson, *Crossing the Next Meridian: Land, Water, and the Future of the West* (Washington, DC: Island Press, 1992). A short, valuable addition is John D. Leshy, *Debunking Creation Myths about America's Public Lands* (Salt Lake City: University of Utah Press, 2018), and several conservation professionals collaborated on their own account in Michael P. Dombeck, Christopher A. Wood, and Jack Edward Williams, *From Conquest to Conservation: Our Public Lands Legacy* (Washington, DC: Island Press, 2003). From these sources, the context emerges for the decisions to create the U.S. Forest Service and National Park Service and their constituent parts. I often found reading the original laws in the *United States Statutes at Large* helpful in seeing original language.

A NOTE ON SOURCES

The scene-setting and context of bison destruction on the Great Plains is in Pekka Hämäläinen, *The Comanche Empire* (New Haven, CT: Yale University Press, 2008); and Andrew C. Isenberg, *The Destruction of the Bison: An Environmental History, 1750–1920* (New York: Cambridge University Press, 2001). The material from George Catlin comes from his own *Illustrations of the Manners, Customs, and Condition of the North American Indians, with Letters and Notes Written during Eight Years of Travel and Adventure among the Wildest and Most Remarkable Tribes Now Existing*, 10th ed. (London: Henry G. Bohn, 1866), found at https://archive.org/details/illustrations maoocatlgoog/page/n4/mode/2up.

The origins of Yosemite and Yellowstone National Parks are found widely. Two classic accounts help provide a working framework: Roderick Nash, *Wilderness and the American Mind*, 5th ed. (New Haven, CT: Yale University Press, 2014); and Alfred Runte, *National Parks: The American Experience*, 4th ed. (Lanham, MD: Taylor Trade Publishing, 2010). Runte is the historian who argued the early parks were traditionally "worthless lands." Scholars who describe park preservation as an outlet for national healing after the Civil War include Leshy, *Debunking Creation Myths*; and Lisa M. Brady, *War upon the Land: Military Strategy and the Transformation of Southern Landscapes during the American Civil War* (Athens: University of Georgia Press, 2012). For more on Yosemite, consult Adam Wesley Dean, *An Agrarian Republic: Farming, Antislavery Politics, and Nature Parks in the Civil War Era* (Chapel Hill: University of North Carolina Press, 2015). The *Hutchings v. Low* (1872) decision can be found at https://www.law.cornell.edu/supremecourt/text/82/77. Several books on Yellowstone establish context, such as Rocky Barker, *Scorched Earth: How the Fires of Yellowstone Changed America* (Washington, DC: Island Press, 2007); John Clayton, *Wonderlandscape: Yellowstone National Park and the Evolution of an American Cultural Icon* (New York: Pegasus Books, 2017); and Marguerite S. Shaffer, *See America First: Tourism and National Identity, 1880–1940* (Washington, DC: Smithsonian Institution Press, 2001). For Native Americans in Yellowstone, see Robert H. Keller and Michael F. Turek, *American Indians and National Parks* (Tucson: University of Arizona Press, 2005).

Besides the overviews listed above and relevant laws, reforming forestry practices is a topic in several sources. Char Miller has produced a number of useful studies, including a biography of Gifford Pinchot, *Gifford Pinchot and the Making of Modern Environmentalism* (Washington, DC: Island Press, 2001); an essay on the relationship between Pinchot and Muir and the internal dynamics of conservation, "A Sylvan Prospect: John Muir, Gifford Pinchot, and Early Twentieth-Century Conservationism," in Michael Lewis, ed., *American Wilderness: A New History* (New York: Oxford University Press, 2007), 131–47; and, with Gerald W. Williams, a study of the National Forest Commission, "At the Creation: The National Forest Commission of 1896–97," *Forest History Today* (Spring/Fall 2005): 32–41. Historians have explored the opposition to national forests in Harold K. Steen, *The U.S. Forest Service: A History*, Centennial Edition (Seattle: University of Washington Press, 2004); Nancy Langston, *Forest Dreams, Forest Nightmares: The Paradox of Old Growth in the Inland West* (Seattle: University of Washington Press, 1995); and the excellent case study of Colorado in G. Michael McCarthy, *Hour of Trial: The Conservation Conflict in Colorado and the West, 1891–1907* (Norman: University of Oklahoma Press, 1977). The Pinchot-Wilson letter is digitized at the Forest History Society website, https://foresthistory.org/research-explore/us-forest-service-history/policy-and-law/agency-organization/wilson-letter/. Firsthand accounts related to timber reform include Franklin Benjamin Hough, *Report on Forestry* (Washington, DC: Government Printing Office, 1878), found at http://archive.org/details/reportonforestro1agri-goog and Carl Schurz, *Report of the Secretary of the Interior, 1877*, found at https://en.wikisource.org/wiki/Report_of_the_Secretary_of_the_Interior/1877.

The early history of ranching and grazing management is critical to understanding the Forest Service and public domain policies. Several accounts by Richard White provide needed context for the livestock industry after the Civil War, including for the Johnson County War: Richard White, *"It's Your Misfortune and None of My Own": A New History of the American West* (Norman: University of Oklahoma Press, 1993); "Animals and Enterprise," in Clyde A. Milner, Carol A. O'Connor, and Martha A. Sandweiss, eds., *The Oxford History of the American West* (New York: Oxford University Press, 1994), 237–73; and *The Republic for Which It Stands: The United States during Reconstruction and the Gilded Age, 1865–1896* (New York: Oxford University Press, 2017). Other sources for overviews of the industry and management include William D. Rowley, *U.S. Forest Service Grazing and Rangelands: A History* (College Station: Texas A&M University Press, 1985); and Christopher Knowlton, *Cattle Kingdom: The Hidden History of the Cowboy West* (Boston: Houghton Mifflin Harcourt, 2017). Case studies of how ranching worked in specific places are helpful; see Leisl Carr Childers on Nevada in *The Size of the Risk: Histories of Multiple Use in the Great Basin* (Norman: University of Oklahoma Press, 2015); and Adam M. Sowards on Arizona in "Administrative Trials, Environmental Consequences, and the Use of History in Arizona's Tonto National Forest, 1926–1996," *Western Historical Quarterly* 31, no. 2 (Summer 2000): 189–214.

A NOTE ON SOURCES

Conflicts on the range constitute a key theme in the history of ranching, whether that conflict concerned violence between grazers, protests against grazing fees, or antagonism toward the federal government and its regulations. In addition to material cited above, early opposition over new rules is a topic in Debra L. Donahue, *The Western Range Revisited: Removing Livestock from Public Lands to Conserve Native Biodiversity* (Norman: University of Oklahoma Press, 1999); Karen R. Merrill, *Public Lands and Political Meaning: Ranchers, the Government, and the Property between Them* (Berkeley: University of California Press, 2002); several essays by Char Miller in *Public Lands, Public Debates: A Century of Controversy* (Corvallis: Oregon State University Press, 2012); and Steen, *The U.S. Forest Service: A History*. For violence and conflict among livestock interests, see Marilynn S. Johnson, ed., *Violence in the West: The Johnson County Range War and Ludlow Massacre: A Brief History with Documents* (Boston: Bedford/St. Martins, 2009); Adam M. Sowards, "Reclamation, Ranching, and Reservation: Environmental, Cultural, and Governmental Rivalries in Transitional Arizona," *Journal of the Southwest* 40, no. 2 (Autumn 1998): 333–61; and Wilkinson, *Crossing the Next Meridian*. The important *Light v. United States* (1911) decision appears here: https://supreme.justia.com/cases/federal/us/220/523/.

For fire, generally see Stephen J. Pyne, *Fire in America: A Cultural History of Wildland and Rural Fire* (Seattle: University of Washington Press, 1997); for the 1910 fires more specifically, see Stephen J. Pyne, *Year of the Fires: The Story of the Great Fires of 1910* (New York: Viking, 2001); and for the Idaho senator, see Timothy Egan, *The Big Burn: Teddy Roosevelt and the Fire That Saved America* (Boston: Houghton Mifflin Harcourt, 2011). Regarding Pinchot's comment about fire and conservation more broadly, see Gifford Pinchot, *The Fight for Conservation* (New York: Doubleday, 1910).

Good overviews of wildlife and predator control are found in Thomas R. Dunlap, *Saving America's Wildlife: Ecology and the American Mind, 1850–1990* (Princeton, NJ: Princeton University Press, 1991); and Donald Worster, *Nature's Economy: A History of Ecological Ideas*, 2nd ed. (New York: Cambridge University Press, 1994). A rich, if racist, primary source is William T. Hornaday, *Our Vanishing Wild Life: Its Extermination and Preservation* (New York: New York Zoological Society, 1913).

Scholars have increased their focus on outdoor recreation in recent years. For a critical and broad background, consult Dorceta E. Taylor, *The Rise of the American Conservation Movement: Power, Privilege, and Environmental Protection* (Durham, NC: Duke University Press, 2016). For the rise of the National Park Service and how it differed from the Forest Service, including the quoted passage from Frederick Law Olmsted Jr., see John C. Miles,

Wilderness in National Parks: Playground or Preserve (Seattle: University of Washington Press, 2009). For Hetch Hetchy, the classic account in Nash, *Wilderness and the American Mind*, has been supplanted by Robert W. Righter, *The Battle over Hetch Hetchy: America's Most Controversial Dam and the Birth of Modern Environmentalism* (New York: Oxford University Press, 2005), and can be supplemented by the study of the complicated Muir-Pinchot relationship in Char Miller, "A Sylvan Prospect," cited above. Readers would benefit from becoming familiar with Muir's own prose, including "Hetch Hetchy Valley," which appeared in *The Yosemite* (New York: The Century Company, 1912). For the ways Indigenous and working-class people suffered from wilderness and parks preservation, see Keller and Turek, *American Indians and National Parks*; Mark David Spence, *Dispossessing the Wilderness: Indian Removal and the Making of the National Parks* (New York: Oxford University Press, 2000), especially for Glacier National Park; and Benjamin Johnson, "Wilderness Parks and Their Discontents," in Michael Lewis, ed., *American Wilderness: A New History* (New York: Oxford University Press, 2007), 113–30.

CHAPTER 3: MANAGING

Most history of public lands focus on the western United States, but conservation in the East has a growing literature. For eastern national forests, start with Christopher Johnson and David Govatski, *Forests for the People: The Story of America's Eastern National Forests* (Washington, DC: Island Press, 2013). The history of these forests is rooted the Weeks Act that Harold K. Steen discusses generally in *The U.S. Forest Service: A History*, Centennial Edition (Seattle: University of Washington Press, 2004), and that Stephen J. Pyne focuses on concerning its firefighting impact in *Fire in America: A Cultural History of Wildland and Rural Fire* (Seattle: University of Washington Press, 1997), which also covers subsequent developments in firefighting and policy. A copy of the Weeks Act appears on the Forest History Society website, https://foresthistory.org/wp-content/uploads/2017/02/WeeksBill.pdf. Another primary source that contextualizes forest history in the region is George Perkins Marsh, *Man and Nature; or, Physical Geography as Modified by Human Action* (London: Samson Low, Son and Marston, 1864), https://www.biodiversitylibrary.org/item/272449.

National parks emerged in the East alongside the national forests. For the Great Smoky Mountains National Park, a good start is Margaret Lynn Brown, *The Wild East: A Biography of the Great Smoky Mountains* (Gainesville:

University Press of Florida, 2001). For the story of the Everglades, start with Ann Vileisis, *Discovering the Unknown Landscape: A History of America's Wetlands* (Washington, DC: Island Press, 1999); Robert H. Keller and Michael F. Turek, *American Indians and National Parks* (Tucson: University of Arizona Press, 2005); and the classic Marjory Stoneman Douglas, *The Everglades: The River of Grass* (New York: Rinehart and Company, 1947). Terry Tempest Williams's celebration of and engagement with national parks, *The Hour of Land: A Personal Topography of America's National Parks* (New York: Sarah Crichton Books, 2016), contains the history of Acadia.

The Appalachian Mountains are a rich place for environmental history. For Skyline Drive, see the beautiful volume by Timothy Davis, *National Park Roads: A Legacy in the American Landscape* (Charlottesville: University of Virginia Press, 2016). The Appalachian Trail helps connect national forest and national park conservation. Sarah Mittlefehldt, *Tangled Roots: The Appalachian Trail and American Environmental Politics* (Seattle: University of Washington Press, 2013) is an outstanding account of the difficulties and opportunities for conservation and tourism in the East. Interested readers should consult Benton MacKaye's original plan for the trail in "An Appalachian Trail: A Project in Regional Planning," *Journal of the American Institute of Architects* 9 (October 1921): 325–30. Silas Chamberlin, *On the Trail: A History of American Hiking* (New Haven, CT: Yale University Press, 2016) offers a fine history of hiking clubs, too. Paul Sutter tells how the Wilderness Society formed on the roadside in *Driven Wild: How the Fight against Automobiles Launched the Modern Wilderness Movement* (Seattle: University of Washington Press, 2002), as well as contextualizing the wilderness movement and the efforts of Aldo Leopold, Bob Marshall, and Benton MacKaye. Neil M. Maher's study of the Civilian Conservation Corps offers a trenchant analysis of the emerging critique of conservation within this context; see *Nature's New Deal: The Civilian Conservation Corps and the Roots of the American Environmental Movement* (New York: Oxford University Press, 2008) for that topic as well as general information about the CCC.

Besides some of the previous work cited, wilderness ideas and policies appear in a range of sources. One of Leopold's classic statements is "The Wilderness and Its Place in Forest Recreational Policy," which originally appeared in the *Journal of Forestry* but can be located conveniently in *A Sand County Almanac & Other Writings on Ecology and Conservation* (New York: Library of America, 2013). Another useful primary source for keeping forests roadless is Elers Koch, "The Passing of the Lolo Trail," *Journal of Forestry* 33, no. 2 (February 1935): 98–104. David Louter, *Windshield Wilderness: Cars, Roads, and Nature in Washington's National Parks* (Seattle: University of Washington Press, 2010) provides a useful framework for seeing the relationship between automobiles and national parks, including Mt. Rainier National Park and the controversies in Olympic National Park. Generally for the National Park Service in this era, see Richard West Sellars, *Preserving Nature in the National Parks: A History* (New Haven, CT: Yale University Press, 1997). For Bernard DeVoto's criticism of the national parks, see his collected essays in Edward K. Muller, ed., *DeVoto's West: History, Conservation, and the Public Good* (Athens: Swallow Press/Ohio University Press, 2005).

The best overviews for the history of grazing on public lands in the West are Christopher McGrory Klyza, *Who Controls Public Lands? Mining, Forestry, and Grazing Policies, 1870–1990* (Chapel Hill: University of North Carolina Press, 1996); Karen R. Merrill, *Public Lands and Political Meaning: Ranchers, the Government, and the Property between Them* (Berkeley: University of California Press, 2002); William D. Rowley, *U.S. Forest Service Grazing and Rangelands: A History* (College Station: Texas A&M University Press, 1985); and James R. Skillen, *Nation's Largest Landlord: The Bureau of Land Management in the American West* (Lawrence: University Press of Kansas, 2013). For some specifics on the early Bureau of Land Management, see Grant McConnell, *Private Power and American Democracy* (New York: Alfred A. Knopf, 1966); and Samuel Trask Dana and Sally K. Fairfax, *Forest and Range Policy: Its Development in the United States*, 2nd ed. (New York: McGraw-Hill, 1980). The case study from Arizona is by Adam M. Sowards, "Administrative Trials, Environmental Consequences, and the Use of History in Arizona's Tonto National Forest, 1926–1996," *Western Historical Quarterly* 31, no. 2 (Summer 2000): 189–214, and also relies on Leopold's "The Virgin Southwest," contained in the previously cited volume. For ecology and range science, see Nathan Freeman Sayre, *The Politics of Scale: A History of Rangeland Science* (Chicago: University of Chicago Press, 2017) for the best account, to be supplemented by Sharon E. Kingsland, *The Evolution of American Ecology, 1890–2000* (Baltimore: Johns Hopkins University Press, 2005); and Donald Worster, *Nature's Economy: A History of Ecological Ideas*, 2nd ed. (New York: Cambridge University Press, 1994).

The history of forestry and the Forest Service is ably told in three key overviews: Samuel P. Hays, *The American People and the National Forests: The First Century of the U.S. Forest Service* (Pittsburgh: University of Pittsburgh Press, 2009); James G. Lewis, *The Forest Service and the Greatest Good: A Centennial History* (Durham, NC: Forest History Society, 2005); and Steen, *The U.S. Forest Service: A History*. Nancy Langston's case study of the forests of northeastern Oregon is outstanding and has provided a model for understanding the environmental history of forests far more broadly than just in the Blue Mountains: *Forest Dreams, Forest Nightmares: The Paradox of Old Growth in the Inland West* (Seattle: University of Washington Press, 1995). Likewise, Paul W. Hirt, *A Conspiracy of Optimism: Management of the National Forests since World War Two* (Lincoln: University of Nebraska Press, 1994), studies the post–World War II Forest Service, focusing on the politics and economy governing forest management. For primary sources, the Copeland Report is worth investigating: United States Forest Service, *A National Plan for American Forestry. Letter from the Secretary of Agriculture Transmitting in Response to S. Res. 175 (Seventy-Second Congress) the Report of the Forest Service of the Agricultural Department on the Forest Problem of the United States* (Washington, DC: Government Printing Office, 1933), http://archive.org/details/nationalplanforao1unitrich.

Several sources help to piece together the history of wildlife refuges. For an overview of the U.S. Fish and Wildlife Service, see Robert Fischman, *The National Wildlife Refuges: Coordinating a Conservation System through Law* (Washington, DC: Island Press, 2003). Some histories of early wildlife conservation include Thomas R. Dunlap, *Saving America's Wildlife: Ecology and the American Mind, 1850–1990* (Princeton, NJ: Princeton University Press, 1991); and John F. Reiger, *American Sportsmen and the Origins of Conservation*, 3rd rev. expanded ed. (Corvallis: Oregon State University Press, 2001). Information on efforts to protect flyways is in Ann Vileisis, *Discovering the Unknown Landscape: A History of America's Wetlands* (Washington, DC: Island Press, 1999); Randall K. Wilson, *America's Public Lands: From Yellowstone to Smokey Bear and Beyond* (Lanham, MD: Rowman & Littlefield, 2014); and Robert M. Wilson, *Seeking Refuge: Birds and Landscapes of the Pacific Flyway* (Seattle: University of Washington Press, 2010). The case of elk in Jackson Hole comes from Robert W. Righter, *Crucible for Conservation* (Moose, WY: Grand Teton Association, 1982), and some of my own archival research in the Olaus J. Murie Papers at the Denver Public Library. Again, Nancy Langston presents a stellar case study in *Where Land and Water Meet: A Western Landscape Transformed* (Seattle: University of Washington Press, 2003). I first encountered the concept of "hybrid landscapes" from Mark Fiege, *Irrigated Eden: The Making of an Agricultural Landscape in the American West* (Seattle: University of Washington Press, 2015). Finally, on the concept of habitat for conservation, see Peter S. Alagona, *After the Grizzly: Endangered Species and the Politics of Place in California* (Berkeley: University of California Press, 2013).

CHAPTER 4: BALANCING

The literature surrounding the wilderness movement is large. An overview written by an activist with a keen sense of history is Doug Scott, *The Enduring Wilderness* (Golden, CO: Fulcrum, 2004). For the movement's emergence, two books by Mark Harvey are central: *A Symbol of Wilderness: Echo Park and the American Conservation Movement* (Seattle: University of Washington Press, 2000) and *Wilderness Forever: Howard Zahniser and the Path to the Wilderness Act* (Seattle: University of Washington Press, 2005). Two biographies of David Brower help contextualize the era: Tom Turner, *David Brower: The Making of the Environmental Movement* (Oakland: University of California Press, 2015); and Bob Wyss, *The Man Who Built the Sierra Club: A Life of David Brower* (New York: Columbia University Press, 2016), as well as the reportage contained in the classic book by John McPhee, *Encounters with the Archdruid* (New York: Noonday, 1971). An excellent case study of wilderness in the Pacific Northwest is Kevin R. Marsh's *Drawing Lines in the Forest: Creating Wilderness Areas in the Pacific Northwest* (Seattle: University of Washington Press, 2007). For the test of mining and the Wilderness Act, see Adam M. Sowards, *An Open Pit Visible from the Moon: The Wilderness Act and the Fight to Protect Miners Ridge and the Public Interest* (Norman: University of Oklahoma Press, 2020). James Morton Turner's *The Promise of Wilderness: American Environmental Politics since 1964* (Seattle: University of Washington Press, 2012) is the single best volume on wilderness politics after the passage of the Wilderness Act in 1964.

Primary sources are useful in framing the wilderness movement. J. Michael McCloskey is an activist whose memoir, *In the Thick of It: My Life in the Sierra Club* (Washington, DC: Island Press, 2005), contains important perspectives. The famous Stegner letter appears in several collections, including Wallace Stegner, *The Sound of Mountain Water: The Changing American West* (New York: Vintage, 2017). The collected writings of Howard Zahniser in Mark W. T. Harvey, ed., *The Wilderness Writings of Howard Zahniser* (Seattle: University of Washington Press, 2014) provide a sense of advocates' perspectives. Key legislation includes the Multiple Use Sustained Yield Act (1960) reproduced at https://www.govinfo.gov/content/pkg/STATUTE-74/pdf/STATUTE-74-Pg215.pdf#page=1, and the Wilderness Act (1964) at https://www.govinfo.gov/content/pkg/STATUTE-78/pdf/STATUTE-78-Pg890.pdf#page=1. The Leopold Report, officially *Wildlife Management in the National Parks* (Washington, DC: Government Printing Office, 1963), is available online at http://npshistory.com/publications/leopold_report.pdf.

A NOTE ON SOURCES 223

Much of this chapter focuses on national parks, and the literature is rich. The best overview, focused on science as the central narrative, is Richard West Sellars, *Preserving Nature in the National Parks: A History* (New Haven, CT: Yale University Press, 1997). See also John C. Miles, *Wilderness in National Parks: Playground or Preserve* (Seattle: University of Washington Press, 2009) for important perspectives. Grand Canyon National Park and its conservation controversies are the subject of many books, including Michael P. Cohen, *The History of the Sierra Club, 1892–1970* (San Francisco: Sierra Club Books, 1988); Robert H. Keller and Michael F. Turek, *American Indians and National Parks* (Tucson: University of Arizona Press, 2005); Byron E. Pearson, *Still the Wild River Runs: Congress, the Sierra Club, and the Fight to Save Grand Canyon* (Tucson: University of Arizona Press, 2002); and Stephen J. Pyne, *How the Canyon Became Grand: A Short History* (New York: Viking, 1998). For the North Cascades, besides my own book cited above, see Lauren Danner, *Crown Jewel Wilderness: Creating North Cascades National Park* (Pullman: Washington State University Press, 2017). In addition to other sources already cited, Darren Frederick Speece's *Defending Giants: The Redwood Wars and the Transformation of American Environmental Politics* (Seattle: University of Washington Press, 2017) offers an excellent account of the Redwoods.

The 1960s and early 1970s saw a host of new laws passed, and their stories are often told in fragments in other books and articles. I have written about several of these (for example, the Land and Water Conservation Act, National Trails System Act, Wild and Scenic Rivers Act, and Endangered Species Act) in my columns for *High Country News*, collected at https://www.hcn.org/topics/reckoning-with-history. In addition, see Sara Dant, "LBJ, Wilderness, and the Land and Water Conservation Fund," *Environmental History* 19, no. 4 (October 1, 2014): 736–43, for the Land and Water Conservation Fund. The National Environmental Policy Act's history is part of James R. Skillen, *Federal Ecosystem Management: Its Rise, Fall, and Afterlife* (Lawrence: University Press of Kansas, 2015); J. Brooks Flippen, *Nixon and the Environment* (Albuquerque: University of New Mexico Press, 2000); and portions of Adam M. Sowards, *The Environmental Justice: William O. Douglas and American Conservation* (Corvallis: Oregon State University Press, 2009). The legislative linchpin during this era was Wayne Aspinall, and his biography by Steven C. Schulte is essential: *Wayne Aspinall and the Shaping of the American West* (Boulder: University Press of Colorado, 2002). On the Endangered Species Act, see Peter S. Alagona, *After the Grizzly: Endangered Species and the Politics of Place in California* (Berkeley: University of California Press, 2013), as well as reading the law itself online at https://www.govinfo.gov/content/pkg/STATUTE-87/pdf/STATUTE-87-Pg884.pdf #page=1 and the key legal decision, *TVA v. Hill* (1978) at https://caselaw.findlaw.com/us-supreme-court/437/153.html.

For the environmental history of forests, start with Paul W. Hirt, *A Conspiracy of Optimism: Management of the National Forests since World War Two* (Lincoln: University of Nebraska Press, 1994), and the appropriate chapters in the overviews cited under chapter 2. Daniel Nelson, *Nature's Burdens: Conservation and American Politics, the Reagan Era to the Present* (Logan: Utah State University Press, 2017) provides key context on lawsuits, and can be usefully paired with Robert B. Keiter, *Keeping Faith with Nature: Ecosystems, Democracy, and America's Public Lands* (New Haven, CT: Yale University Press, 2003).

The reforms related to national rangelands are a focus in James R. Skillen, *The Nation's Largest Landlord: The Bureau of Land Management in the American West* (Lawrence: University Press of Kansas, 2013). In addition, see the history in Michael J. Makley, *Open Spaces, Open Rebellions: The War over America's Public Lands* (Amherst: University of Massachusetts Press, 2017); and in Leisl Carr Childers, *The Size of the Risk: Histories of Multiple Use in the Great Basin* (Norman: University of Oklahoma Press, 2015). Finally, consult the Public Land Law Review Commission's report, *One Third of the Nation's Land; a Report to the President and to the Congress* (Washington, DC: Government Printing Office, 1970).

For Alaska, many of the previously cited works contain key sections, including Turner's *The Promise of Wilderness*. An important book to consult is Stephen W. Haycox, *Battleground Alaska: Fighting Federal Power in America's Last Wilderness* (Lawrence: University Press of Kansas, 2016).

CHAPTER 5: POLARIZING

Many of the sources already cited proved useful in writing this chapter, so only the key repeated sources appear here.

The opening story of the Fallinis is from Leisl Carr Childers, "The Angry West: Understanding the Sagebrush Rebellion in Rural Nevada," in *Bridging the Distance: Common Issues in the Rural West*, ed. David Danbom (Salt Lake City: University of Utah Press, 2015), 269–315, and can be profitably supplemented by Childers's book, *The Size of the Risk: Histories of Multiple Use in the Great Basin* (Norman: University of Oklahoma Press, 2015). The Sagebrush Rebellion and its evolution has found a growing scholarship.

The most recent study is James R. Skillen, *This Land Is My Land: Rebellion in the West* (New York: Oxford University Press, 2020), that promises to reset the debate. But the Sagebrush Rebellion scholarship all started with R. McGreggor Cawley, *Federal Land, Western Anger: The Sagebrush Rebellion and Environmental Politics* (Lawrence: University Press of Kansas, 1996), that remains a critical source. The Nevada Assembly's revolutionary law from 1979 is available at https://www.leg.state.nv.us/Statutes/60th/Stats197907.html#Stats197907page1362. An overview from which I drew many anecdotes and data is Michael J. Makley, *Open Spaces, Open Rebellions: The War over America's Public Lands* (Amherst: University of Massachusetts Press, 2017). The opposition to James Watt and the rise of the New Right are some of the key topics contained in James Morton Turner, *The Promise of Wilderness: American Environmental Politics since 1964* (Seattle: University of Washington Press, 2012). For the Wise Use Movement, in Ron Arnold's own words, consult his "Overcoming Ideology," in Philip D. Brick and R. McGreggor Cawley, eds., *A Wolf in the Garden: The Land Rights Movement and the New Environmental Debate* (Lanham, MD: Rowman & Littlefield, 1996), 15–26. Anthony McCann gracefully explores the most recent opposition by the Bundy family in *Shadowlands: Fear and Freedom at the Oregon Standoff: A Western Tale of America in Crisis* (New York: Bloomsbury, 2019).

Consult Turner's *The Promise of Wilderness* and Kevin R. Marsh's *Drawing Lines in the Forest: Creating Wilderness Areas in the Pacific Northwest* (Seattle: University of Washington Press, 2007) to study how the Roadless Area Review and Evaluation processes worked. Its association with the rise of radical environmentalism is part of Susan Zakin's *Coyotes and Town Dogs: Earth First! and the Environmental Movement* (New York: Viking, 1993), and subject to a superb scholarly treatment in Keith Makoto Woodhouse, *The Ecocentrists: A History of Radical Environmentalism* (New York: Columbia University Press, 2018). The context of conservation biology appears in Michael Lewis, "Wilderness and Conservation Science," in Michael Lewis, ed., *American Wilderness: A New History* (New York: Oxford University Press, 2007), 205–21. Daniel Nelson connects conservation biology and its relationship to the Greater Yellowstone Ecosystem in *Nature's Burdens: Conservation and American Politics, the Reagan Era to the Present* (Logan: Utah State University Press, 2017). Norman L. Christensen offers a useful framework for understanding how managers' old assumptions for public land management were inadequate and provides an updated framework in "Preserving Nature on US Federal Lands: Managing Change in the Context of Change," in Ben A. Minteer and Stephen J. Pyne, eds., *After Preservation: Saving American Nature in the Age of Humans* (Chicago: University of Chicago Press, 2015), 146–53.

The environmental history of Yellowstone offers insights not only regarding the rise of conservation biology but also for wolves and fire. On wolf reintroduction, see Robert B. Keiter, *Keeping Faith with Nature: Ecosystems, Democracy, and America's Public Lands* (New Haven, CT: Yale University Press, 2003); James R. Skillen, *Federal Ecosystem Management: Its Rise, Fall, and Afterlife* (Lawrence: University Press of Kansas, 2015); and Jordan Fisher Smith, *Engineering Eden: A Violent Death, a Federal Trial, and the Struggle to Restore Nature in Our National Parks* (New York: The Experiment, 2019), for which the focus is on bears and also contains excellent context. On fire and its long history, see Stephen J. Pyne, *Fire in America: A Cultural History of Wildland and Rural Fire* (Seattle: University of Washington Press, 1997); Stephen J. Pyne, *Between Two Fires: A Fire History of Contemporary America* (Tucson: University of Arizona Press, 2015); and Stephen J. Pyne, *The Northern Rockies: A Fire Survey* (Tucson: University of Arizona Press, 2016). In addition, consult Rocky Barker, *Scorched Earth: How the Fires of Yellowstone Changed America* (Washington, DC: Island Press, 2007); and Hal K. Rothman, *Blazing Heritage: A History of Wildland Fire in the National Parks* (New York: Oxford University Press, 2007).

One of the most contentious and momentous environmental battles concerned old-growth forests and the northern spotted owl. The works by Keiter, Nelson, Skillen, and Woodhouse cited above are all helpful. In addition, see Erik Loomis, *Empire of Timber: Labor Unions and the Pacific Northwest Forests* (New York: Cambridge University Press, 2016) and James D. Proctor, "Whose Nature? The Contested Moral Terrain of Ancient Forests," in William Cronon, ed., *Uncommon Ground: Toward Reinventing Nature* (New York: W. W. Norton, 1995), 269–97. Nancy Langston examines adaptive management in *Where Land and Water Meet: A Western Landscape Transformed* (Seattle: University of Washington Press, 2003), focusing on a different landscape but with the same political and historical context.

The contentiousness of rangeland politics finds good expression in Donald Snow, "The Pristine Silence of Leaving It All Alone," in Philip D. Brick and R. McGreggor Cawley, eds., *A Wolf in the Garden: The Land Rights Movement and the New Environmental Debate* (Lanham, MD: Rowman & Littlefield, 1996), 27–38. The fights over grazing policies at the federal level are covered well in Christopher McGrory Klyza, *Who Controls Public Lands? Mining, Forestry, and Grazing Policies, 1870–1990* (Chapel Hill: University of North Carolina Press, 1996) and, with a harder edge, in Debra L. Donahue, *The Western Range Revisited: Removing Livestock from Public Lands to Conserve Native Biodiversity* (Norman: University of Oklahoma

Press, 1999). The Childers's chapter cited above and Makley's book tell the story of Wayne Hage.

Stories of collaboration are growing. On the grizzly bears, see Michael J. Dax, *Grizzly West: A Failed Attempt to Reintroduce Grizzly Bears in the Mountain West* (Lincoln: University of Nebraska Press, 2015). Nancy Langston recounts the politics concerning Steens Mountain in *Where Land and Water Meet*. The Malpai Borderlands Group appears in several sources, including these overviews: Robert B. Keiter, *Keeping Faith with Nature*; Daniel Nelson, *Nature's Burdens*; and Randall K. Wilson, *America's Public Lands: From Yellowstone to Smokey Bear and Beyond* (Lanham, MD: Rowman & Littlefield, 2014). More specialized accounts are found in Nathan F. Sayre, *Working Wilderness: The Malpai Borderlands Group and the Future of the Western Range* (Tucson: Rio Nuevo Publishers, 2005); and Thomas E. Sheridan, Nathan F. Sayre, and David Seibert, "Beyond 'Stakeholders' and the Zero-Sum Game: Toward Community-Based Conservation in the American West," in Susan Charnley, Thomas E. Sheridan, and Gary P. Nabhan, eds., *Stitching the West Back Together: Conservation of Working Landscapes* (Chicago: University of Chicago Press, 2014), 53–75. The same book contains an excellent case study of Quivira with Courtney White, "The Quivira Experience: Reflections from a 'Do' Tank," 81–94.

CONCLUSION: THE PROMISE OF THE PUBLIC'S LAND

I have presented some of these ideas before in Adam M. Sowards, "Public Lands and Their Administration," *Oxford Research Encyclopedia of American History*, August 22, 2017, https://doi.org/10.1093/acrefore/9780199329175.013.396; Adam M. Sowards, "Sometimes, It Takes a Table," *Environmental History* 23, no. 1 (2018): 143–51; and Adam M. Sowards, "An Evolving Idea: Perils and Promise of the Federal Landscape," *Desert Report,* September 2020, 8–11, 21. For Bears Ears, consult the Bears Ears Inter-Tribal Coalition website at https://bearsearscoalition.org/about-the-coalition/. The Windigo story is from Robin Wall Kimmerer, "The Windigo," in Simmons B. Buntin, Elizabeth Caroline Dodd, and Derek Sheffield, eds., *Dear America: Letters of Hope, Habitat, Defiance, and Democracy* (San Antonio: Trinity University Press, 2020), 36–39. On the Antiquities Act, see Mark Squillace, "The Antiquities Act and the Exercise of Presidential Power: The Clinton Monuments," in David Harmon, Francis P. McManamon, and Dwight T. Pitcaithley, eds., *The Antiquities Act: A Century of American Archaeology, Historic*

Preservation, and Nature Conservation (Tucson: University of Arizona Press, 2006): 106–36. The policy of termination that led to reduction of Native land in the 1950s can be found in Charles F. Wilkinson, *Blood Struggle: The Rise of Modern Indian Nations* (New York: W. W. Norton, 2006); and Theodore Catton, *American Indians and National Forests* (Tucson: University of Arizona Press, 2016). The concept of "green drift" comes from Christopher McGrory Klyza and David J. Sousa, *American Environmental Policy: Beyond Gridlock*, updated and expanded ed. (Cambridge, MA: MIT Press, 2013). Already, journalists and scholars are exploring the standoff at Malheur, including the following sources: Hall Herring, "The Darkness at the Heart of Malheur," *High Country News*, March 21, 2016; Anthony McCann, *Shadowlands: Fear and Freedom at the Oregon Standoff: A Western Tale of America in Crisis* (New York: Bloomsbury, 2019); James R. Skillen, *This Land Is My Land: Rebellion in the West* (New York: Oxford University Press, 2020); and Peter Walker, *Sagebrush Collaboration: How Harney County Defeated the Takeover of the Malheur National Wildlife Refuge* (Corvallis: Oregon State University Press, 2018). Once again, the Terry Tempest Williams passage comes from *The Hour of Land: A Personal Topography of America's National Parks* (New York: Sarah Crichton Books/Farrar, Straus and Giroux, 2016).

Index

Abbey, Edward, 175
Acadia National Park, 82
Afognak Island, 112–13
Alaska Coalition, 157–58
Alaska Conservation Society (ACS), 157
Alaska National Interest Lands Conservation Act (1980), 156–59
Alaska National Wildlife Refuge (ANWR), 159
Alaska Native Claims Settlement Act (ANCSA), 156–57
Alaska Statehood Act (1959), 157
Albright, Horace, 88
American colonialism, 13–14, 15, 124, 206
American Forestry Association, 48, 80, 86, 106
American National Live Stock Association (ANLSA), 62, 97
Anderson, Harold, 86–87
Andrus, Cecil, 158
Antiquities Act (1906), 158, 159, 205, 206
Appalachian Mountain Club, 79, 89
Appalachian Mountains, 11, 15, 16, 78
Appalachian Trail (AT), 89, 139
Arendt, Hannah, 1, 2–3, 8, 210
Arizona, 23, 98, 127, 196; BLM land, claims to, 167; grass bank plans, 201; range damage in, 57, 61, 95
Arnold, Ron, 171–72
Aspinall, Wayne, 135, 136, 137, 143, 144, 154
Audubon Society, 113
Austin, Stephen, 22

Babbitt, Bruce, 195–96, 197, 200, 201, 209
Baca, Jim, 195, 196
Barnes, Will, 96
Bears Ears Inter-Tribal Coalition, 205, 206
Bears Ears National Monument, 205–7
Beck, Thomas, 115
Beyond the Hundredth Meridian (Stegner), 33
Biden, Joe, 207
biocentrism, 177
bison, 42–43, 46, 57, 75, 113, 187
Blackfeet Reservation, 74
Blue Ridge Mountains, 85, 86
Boag, Peter, 28
Bob Marshall Wilderness Area, 93
Bolle, Arnold, 152
Boone and Crockett Club, 47–48, 74, 113
Borah, William, 99
Bramwell, Lincoln, 192
Brandborg, Guy, 152
Broome, Harvey, 86–87
Brower, David, 126–27, 143, 146
Bundy, Ammon, 208, 209
Bundy, Cliven, 164–65, 208
Bureau of Biological Survey, 66, 112, 114, 116
Bureau of Indian Affairs, 72–73, 92
Bureau of Land Management (BLM), 9, 50, 103, 145, 156, 180, 193, 203; California timber, as managing, 181–82; early agency days, 95, 102, 153–54; grazing concerns, 161, 195–96; livestock industry, influence on,

110; Moab road protest, 170–71; Nevada claims to BLM lands, 166–67; policy and practice overhauls, 138, 150, 155; rancher relations, 163–64, 168, 208–9; *Rangeland Reform '94* impact statement, 197
Bureau of Reclamation, 9, 117, 125–26, 127, 141

California, 44, 144, 181, 200; condors in, 140, 149; Muir as Californian, 50, 68, 70; Nevada land, coveting, 201; Pacific Flyway, 114, 117; redwoods conservation, 142–43; San Francisco water insecurity, 68–70; sheep herding in, 57, 70
Campbell, Molly, 176
Cannon, Joseph, 79, 80
Carhart, Arthur, 87
Carson, Rachel, 148
Carson National Forest, 202
Carter, Jimmy, 157, 158, 159, 174
Catlin, George, 42–43
Church, Frank, 138, 152
Civilian Conservation Corps (CCC), 85, 90–92, 93, 103, 116
Clapp, Earle, 109
Clarke-McNary Act (1924), 81
Classification and Multiple Use Management Act (CMUA), 153–54
Clay, Henry, 26
clearcutting, 111, 121, 123, 143, 150–52, 179, 181, 183, 184
Clements, Frederick, 97–98
Cleveland, Grover, 49, 51–52, 53
Cliff, Edward, 132, 151
Clinton, Bill, 185, 195, 200, 206
Colorado, 50, 125, 135; anti-conservation sentiments, 53, 62; Colorado Plateau survey, 33, 35; Trappers Lake plan for wilderness recreation, 87

Colorado River Storage Project (CRSP), 125–26
Committee on Wildlife Restoration, 115
conservation movement, 36, 53, 68, 123, 135, 142, 174; Alaska, focus on, 157, 159; campaigns, 94, 115, 125–27, 140, 142–43, 147; costs of, 72–75; early days of, 34–35, 39, 44, 46–49; efficiency, grappling with, 66–67, 105; Glen Canyon Dam incident marking turn in, 175; grassroots organizations, enlisting help of, 141; hunters as conservationists, 118; influence, seeking to gain, 79, 158, 160, 161; land grab schemes, opposing, 103; legislation, Nevadans' pushback against, 165; long-term planning, taking pride in, 108; prominent conservationists, 50, 54; "rock and ice" wilderness, disdain for, 128–29
Cooke, Jay, 45
Coolidge, Calvin, 88
Copeland Report, 109, 111
Corps of Discovery, 42
Council on Environmental Quality (CEQ), 144
Cronon, William, 14
Croxen, Fred W., 96–97

Dana, Samuel, 102
Darling, Jay (Ding), 115–16
Death Valley, 93
Deep Ecology (Devall/Sessions), 177
Desert Land Act (1877), 35, 36, 37
Devall, Bill, 177
DeVoto, Bernard, 94, 103
Dinosaur National Monument, 125, 126
Dorr, George, 82
Douglas, Marjory Stoneman, 85
Douglas, William O., 141

INDEX

Drury, Newton, 93
Duck Stamp Act (1934), 116, 118
Dyer, Polly, 130

Earth First!, 175–77, 183, 186, 189, 203
Earth in the Balance (Gore), 185
Eastern Wilderness Area Act (1975), 140
Echo Park controversy, 125–27, 129
Ecological Site Inventory, 196
Eisenhower, Dwight, 133
Eliot, Charles, 82
elk population, 42, 94; Oregon, elk released into, 197–98; of Wyoming, 73, 119, 187; in Yellowstone, 120, 133–34, 187–89
eminent domain, 83, 86
Enclave Clause, 167–68
Endangered American Wilderness Act (1978), 174
Endangered Species Act (ESA), 6, 147, 148–49, 150, 152, 153, 177, 180, 181, 183, 188
Endangered Species Committee, 181–82
Environmental Impact Statement (EIS), 145, 146–47
Equal Footing Doctrine, 168
erosion, 41, 60, 90, 95–96, 103
Everglades, 83, 84–85
The Everglades (Douglas), 85
extinction, 115, 119, 121, 178, 183; bald eagle, protecting from, 148, 149; bison as close to, 75, 113; northern spotted owl as facing, 181
extraction, 136, 154, 177; resource, 135, 165, 169, 178; timber, 152, 179; wasteful practices, identifying, 47

Fairfax, Sally K., 25, 36, 38, 102
Fallini family, 163, 165, 168, 197
Federal Land Policy and Management Act (FLPMA), 156, 160, 170, 181; ecological inventories mandated by, 169; NFMA, not perfectly compatible with, 180; passage of, 150, 154, 194; ranchers, providing security for, 155
Field, Stephen J., 44
Finley, William, 117
fire, 41, 83, 167, 209; Big Blowup of 1910, lingering effects of, 65–66; General Land Office, fire protection provided by, 53; in National Forest Commission report, 50, 51; prescribed, 64, 65–66, 202; restoration ecology theory, applying to management of, 190–91; Selway Fire, deep effect on Forest Service, 91; value of control, 64–67; Yellowstone management, 189, 192
Fish and Wildlife Act (1956), 112
flooding and flood control, 68, 116, 124, 125, 127, 138, 141–42
floods, natural, 41, 79, 83
Ford, Gerald, 154
Foreman, Dave, 175, 176, 183–84, 189
Forest Dreams, Forest Nightmares (Langston), 72
Forest Ecosystem Management Assessment Team, 185
forest reserves, 6, 43, 44, 46; 1897 Organic Act clarifying purpose of, 54; eastern, 78–81, 117; Holy Cross, 62; reserved land, decision-making for, 50–56; roadless areas of, 173–74; timber famine, attempts to hold off, 48–49. *See also* U.S. Forest Service
Forsman, Eric, 179–80, 182
Four Corners area, 205
Frank, Bernard, 86–87
Franklin, Jerry, 184
Free Soil Party, 29
Friends of the Three Sisters, 128

Gabrielson, Ira, 116
Garfield, James, 69–70
Gates, Paul Wallace, 24, 26, 35
General Land Office, 53, 102
General Mining Law (1872), 155
General Revision Act (1891), 49, 113
Gila Wilderness Area, 130
Glacier National Park, 73, 74, 159
Glacier Peak Wilderness, 140–41
Glen Canyon Dam, 126–27, 175
Gore, Al, 185
Grand Canyon, 33, 50, 88, 170; flood threats, 141–42; identity, as source for, 8, 47; protection of, 72, 158
Grand Staircase-Escalante National Monument, 206
Grand Tetons, 47, 88, 119, 120, 189
Gravel, Mike, 158
grazing, 42, 56, 154, 160, 205, 208; environmental damage caused by, 51, 57, 131, 145, 196; fees, 62, 97, 99, 100, 155, 164, 166–68, 170, 194–95, 197; forbidding of, 53, 61, 200; inspectors, 98, 124; overgrazing, 58, 59, 60, 92, 95, 96, 99, 103, 130, 136, 187, 194; permits, 63, 100, 155, 164, 172, 195, 196, 197, 201; Powell proposals for, 33–34; public land, 105, 123, 135, 197; Taylor Grazing Act, 100–104, 153, 155, 161, 163; on western range, 95–104, 109, 198
Great Die-Off, 58
Great Plains, 18, 22, 35, 42, 57, 101
Great Smoky Mountains National Park, 82–84, 85, 86
Greeley, William, 100
Grimaud, Pierre, 63
Grinnell, George Bird, 73
Grow, Galusha A., 31

Haaland, Deb, 207
Hage, Wayne, Jr., 198
Hage, Wayne, Sr., 197–98

Hammond, Dwight and Steven, 208–9
Harney County, defense of, 209
Harrison, Benjamin, 49
Hartzog, George, 135
Hatch, Orrin, 167
Hayden, Ferdinand V., 45
Hedges, Cornelius, Jr., 44
Hetch Hetchy conflict, 67–72, 126
Heyburn, Weldon, 65, 80
Hickel, Walter, 146
High Desert Partnership, 209
Hirt, Paul W., 111, 153
Hitchcock, Ethan, 69
Holman, William S., 31
Homestead Act (1862), 11, 28–32, 34, 35
homesteaders, 31, 32, 34, 59, 61, 193–94, 196
Hoover, Herbert, 85, 99, 100
Hopson, Ruth, 128
Hornaday, William T., 75
Hough, Franklin, 48, 50
Hour of Land (Williams), 8–9, 209–10
Hour of Trial (McCarthy), 53
House Public Lands Committee, 25
"Huckleberries" (Thoreau), 1–2
The Human Condition (Arendt), 1, 2–3
Humphrey, Hubert, 129
Hunter, Celia, 157
hunters and hunting, 42, 113, 117, 134, 147, 151, 189; Bannock rights, 73–74; duck, regulating, 116, 118; elk in Yellowstone, 134; *Forest and Stream*, hunters publishing, 47; FWS-hunter relations, 120, 161; Roosevelt code of conduct for, 74
Hutchings, James Mason, 44

Ickes, Harold, 84, 93, 101
Idaho, 73, 196; float trips on rivers, 138; Idaho-Montana border, 65, 80,

INDEX

91, 191, 199; wolf population of, 188, 199
Indian Removal Act (1830), 83
Interagency Scientific Committee (ISC), 182
Interior Department, 52, 158, 169, 195
Izaak Walton League, 92, 151

Jackson, Henry (Scoop), 144, 160
Jackson, William Henry, 45
Jardine, James, 98
Jefferson, Thomas, 21, 28, 36; as agrarian philosopher, 27, 30; ideals of, 29, 31, 34, 55; sense of land, 14–19; yeomancy visions, 18–19, 20, 25, 29, 35
Johnson, Lyndon B., 129, 136, 137, 138, 142, 143
Johnson, Robert Underwood, 68
Joshua Tree National Park, 158

Kaibab Plateau, 67
Kalmiopsis Wilderness, 175
Keiter, Robert, 202
Kennecott Copper Corporation, 141, 142
Kimmerer, Robin Wall, 207, 210
Klyza, Christopher McGrory, 207
Koch, Elers, 91, 93

Lacey Act (1900), 114
Lafayette National Park, 82
Land and Water Conservation Fund (LWCF), 137, 139, 169
Land Grant College Act (1862), 30
land ordinances, 16, 17, 24, 32–33, 36, 168
Langford, Nathaniel, 44–45
Langston, Nancy, 72, 106, 107
League for the Advancement of States' Equal Rights (LASER), 166, 167
Leek, Stephen, 119

Leopold, A. Starker, 134–35, 190
Leopold, Aldo, 88, 130, 177; as conservationist, 86–87, 115; as land surveyor, 95–96; predators, evolving views on, 134–35, 147; wildlife, taking steps to protect, 91–92
Leopold Report, 134, 187, 188, 190–91
Lewis and Clark expedition, 44
Light, Fred, 62
Lincoln, Abraham, 30, 31, 43
livestock industry, 7, 47, 52, 124, 136; factors in continued prosperity of, 55; Fallini operation, 163–64; marginalizing of small-scale ranching, 96–97; ranching communities, poor view of environmentalists, 165, 167; range fights, 56–63; reforms on the range, 193–98. *See also* grazing
Locke, John, 13–15, 29
Louisiana Purchase, 19, 23
Lujan, Manuel, 182

MacArthur, Robert, 177
MacKaye, Benton, 86–87, 89
Madison, James, 20–21, 29
Malheur National Wildlife Refuge, 116, 117, 208–9
Malpai Borderlands Group, 202
Mammoth Cave, 82
Man and Nature (Perkins), 34–35, 78
Manifest Destiny, 22–23, 27
Mariposa Big Tree Grove, 43
Marsh, George Perkins, 34–35, 41, 47, 78, 79
Marshall, Robert (Bob), 86–87, 92, 127
Mather, Stephen, 82, 84, 88
McCarthy, G. Michael, 53
McKinley, William, 52
Merrell, Harvey, 170
Merriam, C. Hart, 66
Metcalf, Lee, 152

Migratory Bird Hunting Stamp Act (1934), 116
Migratory Bird Treaty Act (1918), 114, 115
Miller, Char, 71
mining industry, 7, 47, 53, 55, 65, 124, 154; BLM, good relations with, 102, 153; damage to land from, 130–31; legislation regarding, 35–36, 52, 155; Superior National Forest, mines near, 75; Wilderness Act and, 135, 136, 140–41
Mission 66 plan, 133, 142, 191
Mississippi: flyway, 114; Mississippi River, 15, 18, 22, 32, 80; Upper Mississippi Wildlife and Fish Refuge, 115
Mittlefehldt, Sarah, 139
Moab road protest, 170–71
Monkey Wrench Gang (Abbey), 175
Monongahela National Forest, 151
Montana, 50, 58, 93; Bitterroot National Forest, 151–52; border with Idaho, 65, 80, 91, 191, 199; Fish and Game Department, 148
Moran, Thomas, 45
Morrill Act, 30
Mortan, Rogers C. B., 157
Mountain States Legal Foundation, 166, 168, 198
Mount Desert Island, 82
Mt. Rainier National Park, 88
Muir, John, 59, 69; as Californian, 68, 70; deep ecology, traces found in writings of, 177; Pinchot and, 50, 71
Multiple Use Sustained Yield Act, 131–32
Murie, Olaus J., 120

Naess, Arne, 177
National Conference on Outdoor Recreation (1924), 88
National Elk Refuge, 119, 120, 187

National Environmental Policy Act (NEPA), 152, 160, 169, 180, 185, 196; environmentalist follow-ups, 181; ESA and, 149–50; establishment of agency, 6, 144–45; legal concerns and, 146, 173; North Slope pipeline, exempting, 146–47; planning process model, 153, 155, 156
National Forest Commission, 50–51, 52
National Forest Management Act (NFMA), 150, 152–53, 155, 160, 175, 180, 181
National Industrial Recovery Act (1933), 119–10
National Oceanic and Atmospheric Administration, 149
National Park Service (NPS), 84, 88, 135, 161, 169, 173; centennial celebration, 8–9; creation of agency, 71, 82; eastern parks, 81–86; mid-century challenges, 125–27, 137, 141–42; new vision for, 134–35; Wirth as director, 132–34
National Trails System Act (1968), 138–39, 142
National Wilderness Preservation System, 87, 136, 138, 139–43, 155, 159, 173
National Wildlife Federation, 92
Nature Conservancy, 202, 205
Nevada, 172, 196, 208; BLM land, claims to, 165–67; elk, wildlife department releasing, 197–98; FLPMA, reacting to passage of, 163–64
New Mexico, 98, 172, 201; BLM land, claims to, 167; Gila, overgrazing, 130; sheep herding in, 59, 96
Newton, Isaac, 14
Nixon, Richard, 146, 147, 157
Norbeck, Peter, 116
North Cascades, 93, 141, 142, 144, 160

INDEX

Northern Pacific Railroad (NPR), 45
Northern Rockies Ecosystem Protection Act, 189
Northwest Ordinances, 11, 16, 26, 33
Notes on the State of Virginia (Jefferson), 17

Obama, Barack, 205, 206
Oberholtzer, Ernest, 86–87
Olmsted, Frederick Law, Jr., 71
Olmsted, Frederick Law, Sr., 29, 43, 44
Olympic National Park, 93–94, 130
One Third of the Nation's Lands (report), 137, 154
"On Property" (Locke), 13
Onthank, Ruth and Karl, 128
Oregon, 61, 72, 114, 116, 138, 185, 200, 210; Earth First! activism in, 175–76; elk, releasing into, 197–98; forests of, 105–8, 179, 181, 183; illegal grazing activities, 208–9; Klamath Basin, 117, 118; Oregon Country, 23, 27–28; Oregon Sheep Shooters Association, 59–60; Three Sisters Primitive Area, 127–28
Oregon Land Donation Act (1850), 28
Organic Act (1897), 52–54, 71, 150, 151, 152
O'Sullivan, John, 22–23
Our Vanishing Wild Life (Hornaday), 75
Outdoor Recreation Resources Review Commission (ORRRC), 129–30, 131, 135, 137

Pacific Crest Trail (PCT), 139
Pacific Flyway, 114, 117
"Passing of the Lolo Train" (Koch), 91
pastoralism, 60, 96
Pelican Island, 113
pesticides, 123, 148
Pinchot, Gifford, 69; as Bureau of Forestry chief, 61, 105; *The Fight for Conservation*, 64; letter, 54–56; Muir and, 50, 71
Potter, Albert, 61
Powell, John Wesley, 33, 34, 35, 38, 41
Powell Survey, 33
Practice of the Wild (Snyder), 8
Preble, Edward A., 119
Preemption Acts, 25–26
private property, 35, 51, 60, 89, 172, 192, 194; beyond, 42–46; colonial understandings of, 13–14, 206; legislation regarding, 24, 52–53, 64; Property Clause, 17, 167; sense of, 1–2, 4, 198; wildlife concerns and, 113, 115, 118
"Problem of the Wilderness" (Marshall), 86
Proclamation Line of 1763, 11, 15
public domain land, 8–9, 35, 41, 50–52, 86, 99–100, 102, 186; acquiring, 5–6, 19–23, 46–49; disposing of, 23–28; extraction on, 71, 177, 179; homestead laws as privatizing, 30–32, 33, 56; livestock grazing on, 57–62, 163; national reserves carved out from, 43, 80, 82, 120; Public Lands Commission as systematizing work on, 36–39; "seeing like a state" and, 16–17; Taylor Grazing Act as applicable to, 101, 163; unclaimed land of, 56, 95
Public Land Law Review Commission (PLLRC), 137, 154
Public Lands Commission, 36–39, 49, 99, 100, 137
Public Land Survey System, 16
Pulaski, Edward, 65

Quivira Coalition, 202

Race Horse, 73
ranching. *See* livestock industry

Reagan, Ronald, 168, 169, 170, 188, 194, 195, 203
Refuge Revenue Sharing Act, 117
Report of the Public Lands Commission (1880), 37–38
Report on Forestry (Hough), 48
Report on Lands of the Arid Region (Powell), 33, 38
Rights-of-Way Act (1901), 69
roads and road-building, 86, 94; activism against, 176; Roadless Area Review Evaluation, 173–74; scenic drives, 85, 92
Robertson, Dale, 181
Rockefeller, John D., Jr., 82, 84
Rocky Mountains, 18, 33, 57, 93; Big Blowup, 65–66; national park, 85, 88; Northern Rockies, 66, 73, 74, 91, 96, 187, 189, 199
Roosevelt, Franklin D., 85, 89–90, 112, 115–16
Roosevelt, Theodore, 74, 94; as conservationist, 54, 71, 99; on Hetch Hetchy Valley, 69–70; Pelican Island, protecting, 113
Roselle, Mike, 176

Sagebrush Collaboration (Walker), 209
Sagebrush Rebellion, 165–73, 186
Sand County Almanac (Leopold), 147
Sargent, Charles Sprague, 50
Save the Redwoods League, 143
Saylor, John, 129
Sayre, Nathan F., 103–4
Schurz, Carl, 48–49
Scott, James C., 16–17
Second Treatise of Government (Locke), 13
"See America First" campaign, 47
Selway-Bitterroot Wilderness, 93
Sequoia National Park, 46
Sessions, George, 177

Seward, William, 29–30
Shafroth, John, 53
sheep industry, 95, 96, 166; cattle interests, conflicts with, 60, 61; grazing fees, 62, 194, 195; introduction of sheep to the west, 57, 59; National Wool Growers Association, 97; sheep herding on public land, 56, 63
Shenandoah National Park, 82, 85, 86
Sierra Club, 92, 126, 128, 173; conservationist movement, role in, 141, 142, 143, 157, 174; growth in membership, 169; Muir as member of, 59, 68, 70; Sierra Club Legal Defense Fund, 176
Sierra South National Forest, 63
Silcox, Ferdinand, 92, 93
Silent Spring (Carson), 148
Simpson, Alan, 196
Skillen, James R., 153, 171, 184–85
Skyline Drive, 85
Smith, Robert, 31
Snyder, Gary, 8, 9
Society for Conservation Biology, 178
Soulé, Michael, 189
Sousa, David J., 207
South Dakota, 73
Spaulding, Henry and Eliza, 27
Speece, Darren, 143
spotted owls, 178–80, 182, 183, 185
Steens Mountain, 200–201, 202, 209
Stegner, Wallace, 33, 34, 126, 130
Stevens, Ted, 159
Stoll, Steven, 17, 29
Storm over Rangelands (Hage), 198
Stuart, Granville, 58
sustained-yield practices, 105, 106–7, 110, 131–32, 183

Taft, William Howard, 80
Taylor Grazing Act, 100–104, 153, 155, 161, 163

INDEX

This Is Dinosaur (Stegner), 126, 130
Thomas, Jack Ward, 182, 185
Thoreau, Henry David, 1–2, 20, 177
Timber and Stone Act, 34–35
Timber Culture Act, 35, 36, 49
timber industry, 6, 52, 71, 123, 136, 164, 172; commercial cutting, lax regulation of, 53; factors in continued prosperity of, 55; in National Forest Commission report, 50, 51; public timber and spotted owls, 178–86; Timber and Stone Act as allowing for logging, 35–36; timber famine, fears of, 48–49; timber mining, 83, 105, 152; USFS, close ties with, 127–29, 142, 161
Tongass National Forest, 159
Tonto National Forest, 95
Trans-Alaska Pipeline, 157
Transfer Act (1905), 54
transhumance, practice of, 60, 63
Treaty of Guadalupe Hidalgo (1848), 23, 27
tribal lands, dispossession of, 3, 19, 23, 32, 43, 72
Truman, Harry, 84, 102
Trump, Donald, 206, 207
Turner, Frederick Jackson, 24, 25

U.S. Department of Agriculture (USDA), 30, 54, 61, 63, 71, 112
U.S. Department of the Interior, 54, 71, 102, 168–69
U.S. Fish and Wildlife Service (FWS), 66, 112, 119, 120, 145, 148, 149, 161, 164, 180–81, 189, 202, 208
U.S. Fish Commission, 112
U.S. Forest Service (USFS), 9, 50, 54, 90, 95, 100, 124, 141, 148, 153, 172, 191, 193; BLM, working with, 197–98; Clementsian succession, embracing concept of, 98, 103, 105–6; grazing allotments on, 98, 201–2; industrializing of forests, 105–12; infrastructure, limiting development of, 92–93; large-scale ranchers, cooperating with, 96; multiple use, reforming, 131–32, 150–56; New Forestry approach, 184; Northwest Forest Plan, implementing, 185–86; NPS-USFS rivalry, 71, 88; orientation and goals of, 56, 65–66, 190; purity standards, application of, 139–40; range, regulation of, 62–63; reclassification strategies, 127–28, 129; timber industry–USFS relations, 127–29, 142, 161, 180–81, 183; Weeks Act, agency made national with, 80
U.S. Grazing Service, 100, 102, 104
Udall, Morris, 158
Udall, Stewart, 134, 146, 158
"A University View of the Forest Service" (Bolle Report), 152
Unlawful Enclosures Act (1885), 58
untrammeled land, concept of, 130–31, 133, 139
U-Regulations, 92–93, 127
Utah, 82, 99–100, 119, 125, 127, 210; anti-conservation sentiment in, 205, 206; BLM land, claims on, 167; Great Salt Lake Valley, 33; Moab road protest, 170–71; poor soil conditions in, 196–97; Sagebrush Rebellion, 170–71

Walker, Peter, 209
Warren, Louis, 19
Washburn-Langford Expedition, 45
Washington's Birthday Reserves, 51
Watt, James, 168–70, 171, 198
Weeks Act, 80–81, 89
western range: grazing on, 95–104; sheep herding on, 59–60

The Western Range study, 100, 101–2, 109
western vigilantism, 59
White, Elijah, 27
White, Richard, 57, 59
Whitman, Marcus and Narcissa, 27
Wichita Forest Reserve, 113
Wild and Scenic Rivers Act (1968), 138, 142
wilderness, 124–43, 175; preservation of, 87, 136, 138, 139–43, 155, 159, 173; protection of, 123, 125–29, 167; recreation and, 86–94, 121, 124; "rock and ice," 128–29, 173; "The Wilderness Letter," 130; wild forest lands, 78, 128
Wilderness Act (1964), 6, 138, 140, 150, 152; creation and passing of, 124, 129–36, 137, 151; roadless lands, requiring inventory of, 173–74; USFS as administering, 169, 191
"Wilderness and Its Place in Forest Recreational Policy" (Leopold), 87
Wilderness Society, 92, 128, 140, 157, 169, 174; Earth First! as inspired by, 175; founding of, 86–88; wilderness protection as main goal of, 129
Wild Free-Roaming Horses and Burros Act (1971), 163
Wildlands Project, 189
wildlife conservation, 117, 118, 124
Wildlife Coordination Act (1934), 116
wildlife refugees, 6, 112–21, 123, 156, 158, 206, 221
Wilkinson, Charles, 56
Williams, Terry Tempest, 4, 8–9, 82, 209–10
Wilson, E. O., 177
Wilson, James, 54–55
Wilson, Woodrow, 82, 94

Windigo, 207
Winthrop, John, 14
Wirth, Conrad, 132–133, 134, 137
Wise Use Movement (WUM), 171–72, 198, 209
wolves: government eradication of, 66, 133, 134; reintroduction of, 186–89, 197, 199; wolf-pack death, Leopold moved by, 147
Wyoming, 61, 125, 167, 196; elk population of, 119, 187; Johnson County War of 1892, 59; public land hunting, Fort Bridger Treaty allowing, 73. *See also* Yellowstone
Wyoming Stock Growers Association (WSGA), 59, 61

Yard, Robert Sterling, 86–87
Yellowstone, 5, 46, 49, 72, 113; elk population, 120, 133–34, 187–89; fire management in, 189–92; greater ecosystem of, 119, 133–34, 188, 189; Native American presence, 73–74; origin story, 44–45; wolves, reintroducing to, 186–89, 199
Yosemite Valley, 5, 45, 46, 71, 73; Hetch Hetchy Valley controversy, 67–72, 126; pride of place, providing, 8, 72; state management of, as contentious, 43–44; tungsten mining, temporarily allowing in, 93

Zahniser, Howard, 128; CRSP, working to stop, 125–26; grazing, making concessions for, 135–36; NPS support, as seeking, 132–33; wilderness legislation, helping to craft, 127, 129, 130–31
Zinke, Ryan, 206
Zion National Park, 88